NOW, ACTING STUDENTS, SEASONED
ACTORS—EVEN PUBLIC SPEAKERS AND
BUSINESS PROFESSIONALS—CAN
LEARN TO:

- Increase confidence on and off the stage
- Heighten concentration
- Improve memory
- Broaden their range
- Polish their performance
- And much, much more!

GREAT SCENES AND MONOLOGUES FOR ACTORS

THE ULTIMATE COLLECTION FOR TODAY'S ACTOR

GREAT SCENES
and
MONOLOGUES
for ACTORS

Michael Schulman

and Eva Mekler

St. Martin's Paperbacks

"Creating a Character" was previously published in the *Actor's Scene Book*, volume 2, by Michael Schulman, (copyright © 1987 Bantam Books). All rights reserved.

GREAT SCENES AND MONOLOGUES FOR ACTORS

ISBN: 0-312-96654-7

Printed in the United States of America

St. Martin's Paperbacks edition/September 1998

St Martin's Paperbacks are published by St Martin's Press, 175 Fifth Avenue, New York, NY 10010.

10 9 8 7 6 5

CONTENTS

SCENES FOR TWO WOMEN

SCENES FOR TWO MEN

MONOLOGUES FOR WOMEN

MONOLOGUES FOR MEN

CREATING A CHARACTER

by Michael Schulman

We can think of actors as falling into two categories: character actors and personalities. To illustrate, imagine both George C. Scott and Marlon Brando playing Richard III. Both are fine actors and have had long and distinguished careers. And anyone would love to have seen either of them play the part when they were the appropriate age. But if your impression of these two actors is similar to mine, you already have quite a good picture of how Scott's performance would have looked and sounded—much like almost all of his other roles. But there is no way to know what Brando's version of Richard III would have been like, because in most of Brando's roles he sought to create a unique character, one unlike any he had played before. He is, as I am using the term here, a *character actor*. In contrast, Scott's characters were all shaped to fit much the same mold—his own impressive personality (or at least the personality he displays in his film and stage work; it may not really be what he is like in his private life).

Many of our most successful film stars have fallen into the personality category. Katharine Hepburn and Jimmy Stewart have been two extraordinarily fine actors of this type, as are Gene Hackman and John Travolta. Among the best known "character actors" have been Laurence Olivier, Meryl Streep, Dustin Hoffman, Swoosie Kurtz, and Robert DeNiro (which does not necessarily mean that they have sought to create a unique and particular character for every role).

All actors must master certain aspects of their craft, regardless of whether they approach a role by trying to create a unique character or by attempting to express their own personalities. For instance, all actors must learn how to create what I call "basic realities," whatever their personal performing styles or the style and period of the play or film. *All* characters take actions in pursuit of objectives and all characters react to stimuli. Actions and reactions are two essential aspects of all human beings, on stage and off.

Hamlet, for example, takes the action of asking the visiting players to enact a play about murder as a way to resolve his doubts about whether his uncle killed his father. In order to play the reality of Hamlet's action, the actor, regardless of whether he is a character or personality actor, must know how to create the anguish that those doubts have inflicted on Hamlet, the anguish that drives his action. Otherwise he will make empty sounds and gestures.

Similarly, whenever Hamlet talks of his father, the actor playing him must bring to mind actual images and remembrances of a father. These may be of a father he has created in his imagination, or memories of his own father. He may even use another person as a substitute father, or he may use a combination of all three approaches, but he *must* have a father-stimulus and he must have those images of his father in mind *on stage* as he speaks Hamlet's lines; otherwise, he can not authentically experience the life of Hamlet. Try talking about your own father without images of him; you'll find that it is impossible.

So all actors must learn how to create realities that lead to authentic physical and verbal actions and reactions, but only some actors are concerned with the question of how to create unique characters.

There are three main ingredients for creating authentic characters. The first is commitment. Most actors don't think about how to make their portrayals unique and specific to each role they play, but great actors do. Olivier spoke of this attitude in an interview some years ago. He was discussing the important influence Clare Eames had on his approach to acting and he said, "I used to talk about a straight part or a character part and she said, 'What's the difference? Don't tell me there's such a thing as a straight part. There isn't a part in the world that isn't a character part.' And it was she who gave me that attitude."[1]

---

[1]Hal Burton, ed., *Great Acting* (New York: Bonanza Books, 1967), p. 16.

In another part of the interview, Olivier revealed that initially he wasn't enthusiastic about playing Richard III—a role for which he received great acclaim—because he felt he had nothing unique to offer in the role. As he put it, "One thing that may lead an actor to be successful in a part, not always, but it may, is to try to be unlike somebody else in it."[2] Marlon Brando appears to have the same attitude. In an interview on his work in the western film *Missouri Breaks*, he described his interest in creating a cowboy unlike any he had ever created before and unlike any he had seen other actors portray. In general, character actors are committed to creating unique and authentic lives.

Perhaps the strongest statements about character acting were written by Constantin Stanislavski:

> I claim that all actors must be character actors.... This does not mean [the actor] must lose his own individuality and his personality; it means that in each role he must find his individuality and his personality, but nevertheless be different in every role.
>
> Any role that does not include a real characterization will be poor, not lifelike, and the actor who cannot convey the character of the roles he plays is a poor and monotonous actor. As a matter of fact, there is no person on earth who does not possess his own individual character.... That is why I propose for actors a complete inner and external metamorphosis.
>
> There are actors and especially actresses who do not feel the need of preparing characterizations or transforming themselves into other characters because they adapt all roles to their own personal appeal.
>
> Characterization, when accompanied by a real transposition, a sort of re-incarnation, is a great thing.... In other words all actors who are artists should make use of characterization. A capacity to transform himself, body and soul, is the prime requirement for an actor.[3]

[2]*Ibid*, p. 23.
[3]Constantin Stanislavski, *An Actor's Handbook*, ed. Elizabeth Reynolds Hapgood (New York: Theatre Arts Books, 1963), pp. 32–34.

The second ingredient for successful character acting is to base your characters on real people. Olivier finally realized that he could bring something special to the role of Richard III by basing his character on Jed Harris, the American producer (the same person that Disney modeled the Big Bad Wolf after). Another of Olivier's major roles, Archie Rice in *The Entertainer*, was, it has been said, based on the English vaudevillian Vic Oliver.

Most character actors, when they talk about their work process, talk about spending lots of time observing other people, and either base a character on one particular individual or piece a character together by drawing various aspects from different people. Meryl Streep once commented that one of her problems in becoming a star was that it became difficult to watch people since now everyone was watching her. Olivier put it this way:

> You've got to find, in the actor, a man who will not be too proud to scavenge the tiniest little bit of human circumstance; observe it, find it, use it some time or another. I've frequently observed things, and thank God, if I haven't got a very good memory for anything else, I've got a memory for little details. I've had things in the back of my mind for as long as eighteen years before I've used them. And it works sometimes that, out of one little thing you've seen somebody do, something causes you to store it up. In the years that follow you wonder what it was that made them do it, and, ultimately, you find in that the illuminating key to a whole bit of characterization.[4]

There has been a lot of confusion among acting teachers about using people as character models. I believe that most of this confusion stems from Lee Strasberg's dictum to his students that one never bases a character on people. I studied with Lee and then taught in his school for a number of years, and I must say that characterization was one of the areas he never really came to grips with. He almost never dealt with it in his classes, either in his own school or at The Actors Studio,

[4]Burton, *loc. cit.*, p. 23.

at least not during the eight or so years that I saw his classes on a regular basis.

Indeed, at The Actors Studio, auditioners are discouraged from presenting anything but a role that is "close" to themselves, as if playing a role that is like you is a higher form of acting or reveals more of an actor's true ability than does creating a character. In actuality, many actors are not very good at playing parts that are close to themselves but are truly brilliant when they play characters. John Gielgud, who has done both with great success, described the "release" he found the first time he created a character that was very different from himself:

> It was when I played Trofimov, the student in *The Cherry Orchard* . . . and suddenly having to put on a bald wig and glasses and a shambling walk, I found a kind of impersonating release from my own personality that seemed to give me a freedom of expression which I had never found before . . . and I was able to lose myself completely in the role. I was relaxed for the first time.[5]

Lee Strasberg was a powerful influence on many of today's teachers and, unfortunately, many have blindly accepted his rule against using people as models. He did have one character exercise and it did involve observation—the observation of animals. Actors certainly have found animals useful as character models, but such study is a much slower and more difficult process than using people and more likely to lead to conventional, "archetypal" choices. People, with all their quirks and idiosyncracies, provide much more varied and individualized models. The question of using people as models should never have become a theoretical issue at all, not when great actors tell us that they are constantly observing people and basing their characters on what they've observed. The only sensible question for the acting student to ask is how to do it, not whether the process fits into his or her teacher's theory. (One recent actor's manual goes so far as to say that there is no such thing as character acting, as if all it takes to

[5]Lewis Funke and John E. Booth, eds., *Actors Talk About Acting* (New York: Avon, 1963), p. 15.

get acting students to deny what they see with their own eyes is to make a nonsensical assertion boldly.)

CHARACTER EXERCISES

The best way I've found to describe the process of creating a character is with the phrase, "getting possessed by a life." That is what the actor who strives to create characters must learn to do. There is a standard character exercise I do with students to help them learn this process of "getting possessed." It provides a structured procedure for learning and practicing the craft of character acting.

Start by thinking of five people you know who are very different from each other. To help select individuals who are very contrasting, pick one person who is easily irritated, one who is funny, one who is shy, one who appears very confident, and one who is overtly sexual. The people must be real and be recalled with a fair degree of clarity. The character labels (irritable, funny, shy, etc.) are only used to prompt thought. You must never merely play the general quality of irritability or shyness or any other personality label. If you do, your portrayal will rarely rise above the most obvious and conventional character choices. It is also important not to base a character on other actors' portrayals. For example, you should not choose Jackie Gleason's Ralph Cramden as a character model. If you do, your character will be two steps removed from life and almost certainly will be a caricature.

After selecting your five models, choose an "ongoing activity," something like painting a wall or vacuuming the house—an activity that involves your whole body and that can continue for a fairly long time. You will also need to memorize a monologue to use when working on the character's voice.

Start the exercise as yourself, engaging in the ongoing activity. Give yourself a good reason for doing it. Walls, carpets, paintbrushes, and the rest will all be created "sensorially"—through your imagination. It is important to provide yourself with obstacles to the task (the paint drips, the wall cracks, the paintbrush leaves hairs in the paint, the carpet has gum in it, and so on). These obstacles will intensify your sense of reality as you pantomime the activity. Obstacles will also allow you to experience the differences in temperament of each of your characters, because each will react to the obstacles in his or her own very particular way. After working on the activity for about three minutes, begin to recite your monologue as you work, speaking it as if you were practicing it in a fairly casual way.

After another couple of minutes it will be time to "get possessed" by the first character, say the irritable one. Stop the activity and feel the character "take over" your body. In class I will say, "Feel the character move right inside you and take over your body. Feel how the distribution of your weight changes, and how your posture and stance change. Feel the change in the rhythm in your body. Now let the character take over your eyes. You are seeing the room and the people in it through his or her eyes now. Feel the character take over your lips and face muscles, then your arms and fingers. Begin to walk around as the character. Feel how different your stride is. Feel what that stride is saying."

If there are odd aspects of a character or apparent infirmities, try to understand the physical or emotional causes that lie behind those behaviors. For example, a particular stride or posture may be a compensation for a physical infirmity or for a feeling of insecurity.

As the exercise continues, check all parts of the body and try to find which elements (eyes? stride?) seem most effective in triggering your sense of becoming the character. Then start your activity again, but now *as the character*. When working on a character, never ask yourself "How would my character do this (paint or vacuum or any other activity)?" You will usually have no idea and begin to worry about whether you are getting it right. Don't be concerned about getting it right; your only goal is to *feel* as if you are the character as you do it. Simply take your character into the situation and discover how he or she wants to behave. It doesn't matter whether your character model would actually carry out the task in the same way.

There is, though, one important way in which you must be true to your character. You must be faithful to your character's reactions, whatever they are, and not to the label you have applied to him or her. For example, you may find in working on your "funny" character, that he or she may not react with any humor to a paintbrush that falls. That's fine. Just express what seems true for your character at that moment.

After awhile, try to find the voice of the character, using the memorized monologue. Find the areas of resonance, the rhythms of the voice, and the way consonants are hit and vowels held. You are likely to find that the very meanings of the words change when you speak them while you are possessed by someone whose temperament and self-image are very different from your own.

Work on a character for about ten minutes, then switch to a second character and repeat the process. Do the same for all five. In class, after we go through all the characters, I will have students do a group improvisation in which each participates as one of his or her characters. Some will work on their funny characters, others will do their irritable one, etc., so that all five types are represented in the improvisation. Sometimes I will strand them all in a bus station during a snowstorm or put them in a barn that they are converting to a summer theater. After a few minutes I will ask them to switch to a second character. They switch every five minutes or so until each student has tried all his or her characters in the improvisation. As they improvise, if I see a character slipping or becoming too general, I will remind the actor to go back to the "triggers" that will help him or her get possessed again.

Consider the exercise a success even if you experienced only a few seconds when you felt that you were taken over by another life. Once you know the experience of reacting spontaneously as another authentic human being, you can sort out the elements that worked for you and apply them more systematically the next time you practice the exercise.

You are likely to discover that you were more comfortable with some characters than others. Some people, for example, have trouble being assertive or expressing anger. Sometimes when they work on the irritable character, their own fears about anger conflict with their attempts to express the impulses rising up in them as the character. If you do experience a conflict between your own personality and the character's, you can overcome your fears and inhibitions by using some of the concentration and confidence-building techniques that I describe in my chapter, "Overcoming Stage Fright," in the first volume of *The Actor's Scenebook.*[6]

While some actors experience discomfort playing certain kinds of characters, others find it liberating to play a character who is very different from themselves; in the guise of the character they feel free to express passions that they ordinarily inhibit in life.

The last phase of the character exercise teaches the actor how to use incidents, relationships, and objects from his own life (I call them "personal stimuli") in combination with character work. Many actors use personal stimuli to arouse strong emotions in themselves and have done so throughout the history of theater. Perhaps the most powerful example of this process is the story of the ancient Greek actor Polus, who, when playing Electra's mourning scene over the ashes of her brother, carried onstage the urn and ashes of his own recently deceased child.[7] (Students who have a misconception of British acting technique are usually surprised when they learn that John Gielgud uses personal stimuli.)[8]

When playing a character, you can use personal stimuli, but your reactions should be expressed in a form appropriate for your character. Start by imagining yourself in an emotionally arousing situation, for example, talking with someone who makes you very angry. Express your feelings to that person. Use words or even gibberish (random sounds), or put the feeling into the words of a memorized monologue. After a few minutes "get possessed" by one of your characters and repeat the exercise, again expressing your anger. The emotional stimuli will come from your own experience, but its expression should now be the character's. Try this exercise with all five characters. The form of your anger should be different for each.

When using the process of character creation in a play, there will be times when you want to create a fairly close facsimile

---

[6]Michael Schulman and Eva Mekler, eds., *The Actor's Scenebook* (New York: Bantam Books, 1984).

[7]Aulus Gellius, "Attic Nights," in *Actors on Acting*, ed. by Toby Cole and Helen Krich Chinoy (New York: Crown, 1970), pp. 14–15.

[8]Funke and Booth, *op. cit.*, p. 26.

of your character model, incorporating all the details of the person's voice and movements, all of his or her mannerisms and gestures. To accomplish this you'll need to observe the person very carefully. (Don't confuse this process with what nightclub impersonators do; they are caricaturists and are only concerned with copying—and usually magnifying—the externals of a character, not the feelings and thoughts that lie behind a person's particular style of expression.) For some roles you will only want to incorporate a more global sense of your character model, such as aspects of temperament or just stance and stride, but not particular mannerisms. Sometimes you may wish to capture aspects of a model's voice such as its resonance or rhythm without incorporating the accent or melody. And sometimes you will want to combine elements from two or more character models. In his autobiography, Olivier notes that "by the alteration of one major characteristic, not hitherto associated with you, you can become another person with a different personality."[9]

The third ingredient for successful character acting is finding aspects of yourself that are similar to the character you are playing. Even when playing a character who experiences and expresses emotions very differently from the way you do, you can still draw on your own feelings and behavior. Your character may be easily aroused to violence while you may be a pacifist who tries to handle conflicts reasonably. Yet you will still have had strong feelings of anger and have imagined yourself engaging in acts that are far more aggressive than any you've actually carried out. Also, you can probably imagine circumstances in which you would act violently, even if just to protect yourself or someone else. By using situations from your own life that have angered you—both real and imagined—and incorporating them as personal stimuli into your onstage thoughts and images, and by allowing your body and voice to express the violent behavior that you have imagined yourself engaging in, you will be putting your personal experiences in the service of your character.

The lesson here is that you create convincing characters by

---

[9]Laurence Olivier, *Confessions of An Actor: An Autobiography* (New York: Simon and Schuster, 1982), p. 165.

combining a character model and appropriate aspects of yourself. Say you are playing someone who is more suave than you are, and you pick a suave character model. It will help if you also find the suave aspects of yourself. The suave person is comfortable in his environment; he knows the social rules and what to talk about and what words to use.

Now you may not be suave in the usual sense of the term, which generally refers to polished and polite behavior in sophisticated circles. But there may be environments where you do, in fact, display many of the essential ingredients—where you are comfortable, know the social rules, and make good conversation. Perhaps you experience all these elements when you are in a locker room. Even though your character's suavity is expressed in very different ways and in very different surroundings—in elegant salons and restaurants—you can use your own experiences (*in conjunction with your character model*) to help you achieve the proper behavior and feelings. A useful way to do this is to place onstage, via your imagination, objects from your own life that will help give you the proper reactions. For example, you might imagine a part of the locker room in a corner of the stage set, or a particular locker room buddy seated among the patrons of the elegant restaurant.

HOW DO YOU CHOOSE A CHARACTER MODEL FOR A ROLE YOU ARE PLAYING?

The playwright has given you the lines the character speaks and some of his or her actions. You must decide what kind of person would speak those lines and take those actions. Think of who you have known that might say and do the things your character says and does. Consider more than one person: different people will highlight different aspects of the character, and you may discover interesting facets of the person you are playing that you hadn't thought of before.

In a sense, you are casting the role with the people you have known in your life. When a director of a play or film casts a role and sees a lot of different actors, he or she usually comes up with a clearer idea of what the essential characteristics of that role are. The same thing will happen to you as you think about who you have known in your life who seems like the character in the play. All your years of observing people will now help you define who this person you are playing really is.

To illustrate, let's say you are playing Shakespeare's Coriolanus. Most actors simply play his haughtiness and disdain for the populace in a very general way, shouting from beginning to end, never revealing the human nature that lies behind all this anger (in a recent highly touted TV version from the BBC, the actor just brayed for three hours). But perhaps as you read the play you find yourself focusing on the side of Coriolanus's character that is extremely uncomfortable with being a public figure. In thinking about who you know that is uncomfortable like that, perhaps someone will come to mind. This will help you root the character in a real life. For instance, when I think of who I know that has that kind of discomfort someone comes to mind who is somewhat of a cross between Robert Stack (who played Eliot Ness in *The Untouchables* series) and Gary Cooper—a man whose system seems to recoil when he is the center of attention and who will rarely engage in any kind of superficial social exchanges. By having a specific character model, a whole personality begins to take shape. Then begin to explore what you, in your own life, have experienced that is similar to what you have chosen for your character (such as discomfort that you have felt when public attention is focused on you).

In searching for a character model you may find that someone you know has many of the characteristics that are perfect for the character, but others that don't fit—someone who perhaps has the temperamental aspects that seem right for Coriolanus, but who uses his body in ways that seem inappropriate for a great warrior. The solution is to combine elements from different models.

Thinking of a role in terms of actual people will ground you in the realities of the events your character goes through and help you define the psychological attributes that lie behind his or her actions. In his autobiography, Olivier describes Jed Harris (his character model for his Richard III) as sadistic, arrogant, and charming. Those characteristics are all evident in Olivier's Richard. Any actor playing Richard will play the sadistic and arrogant qualities. But it is the charming side of Olivier's Richard that makes his rendering so unique and fas-

:inating. That is the aspect that was brought to life by his
:hoice of Jed Harris as a character model.

One doesn't *always* need a specific character model to create a fully defined character. Many times as you read a script
a very specific life will emerge from the dialogue without any
:onscious effort on your part to define the character. You will
simply know intuitively how that person moves and talks and
feels. Sometimes you may realize that your intuition about this
:haracter comes from having known someone in your past
who is like the person the author has described. At other times
you won't have any idea where your sense of the character
:omes from. If, as you play the character, he or she feels like
a real person to you, then you may not have to use a specific
:haracter model at all.

Sometimes, though, a character can feel real, while in ac-
:uality you will be playing a "type" (for example, a "Southern belle" or a "tough guy") that is based on what you have
seen other actors do. It's a pretty good sign that you are playing a type and not a person when your emotional reactions are
missing their normal bodily component, as when you express
anger but don't experience the physiological sensations that
accompany real feelings of anger. If you find yourself playing
a type, it is time to do your character work in a more conscious
and systematic way.

Some teachers mistakenly refer to physical character work
as an "external" process, in contrast to the "internal" process
of working on a character's stimuli and motivation. But physical character work, properly done, does not only deal with
the externals of a character. One chooses the particular walk
or voice or facial features of a character only because one has
some sense of the character's inner life—of his or her temperament and needs and vulnerabilities—and because those
physical characteristics help one experience and reveal that
inner life more fully.

Creating a character takes a lot more thought than simply
playing one's personality. Finding just the right character to
fit what a playwright has written is no easy task. It is an act
of creativity. I have favorite personality actors and I see most
of what they do because I enjoy spending a few hours with
them and they always do a fine job. But I don't rush to see
their latest efforts with the same enthusiasm and excitement

as I do when one of my favorite character actors is in a new production or film. Then I rush to see the mind of an actor at work, trying to create a life that reveals what is essential about the particular human experience of a specific character.

CHARACTERS IN SHAKESPEARE AND OTHER PERIOD PLAYS

When creating a character for a period play, you will need to understand the behavioral conventions that prevailed at that period, or at least the conventions as they have been handed down to us through theatrical tradition. We can learn something about how people behaved in other periods from the painting and literature of the time, but to a large degree what is considered acceptable period playing is based on a tradition that is passed down from one generation of actors to the next.

Sometimes what is passed down goes through sizable changes from the original. For example, if you see films or hear tapes of Noël Coward's original productions, the actors—including Coward himself—were much more naturalistic and less eccentric than the performers you are likely to see in a current production of a Coward script. Today's Coward players work so hard trying to be ever and ever more arch, whereas the original players had an ease and effortlessness that bore a closer resemblance to actual human beings.

Similarly, many of Shaw's plays are about men pursuing women, and in his notes on directing, Shaw wrote that he wanted his actors to play his characters as real people ("[make] the audience believe that real things [are] happening to real people").[10] But in many contemporary productions of Shaw in both the U.S. and London, masculine sexuality is in short supply and the actors are working so hard at being eccentric Englishmen and -women that nothing Shaw would have recognized as a real person is to be seen. Here, too, if one watches some of the fine old film versions of Shaw plays, such as *Pygmalion* with Leslie Howard and *Major Barbara* with Wendy Hiller, one sees acting that is far less ornate than contemporary versions and much closer to what Shaw described.

Perhaps the greatest alterations from what appear to be the

---

[10]George Bernard Shaw, *The Art of Rehearsal* (New York: Samuel French, 1928), p. 5.

playwright's original intention are found in contemporary productions of Molière. Molière praised the actor who played "in the most natural manner he could," and he derided the use of artificial emphases for theatrical effect.[11] Yet it is rare to see characterizations that resemble human beings in Molière's plays. Unfortunately we have no films to show us what "natural" meant to Molière.

Regardless of the particular behavioral conventions you adopt to represent a period, and regardless of whether the author intended the play to be naturalistic (for its time) or stylized (as, say, Goethe did), you must still play your character's basic realities; that is, every character in every play in every period and style takes actions in pursuit of objectives and reacts to stimuli. And even in period plays you can still develop a character through observation. It is not hard to find characteristics in people you meet today that are useful for fleshing out characters from other periods.

Basing your character in a period play on a real person will help root the character's "period" behavior in a human reality. It's important to keep in mind that the behavioral conventions of any period have a psychological basis. For example, Restoration male characters walked and held their arms in distinctive ways, often with a hand held up. Many acting students feel awkward and artificial trying to use their bodies this way. The reason may be that the only reason they are usually given for why Restoration characters held their hands up was because they wore large shirt sleeves that would get soiled if they lowered their arms. This is nonsensical and totally useless to the actor. If you hold your arms up simply to keep your sleeves clean, rest assured that you will not look anything like a Restoration character.

No one in any period would let a fashion designer give him overflowing sleeves or any other uncomfortable clothing *unless* that style helped the person express something he or she wanted to express. The Restoration male held his hands and body in particular ways in order to express his virility and his elegance. He was a peacock and his flowing sleeves helped him convey that image. The only way an actor will impart the distinctive and unusual Restoration style of movement is by

---

[11]Cole and Chinoy, *op. cit.*, pp. 156–57.

playing the intentions that lay behind that style. Most actors today find it much easier to adopt the characteristic swagger of a ghetto youth, even though this walk is just as distinctive and unusual as the Restoration walk. But the contemporary actor is likely to understand, at least intuitively, what that walk is saying, that its message is, "I'm tough. I'm cool. I know my way around." By playing that message, the walk makes sense.

One of the problems in developing characters for Shakespeare's plays is that it is hard to locate his characters in a particular period and place. Many other English "period" playwrights wrote about their own times, often satirizing the style and manners of their contemporaries. So when we do their plays, we do our best to convey the behavior of those times. But none of Shakespeare's plays takes place in Elizabethan England and none are primarily social satires. So when an actor plays Mercutio in *Romeo and Juliet*, does he play him as a fourteenth century Veronese, a seventeenth century Elizabethan, or as a modern young man? There are no right or wrong answers. Audiences would be startled to hear Mercutio's lines spoken with a modern Brooklyn dialect, but perhaps less because of the particular speech sounds than because one doesn't associate the brilliance and complexity of Mercutio's words with a youth who speaks in a typical Brooklyn dialect.

Most contemporary American actors use a "standard" American dialect when playing Shakespeare, except when portraying his rustics and certain other regional characters. For these they use one or another British regional dialect. There is a danger in using a "standard" dialect, whether it is standard American or English: you may sound like everybody else, with no individuality to your voice. In most Shakespeare productions the stars (Laurence Olivier, John Gielgud, Derek Jacobi, Ralph Richardson, Richard Burton) all have very distinctive speaking styles. The rustics and regional characters, like the gravedigger in *Hamlet*, speak with various regional dialects. And then there are the assortment of dukes, messengers, and courtiers who all sound alike, fresh from their voice and speech classes. Even worse, they often all behave alike too, adopting a kind of "standard" Shakespearean demeanor—which "neither having the accent of Christians nor the gait of Christian, pagan, nor man" would not likely have pleased the author. Even when using a standard American or English dialect, you should give your characters their own personal voices and their own distinctive *human* qualities.

Some of our finest Shakespearean actors, like Richard Burton, pretty much play their own personalities from role to role. Others, like Olivier, apply their process of characterization to Shakespeare's characters just as they do when playing any other characters. They look for the unique physical, vocal, and temperamental attributes of the life they are creating. Some actors may be so appealing as personalities that audiences forgive the fact that their Hamlet, Macbeth, and Benedick are identical, but most actors are not that compelling. A couple of years ago I rushed with great enthusiasm to Stratford, England, to see a production of *Macbeth* starring an actor I'd seen in the Royal Shakespeare Company's *Nicholas Nickleby*. In *Nicholas* he played two characters that were so distinctive that most members of the audience didn't realize they were played by the same man. Both performances were brilliant.

But it was apparent that this actor had not used the same process of characterization for his Macbeth (perhaps because he did not have the precision and clarity of Dickens's character descriptions to guide him). Unfortunately his Macbeth had not been formed into a particular person with a distinctive manner and temperament. He played the *moments* that Macbeth lives through, but not the *life* that lives those moments in a particular way. This is a common problem in Shakespearean productions, even with fine actors.

When I say look for the unique attributes of your character, I don't mean that there is any single correct solution to this search—and don't believe any teachers who say otherwise, no matter how distinguished their credentials or authoritative their tone. There is no one correct way to play a Shakespearean character or to speak his or her lines. If you see both Laurence Olivier's and Orson Welles's film versions of *Othello* you will get a wonderful demonstration of how differently Shakespeare's characters can be played. Olivier's Othello is a powerful, confident, and warm "negro." When he finally succumbs to suspicion—after some resistance—it is like a giant oak falling. Welles's Othello is more "Moorish" in physiognomy and more mistrusting from the start. He is a man who knew all the time that he should never have trusted any of these Venetians. But he let his guard down with Desdemona and when he believes she has betrayed him, it confirms his worst fears. Virtually every line in the play is spoken differently by these two actors.

When creating a Shakespearean character, use all the same basic acting elements that you would use for any character, such as objectives, obstacles, and imagery (see my chapter "How to Approach a Scene," for a discussion of these).[12] But also pay attention to physical behavior and language in a more systematic way than you usually need to in contemporary plays. We know how people behave in the kitchens and living rooms in which today's authors place their characters. But how does one behave in a castle?

One of the great challenges in playing Shakespeare is to find behavior that illuminates the actions and personalities in the play. On one side one can err by overwhelming the events of the play with a flood of mundane behavior that may be authentic but is totally extraneous to the scene as written (and tends to make productions intolerably long). On the other side, in many productions the actors just rush on, take their positions, and recite their lines. The goal is to find actions that clarify the human events of the play. In *Richard II*, Bolingbroke launches a rebellion against Richard while the king is in Ireland. In "a camp in Wales" the Welsh Captain tells a duke who is still aligned with Richard that he and his army will not wait any longer for Richard to return to lead them against Bolingbroke:

> My Lord of Salisbury, we have stay'd ten days,
> And hardly kept our countrymen together,
> And yet we hear no tidings from the king;
> Therefore we will disperse ourselves: farewell.
>
> (Act II, iv, 1–4)

How might the actor playing the captain convey why he is leaving? What does waiting in the field for ten days actually mean to him and his men? If, before he speaks, the captain—

---

[12]Michael Schulman, "How to Approach a Scene" in *Contemporary Scenes for Student Actors*, ed. by Michael Schulman and Eva Mekler (New York: Penguin, 1980).

seated perhaps with his shirt open—makes some gesture indicating heat, then swats a mosquito on his forehead, and finally reaches for a water skin and finds it empty, the audience will get a sense of what the waiting has come to. Then if he says his lines as he rises and gathers his belongings to leave, they will understand his motivation more fully than if the actor simply enters and says his lines.

The best way to deal with Shakespeare's language is not through any external devices, but by realizing that the language is *intrinsic* to the character you are playing. You need to create a life that is totally at home with the words you speak. Shakespeare's plays are stylized. His characters have real feelings and desires, but do not express them in naturalistic ways. You must accept that you are playing people who express their passions in language that has a richness far beyond ordinary speech. They are clearer about their feelings and describe them in more detail than people in everyday life. To "own" the language, your characters need to experience that clarity. And if your characters say things that are brilliant and perceptive, then, as in any play, they must be played as people who have the intelligence that allows them to make those statements.

I have seen a number of fine American actors (and recently some English ones too) fall on their faces when doing Shakespeare by trying to make their characters sound "natural," like ordinary people. In so doing they produce a totally unnatural effect. They are so afraid to sound artificial that they overly constrict the melody of their voices and stress virtually no words or phrases. They are so busy trying not to sound phony that they forget to apply their basic acting craft to the role. They forget that a particular image or stimulus *does* make one stress or isolate particular words. And they forget that we use words as actions and in so doing we (even we moderns) use emphasis, melody, pauses, and all sorts of vocal dynamics.

Richard II says, "What must the king do now? Must he submit?" If, in playing Richard, the actor experiences shame or disbelief at hearing himself use the word "submit," perhaps wanting to take the word back as it is spoken, then the actor should convey that experience by how he speaks that word. If, however, he is preoccupied with how Shakespeare's words should be spoken (Do they sound natural enough? Do they sound "Shakespearean" enough?), then he will never engage his acting process fully enough to discover and experience his Richard's particular relationship to the word "submit."

Whether you are playing in a Shakespeare play or any other play, never ask yourself how to say the words. In life, how our words come out depends on what we are reacting to and why we are saying them. The same principle should hold in theater. Focusing on trying to speak "naturally" is as useful to an actor as focusing on trying to walk "naturally." Both are guaranteed to produce artificial behavior.

Benedick, in a soliloquy in *Much Ado About Nothing*, says,

> I do much wonder that one man, seeing how much another man is a fool when he dedicates his behaviors to love, will, after he hath laughed at such shallow follies in others, become the argument of his own scorn by falling in love: and such a man is Claudio.

> (Act II, iii, 7–12)

The only *natural* way to speak these nested clauses with clarity is by isolating each clause through melody, emphasis, and pauses. An actor who, in the hope of sounding natural, runs the phrases together will sound highly unnatural. He won't sound as if he owns the character's speech and thoughts, and no one will know what he is talking about.

Moreover, if the actor playing Benedick actually remembers Claudio laughing in mockery at another companion who had fallen in love, then when he gets to the word "laughed" the actor will do something specific with it, or, to put it more correctly, the image of Claudio laughing will do something to the actor's voice (and body) as he speaks that part of the speech.

In addition, *all* of Benedick's words must reflect the particular motivation that lies behind his criticism of Claudio. In other words, an actor plays an *event*, not words or lines. Perhaps right now Benedick is feeling especially irritated as he speaks because he's lost his last pal and must spend his afternoons alone (he's just sent for a book to read in his garden—not the most exciting afternoon's activity for a man of action).

If that's what the actor chooses to play, then all his words must reflect this condition.

Shakespearean and other stylized plays often call for a character to speak directly to the audience. Many actors find this difficult, primarily because they don't establish a relationship to the audience. Perhaps they have had a teacher who advised them to speak to the exit sign or doorway or some other spot that has nothing to do with their character's life. If you address the audience, establish what your relationship is to them and what you want from them, just as you would for anyone else your character speaks to. In other words, you must know why you are speaking to them. Do you need their support or want to justify your behavior to them? Do you want to charm them or perhaps teach them something? Do they start out on your side, or do you have to win them over?

Talk *to* them, not just toward them. Even if the stage lights prevent you from seeing their faces, you must sense their reactions to what you are saying.

Olivier's film of *Richard III* provides an extraordinary example of an actor thoroughly defining his character's relationship to the audience. His Richard makes us his confidants. He mocks the gullibility of the other characters to us, as if he is baiting them for our entertainment. He lets us know he has exciting plans and that if we stick with him we will have an exciting time. At times he frightens us, perhaps to let us experience directly what we are about to witness him doing to others. That he manages to create this level of intimacy with an audience *in a film* is quite an achievement.

Sometimes it is obvious that a monologue is intended to be directed to the audience, as in the opening speech of *Richard III* ("Now is the winter of our discontent . . ."). Sometimes you will have a choice as to whether to direct a monologue to the audience or speak it as a private airing of your thoughts. Some soliloquies, such as Hamlet's "To be, or not to be" speech, can be spoken all to oneself, all to the audience, or a combination of both.

If you decide that a soliloquy is private, create your environment very fully and include the fourth wall between you and the audience. If your character truly inhabits an environment while speaking his or her innermost thoughts, there is a good chance that interesting behavior will emerge from you quite spontaneously. I once saw an actor produce a marvelous effect by shrinking back toward a wall as he began to speak a soliloquy. Although he spoke only for himself, he was so troubled by where his thoughts were leading him that it appeared as if he wished to find a crevice in the wall in which to hide. Without a clear sense of his environment the actor could not have come upon this interesting physical expression of his feelings.

Some Shakespeare teachers will consider my next point heretical: Do not pay any attention to the iambic pentameter. When we read any other poet, there is no footnote to tell us what meter to use. If we read the lines sensibly, the meter is there automatically. Only with Shakespeare are we supposed to do something special with the meter. It makes no sense and it stifles the actor. Many of Shakespeare's lines break the iambic pentameter. How do we know which lines keep the meter and which break it? Simply by speaking them sensibly. Nothing else need be done.

You will hear some teachers say that by scanning the meter, special meanings that Shakespeare intended are revealed. I've heard many of their examples and found that the "hidden" meanings were usually obvious, without any special attention to the meter, or that they had come up with some bizarre interpretations that made no sense in the context of the play. Normal English speech is, on average, stressed on every other syllable; that is, it naturally falls into an iambic pattern. So, when playing Shakespeare, if you make sense of what your character is saying, you will have no trouble with the meter and will be speaking in a rhythm quite close to your natural speech.

I've also heard teachers tell students that in Shakespeare emotions are conveyed by long vowels and intellectual ideas by consonants, and they have their students stretch the vowels during emotional moments and smash the consonants when conveying ideas. This leads to highly artificial playing and puts the actor's focus in precisely the wrong place—on how the lines should sound. Even if the formula about vowels and consonants made sense (and I don't believe it does), if your emotions are properly aroused and authentic and you are expressing your character's ideas for a purpose, then your voice will handle the vowels and consonants appropriately.

As you study a Shakespeare part, you'll find that your character's experiences won't divide neatly into such discrete entities as the "emotional" and the "intellectual." People are emotional about ideas and have ideas while in the throes of emotion. Besides, one can find endless counter-examples to the formula, such as the line from *Richard II* quoted above: "What must the king do now? Must he submit?" These words are said at a highly emotional moment yet are filled with short vowels and strong consonants.

Every so often I come across an actor who refuses to experience real feelings while doing Shakespeare. "What, cry during a Shakespeare speech? That ruins the poetry!" is their attitude. Sometimes merely letting them listen to John Gielgud's highly poetic, tear-filled, and exquisite rendering of Richard II's soliloquies from his *Ages of Man* production is enough to change their minds. Shakespeare himself had something to say on the subject of real emotions in acting. Hamlet refers to the high esteem in which the players who come to Elsinore are held and he immediately asks to hear a favorite speech that he has heard the First Player do before. The player's eyes fill with tears as he delivers the speech. As Polonius puts it, "Look, whether he has not turned his color and has tears in's eyes." This upsets Polonius who Hamlet has mocked as "for a jig or a tale of bawdry, or he sleeps."

Polonius stops the speech, but Hamlet is impressed and says " 'Tis well; I'll have thee speak out the rest of this soon." Later Hamlet will puzzle over the actor's ability to arouse real emotions in himself. Assuming that Hamlet was speaking for Shakespeare, we have a good idea of the kind of "organic," emotional acting that Shakespeare wanted for his plays.

Another caution: Be wary of what nowadays passes for what the English call "text analysis." Too often a teacher or director will go through the text of a Shakespeare play making isolated associations to words and phrases. One teacher in a well-known academy insisted that a student play Hamlet's "O, what a rogue and peasant slave am I" soliloquy with a wry chuckle because the word "rogue," he said, connotes "a likeable though slightly naughty chap." His argument was that if

Hamlet has chosen that word then he must be giving himself a fairly lighthearted reprimand.

Of course the actor must decide why the character speaks precisely the words the playwright has given him. But the connotation of most words has a good deal of latitude and should be determined by the overall events that the character is experiencing. Given the moment in the play that Hamlet speaks that soliloquy, an actor could make a pretty good case for interpreting those lines as filled with self-loathing (besides, a "peasant slave" is a pretty severe condemnation).

A "good" example of the kind of harmful text analysis I am talking about was provided by the English actor Ian McKellen in a television presentation called *Ian McKellen Acting Shakespeare*. Phrase by phrase, McKellen went through Macbeth's speech that begins:

> Tomorrow, and tomorrow, and tomorrow,
> Creeps in this petty pace from day to day,
> To the last syllable of recorded time . . .
>
> (Act V, v, 19–21)

For each phrase the actor had a specific association that led to a particular reading. Some of the associations led to odd deliveries (particularly, his idiot-like intonation of the phrases following "It is a tale told by an idiot") that, I believe, would not have been understood by an audience that didn't have the actor's running commentary as a guide to his substitutions. Not one of the actor's associations had anything to do with the context of that moment in the life of Macbeth. The speech comes right after Macbeth learns that his wife has died. McKellen's phrase by phrase substitutions did not deal with that fact at all. Surely it should have some bearing on how this speech comes out.

By doing this kind of text analysis you will find that all you are playing is a series of disconnected ideas based on your personal associations to Shakespeare's lines. You certainly won't find it any easier to play these associations than to play what the lines mean in the context of the character's life. When the great British actors of an earlier generation discussed their approaches to Shakespeare, they didn't talk about anything resembling this kind of text analysis.

For example, when Olivier described his approach to playing Macbeth, he mentioned that a key choice for him was that from the moment Macbeth encounters the first witch he knows what will befall him,[13] and then finds himself powerless to alter his fate, though he continues to try. This kind of choice provides an overall context for the events of the play, and every line is affected by it. No line should find its meaning through isolated and arbitrary associations.

In playing plays from other periods it is useful to research the period, to read about it in histories and novels, to look at paintings and sculpture of the time, and to familiarize yourself with the clothes, furnishings, and artifacts of the time. But don't let what you read lead you to distort what the playwright has written. Shakespeare was a sixteenth century Englishman, and his Joan of Arc (LaPucelle in *Henry VI—Part 1*) is a vicious young woman. It would violate his writing to turn her into the saintly heroine depicted by modern writers. Similarly, contemporary historians view Richard III in a much more flattering way than Shakespeare did. If you are doing his play, do *his* Richard. Otherwise, the dialogue will make no sense.

Sometimes academicians get caught up in historical details that have little bearing on an audience's response to a play. One expert argued that Hamlet should always wear a hat because a young man in his day would never have appeared in court hatless; indeed Ophelia even describes her fright when Hamlet came into her chamber with disheveled clothes and "no hat upon his head." Contemporary audiences don't know these kinds of details. For centuries audiences have gone to Shakespeare plays for the power of his imagination, for his language, and for his insight into what is universal about mankind. It is questionable that complete faithfulness to historical details adds to the experience of a contemporary audience.

Remember, remember, remember: There is no one correct way to say a Shakespeare line. I come back to this because I have seen so many Shakespeare teachers force readings on their students. When Hamlet says, "Now I am alone," he might mean, "Now I am *finally* alone," if he had been impatient for the players to leave so he could vent his rage at

---

[13]Burton, *op. cit.*, p. 21.

himself. On the other hand, he might mean, "Oh God, I'm left alone now," if he had been enjoying himself with the players, but then found himself thrust back into his agony as soon as they left. Each of these interpretations (and these are only two out of many possible ones) will lead to very different deliveries.

It is a useful classroom exercise to give students this single line to act and to ask each student to work out a context that motivates Hamlet to speak it. Each context should produce its own particular rendering.

SCENES FOR ONE MAN
AND ONE WOMAN

THE DINING ROOM

by A.R. Gurney

ACT II

This play consists of a number of intense, short scenes connected only by the fact that they take place in the dining room of a well-to-do family (the characters and families change from scene to scene). As a collection these scenes illuminate both the comic and tragic aspects of the "traditional" American family. In the following exchange, Jim's daughter ("about thirty") has returned home with her children and a lot on her mind. She corrals her father in the dining room, imploring him to pay some attention to her.

....

(An Older Man, called JIM, *comes in from the hall, followed by his daughter,* MEG. *He is in his late sixties, she is about thirty.)*

MEG: Where are you going now, Daddy?

JIM: I think your mother might want a drink.

MEG: She's reading to the children.

JIM: That's why she might want one.

MEG: She wants no such thing, Dad.

JIM: Then I want one.

MEG: Now? It's not even five.

JIM: Well then let's go see how the Red Sox are doing. (*He starts back out, R.*)

MEG: Daddy, *stop!*

JIM: Stop what?

MEG: Avoiding me. Ever since I arrived, we haven't been able to talk.

JIM: Good Lord, what do you mean? Seems to me everybody's been talking continuously and simultaneously from the moment you got off the plane.

MEG: Alone, Daddy. I mean *alone*. And you *know* I mean alone.

JIM: All right. We'll talk. (*Sits down.*) Right here in the dining room. Good place to talk. Why not? Matter of fact, I'm kind of tired. It's been a long day.

MEG: I love this room. I've always loved it. Always.

JIM: Your mother and I still use it. Now and then. Once a week. Mrs. Robinson still comes in and cooks us a nice dinner and we have it in here. Still. Lamb chops. Broilers—

MEG: (*Suddenly.*) I've left him, Daddy.

JIM: Oh well now, a little vacation . . .

MEG: I've left him permanently.

JIM: Yes, well, permanently is a very long word . . .

MEG: I can't live with him, Dad. We don't get along at all.

JIM: Oh well, you may think that now . . .

MEG: Could we live here, Dad?

JIM: Here?

MEG: For a few months.

JIM: With three small children?

MEG: While I work out my life. (*Pause. JIM takes out a pocket watch and looks at it.*)

JIM: What time is it? A little after five. I think the sun is over the yardarm, don't you? Or if it isn't, it should be. I think it's almost permissible for you and me to have a little drink, Meg.

MEG: Can we stay here, Dad?

JIM: Make us a drink, Meggie.

MEG: All right. (*She goes into the kitchen; the door, of course, remains open.*)

JIM: (*Calling to her.*) I'd like Scotch, sweetheart. Make it reasonably strong. You'll find the silver measuring gizmo in the drawer by the trays. I want two shots and a splash of water. And I like to use that big glass with the pheasant on it. And not too much ice. (*He gets up and moves around the table.*)

MEG'S VOICE: (*Within.*) All right.

JIM: I saw Mimi Mott the other day . . . Can you hear me?

MEG'S VOICE: (*Within.*) I can hear you, Dad.

JIM: There she was, being a very good sport with her third husband. Her third. Who's deaf as a post and extremely disagreeable. So I took her aside—can you hear me?

MEG'S VOICE: (*Within.*) I'm listening, Dad.

JIM: I took her aside, and I said, "Now Mimi, tell me the truth. If you had made half as much effort with your first husband as you've made with the last two, don't you think you'd still be married to him?" I asked her that. Point blank. And you know what Mimi said? She said, "Maybe." That's exactly what she said. "Maybe." If she had made the effort. (*MEG returns with two glasses. She gives one to JIM.*)

MEG: That's your generation, Dad.

JIM: That's every generation.

MEG: It's not mine.

JIM: Every generation has to make an effort.

MEG: I won't go back to him, Dad. I want to be here.

JIM: (*Looking at his glass.*) I wanted the glass with the pheasant on it.

MEG: I think the kids used it.

JIM: Oh. (*Pause. He drinks, moves away from her.*)

MEG: So can we stay, Dad?

JIM: I sleep in your room now. Your mother kicked me out because I snore. And we use the boys' room now to watch TV.

MEG: I'll use the guest room.

JIM: And the children?

MEG: They can sleep on the third floor. In the maid's rooms.

JIM: We closed them off. Because of the oil bills.

MEG: I don't care, Dad. We'll work it out. Please. (*Pause. He sits down at the other end of the table.*)

JIM: Give it another try first.

MEG: No.

JIM: Another try.

MEG: He's got someone else now, Dad. She's living there right now. She's moved in.

JIM: Then fly back and kick her out.

MEG: Oh, Dad . . .

JIM: I'm serious. You don't know this, but that's what your mother did. One time I became romantically involved with

Mrs. Shoemaker. We took a little trip together. To Sea Island. Your mother got wind of it, and came right down, and told Betty Shoemaker to get on the next train. That's all there was to it. Now why don't you do that? Go tell this woman to peddle her papers elsewhere. We'll sit with the children while you do.

MEG: I've got someone too, Dad. (*Pause.*)

JIM: You mean you've had a little fling.

MEG: I've been going with someone.

JIM: A little fling.

MEG: I've been living with him.

JIM: Where was your husband?

MEG: He stayed with his girl.

JIM: And your children?

MEG: Oh they . . . came and went.

JIM: It sounds a little . . . complicated.

MEG: It is, Dad. That's why I needed to come home. (*Pause. He drinks.*)

JIM: Now let's review the bidding, may we? Do you plan to marry this new man?

MEG: No.

JIM: You're not in love with him?

MEG: No. He's already married, anyway.

JIM: And he's decided he loves his wife.

MEG: No.

JIM: But you've decided you don't love him.

MEG: Yes.

JIM: Or your husband.

MEG: Yes.

JIM: And your husband's fallen in love with someone else.

MEG: He lives with someone else.

JIM: And your children . . . my grandchildren . . . come and go among these various households.

MEG: Yes. Sort of. Yes.

JIM: Sounds extremely complicated.

MEG: It is, Dad. It really is. (*Pause. He drinks, thinks, gets up, paces.*)

JIM: Well then it seems to me the first thing you do is simplify things. That's the first thing. You ask the man you're living with to leave, you sue your husband for divorce, you hold onto your house, you keep the children in their present schools, you—

MEG: There's someone else, Dad. (*Pause.*)

JIM: Someone else?

MEG: Someone else entirely.

JIM: A third person.

MEG: Yes.

JIM: What was that movie your mother and I liked so much? *The Third Man*? (*He sits, D.L.*)

MEG: It's not a man, Dad. (*Pause.*)

JIM: Not a man.

MEG: It's a woman.

JIM: A woman.

MEG: I've been involved with a woman, Dad, but it's not working, and I don't know who I am, and I've got to touch *base*, Daddy. I want to be here. (*She kneels at his feet. Pause. JIM gets slowly to his feet. He points to his glass.*)

JIM: I think I'll get a repair. Would you like a repair? I'll take your glass. I'll get us both repairs. (*He takes her glass and goes out to the kitchen, leaving the door open.*)

MEG: (*Moving around the dining room.*) I'm all mixed up, Dad. I'm all over the ball park. I've been seeing a Crisis Counselor, and I've taken a part-time job, and I've been jogging two miles a day, and none of it's working, Dad. I want to come home. I want to take my children to the Zoo, and the Park Lake, and the Art Gallery, and do all those things you and Mother used to do with all of us. I want to start again, Dad. I want to start all over again. (*JIM comes out from the kitchen, now carrying three glasses.*)

JIM: I made one for your mother. And I found the glass with the pheasant on it. In the trash. Somebody broke it. (*He crosses for the doorway, R.*) So let's have a nice cocktail with your mother, and see if we can get the children to sit quietly while we do.

MEG: You don't want us here, do you, Dad?

JIM: (*Stopping.*) Of course we do, darling. A week, ten days. You're most welcome.

MEG: (*Desperately.*) I can't go back, Dad!

JIM: (*Quietly.*) Neither can I, sweetheart. Neither can I. (*He shuffles on out. MEG stands for a moment in the dining room, then hurries out after him.*)

A MONTH IN THE COUNTRY
by IVAN TURGENEV

translated by Richard Freeborn

ACT IV

*It is the 1840s in Russia on the country estate of Arkady
Sergeich Islaev. His wife Natalya Petrovna, bored with her
idle life, has fallen in love with her son's tutor, Aleksei
Nikolaich Belyaev, a poor student. She has tried to suppress
her passion but her seventeen-year-old ward, Verochka
(Vera), who also loves Belyaev, has become aware of Na-
talya Petrovna's feelings. Vera told Belyaev of her suspi-
cions but he didn't believe her, instead believing that
Natalya Petrovna is upset with him for leading Vera on. In
the scene that follows, Vera has just confronted Natalya
Petrovna with her suspicions about her feelings for
Belyaev, and has run off in tears. Belyaev, who had drifted
off to let the two women talk privately, approaches Natalya
Petrovna.*

....

BELYAEV: (*Approaching* NATALYA PETROVNA.) I can assure
you, Natalya Petrovna . . .

NATALYA PETROVNA: (*Staring motionlessly at the floor and
stretching a hand out in his direction.*) Stop, Aleksei Nikolaich. It's true. Vera's right, it's time . . . it's time for me
to stop pretending. I'm guilty before her, before you—and
you have every right to despise me. (BELYAEV *makes an
involuntary gesture.*) I've debased myself in my own eyes.
I've only got one way of earning your respect again—to be
frank, completely frank, no matter what the consequences

are. In any case, I am seeing you for the last time and I am speaking to you for the last time. I *am* in love with you. (*She still does not look at him.*)

BELYAEV: You, Natalya Petrovna!

NATALYA PETROVNA: Yes, me. I *am* in love with you. Vera wasn't mistaken and didn't mislead you. I fell in love with you the day you arrived, but I didn't admit it to myself until yesterday. I have no intention of justifying my conduct . . . It was unworthy of me. But at least now you can understand and forgive. Yes, I was jealous of Vera. Yes, I thought of marrying her off to Bolshintsov, so as to put her out of reach of me and you. Yes, I made use of my superiority in age and position to worm her secret out of her and, of course, I hadn't expected it and I gave myself away. I *am* in love with you, Belyaev. But you must realize it's only pride that makes me admit it . . . The comedy I've been playing out until now has finally disgusted me. You can't stay here any longer . . . However, after what I've just said to you, you'll probably feel extremely embarrassed in my presence and will want to leave as soon as possible. I'm certain about that. This certainty has given me courage. I confess I wouldn't want you to take away with you unpleasant memories of me. You know everything now . . . Perhaps I spoiled things for you, perhaps if this hadn't happened you'd have fallen in love with Verochka . . . I've only got one excuse, Aleksei Nikolaich: it was all beyond my control.

(*She falls silent. She has said all this in a fairly level and calm voice, without looking at* BELYAEV. *He has said nothing. She continues with a certain excitement, still not looking at him.*)

Can't you say something? Still, I understand. There's nothing left for you to say. The position of someone who is not in love and has a confession of love made to him is altogether too painful. I thank you for your silence. Believe me, when I said I was in love with you I wasn't pretending . . . as I had been. I wasn't counting on anything. On the contrary, I wanted to tear from myself the mask which, I can assure you, I'd never got used to . . . And anyhow there's no point in putting on a great show when everything's out in the open. What's the point of pretending when there's no one there to be fooled? Everything's now over between us. I won't keep you any longer. You can go away from here without saying a word to me, without even saying goodbye. I not only won't consider that impolite, on the contrary I'll be grateful to you. There are times when delicacy is inappropriate—even worse than rudeness. Evidently we weren't intended to get to know one another. Goodbye. Yes, we weren't intended to get to know one another . . . But at least I hope that I've now ceased to be in your eyes the oppressive, secretive and sly creature I was . . . Goodbye, for ever. (*BELYAEV, in his excitement, tries to say something and cannot.*) Why aren't you going?

BELYAEV: (*Bows, makes as if to go and after a certain struggle with himself returns.*) No, I can't go . . . (*NATALYA PETROVNA looks at him for the first time.*) I can't go just like this! Look, Natalya Petrovna, you've just told me . . . you wouldn't want me to take away with me unpleasant memories of you, but I also wouldn't want you to remember me as a man who . . . My God, I don't know how to put it! . . . Natalya Petrovna, forgive me, I don't know how to talk to ladies. Until now I've only known . . . a completely different sort of woman. You say we weren't intended to get to know one another, but, I ask you, could I, a simple, almost uneducated boy, even so much as think of having a relationship with you? Think who you are and who I am! Think a moment, could I dare to imagine me . . . and someone with your background? I mean background, so just look at me— this old coat of mine and your perfumed dresses! I ask you! Yes, of course I was frightened of you and I'm frightened now! Without any exaggeration I looked up to you as a higher being and now you say . . . you say you're in love with me, you, Natalya Petrovna, in love with *me*! I feel my heart beating inside me as it's never beaten before in my entire life and it's not just out of astonishment, it's not that I'm flattered—it's got nothing to do with feeling like that! But I can't just go! It doesn't matter what you say!

NATALYA PETROVNA: (*After a pause, as if to herself.*) My God, what have I done!

BELYAEV: Natalya Petrovna, in God's name, believe me . . .

NATALYA PETROVNA: (*In a changed voice.*) Aleksei Nikolaich, if I didn't know you were a man of honour, someone devoid of falsehood, I could have God knows what thoughts now! Perhaps I would regret my frankness. But I believe you. I don't want to hide my feelings from you and I tell you I am grateful to you for what you've just said. I know now why we didn't become friends . . . It wasn't anything about me personally that put you off, it was only my position . . . (*Stops.*) All's for the best, of course, but it'll be easier now for me to say goodbye . . . Goodbye. (*Is on the point of leaving.*)

BELYAEV: (*After a pause.*) Natalya Petrovna, I know I can't stay here, but . . . but I can't tell you everything that's happening inside me. You're in love with me . . . it's terrible for me even to say the words, it's all so new to me! I think I'm seeing and hearing you for the very first time, but I feel only one thing—that I must go, I feel I can't be responsible for what may . . .

NATALYA PETROVNA: (*In a weak voice.*) Yes, Belyaev, you must go. Now, after being so frank, you can go . . . I mean, despite everything I've done, maybe it could be possible . . . Oh, believe me, if I could only have had an inkling of everything you've just said, what I've confessed, Belyaev, would have died inside me . . . I simply wanted to put an end to any misunderstandings, I wanted to be penitent, to punish myself, I wanted to cut the final link at one stroke. If I'd had any idea . . . (*She covers her face.*)

BELYAEV: I believe you, Natalya Petrovna, I believe you. I myself, just a quarter of an hour ago—could I have imagined, after all . . . It was only today, during our meeting before lunch, that I felt for the first time something extraordinary, something unforeseen happening to me, like a hand squeezing my heart, and I grew all hot . . . Before that I'd really kept away from you, as I didn't even like you. But when you told me today that Vera Aleksandrovna didn't feel indifferent . . . (*Stops.*)

NATALYA PETROVNA: (*Smiling unwillingly despite herself.*) Enough's enough, Belyaev, we mustn't think about that. We mustn't forget that we're talking together for the last time . . . and that tomorrow you're leaving . . .

BELYAEV: Oh, yes, I'll be leaving tomorrow! Now I've still got the chance of going away . . . and all this'll be over!

You see I don't want to exaggerate—I'll be going, and that'll be that! I'll take away one memory, I'll remember for ever and ever that you were in love with me . . . How come I didn't know you till this moment? Look—look at me now! Could I really have tried to avoid looking at you? Could I really have been afraid of you?

NATALYA PETROVNA: (*With a smile.*) You've only just told me you were frightened of me.

BELYAEV: I have? (*A pause.*) True, I did . . . I'm astonished at myself. I mean, how can I dare to talk to you like this! I don't know what's happened to me.

NATALYA PETROVNA: Are you sure you don't?

BELYAEV: How do you mean?

NATALYA PETROVNA: That you and me . . . (*Shudders.*) Oh, God, what am I doing! Listen, Belyaev, please help me . . . No woman has ever found herself in a situation like this. I really can't stand it any longer! Perhaps it's a good thing it's being ended now once and for all, but at least we've got to know each other . . . Give me your hand—and let's say goodbye for ever.

BELYAEV: (*Taking her hand.*) Natalya Petrovna, I don't know what to say . . . my heart's so full . . . God grant you . . . (*Stops and presses her hand to his lips.*) Goodbye. (*Starts to exit through the garden door.*)

NATALYA PETROVNA: (*Watching him go.*) Belyaev . . .

BELYAEV: (*Turning round.*) Natalya Petrovna . . .

NATALYA PETROVNA: (*After a moment's silence, in a weak voice.*) Don't go . . .

BELYAEV: What?

NATALYA PETROVNA: Don't go! May God be our judge! (*She hides her head in her hands.*)

BELYAEV: (*Going quickly up to her and holding out his hands to her.*) Natalya Petrovna . . .

(*At that moment the garden door opens and* RAKITIN *appears.*)

THE FOURPOSTER

by Jan de Hartog

ACT II, SCENE 1

It is 1901 and Michael and Agnes (He and She in the script) have been married for eleven years. They have had a wonderful marriage, but now there are strains, serious strains. They are both feeling unappreciated. Michael has finally become a successful author, doted upon by admirers. And Agnes, who has been his muse and honest critic, is feeling pushed aside.

It is the evening in their bedroom, which has new furniture and amenities, and their fourposter bed is now "fitted out with new brocade curtains," reflecting the general improvement in their standard of living.

....

(AT RISE, there is no one in the room. SHE enters door Center and slams the door behind her. SHE stands at the foot of the bed, removing her evening gloves. Crosses up Right to dressing table, throws gloves on the table, crosses Left Center and is stopped by a KNOCK at the door. SHE stands Left Center for a moment. The KNOCK is repeated, more insistently.)

SHE: *(After a pause.)* Come in.

HE: *(Enters, closes door.)* Excuse me. *(Goes to the dressing room Left, gets his night clothes, re-enters and crosses to door up Center.)* Good night.

SHE: *(As HE opens door.)* You were the life and soul of the party this evening, with your interminable little stories.

HE: (*Starts out, stops, turns.*) My dear, if you don't enjoy playing second fiddle, I suggest you either quit the orchestra or form one of your own. (*Goes out and shuts door.*)

SHE: (*Mutters after a moment's stupefaction.*) Now, I've had enough! (*Runs to door, rips it open, stands in hallway and calls off.*) Michael! (*Then bellows.*) Michael! Come here! (*Re-enters, crosses Left Center, takes off evening wrap, throws it on bed.*)

HE: (*Pops in. At up Center. Has top hat and cane in hand and evening cape over arm.*) Have you taken leave of your senses? The servants?

SHE: (*At Left Center.*) I don't care if the whole town hears it. (*HE exits*) Come back, I say!

HE: (*Re-enters.*) All right. This situation is no longer bearable! (*Closes door.*)

SHE: What on earth is the matter with you?

HE: Now, let me tell you one thing, calmly. (*SHE crosses below him to dressing table up Right. Takes off plume, throws it on table.*) My greatest mistake has been to play up to you, plying you with presents—

SHE: I like that! (*Picks up gloves.*)

HE: Calmly! Do you know what I should have done? I should have packed you off to boarding school, big as you are, to learn deportment.

SHE: (*Turns to him.*) Deportment for what?

HE: (*Crossing down Center.*) To be worthy of me.

SHE: The pompous ass whose book sold three hundred thousand copies!

HE: That is entirely beside the point.

SHE: It is right to the point! (*Carrying gloves.*) Before you had written that cursed novel, the rest of the world helped me to keep you sane. (*HE crosses Left.*) Every time you had finished a book or a play or God knows what, and considered yourself to be the greatest genius since Shakespeare— (*HE says, "Now really!" HE puts cape, hat, gloves on wall chair Left.*) —I was frightened to death that it might turn out to be a success. (*SHE crosses to him.*) But, thank Heaven, it turned out to be such a thorough failure every time, that I won the battle with your megalomania. But now, now this book, the only book you ever confessed to be trash until you read the papers—oh, what's the use! (*Crosses down Right Center, rolls up gloves.*)

HE: My dear woman, I may be vain, but you are making a tragic mistake.

SHE: (*Crossing up Center. Laughs.*) Now listen! (*Laughs.*) Just listen to him! To be married to a man for eleven years, and then to be addressed like a public meeting. (*Throws gloves on dressing table.*) Tragic mistake! (*HE sits Left center. SHE crosses down to him.*) Can't you hear yourself, you poor darling idiot, that you've sold your soul to a sentimental novel?

HE: Agnes, are you going on like this, or must I—

SHE: Yes, yes, you must! You *shall* hear it. (*HE pounds floor with cane.*) And don't interrupt me! There is only one person in this world who loves you in spite of what you are, and let me tell you— (*SHE crosses Center.*)

HE: You are mistaken. There is a person in this world who loves me—because of what I am.

SHE: (*At Center.*) And what are you, my darling?

HE: Ask her.

SHE: Her—

HE: Yes.

SHE: Oh— (*Crosses up Center, holds onto bed post.*) Who is she?

HE: You don't know her.

SHE: Is she—young? (*Turns upstage.*) How young?

HE: No. (*Rises. Crossing Left. Picks up clothes.*) I'll be damned if I go on with this. You look like a corpse.

SHE: A corpse?

HE: (*Crossing up to arch.*) So pale, I mean. (*At door.*) Agnes, I'm not such a monster, that— (*Crossing down Center to her.*) Sit down. Please, Agnes, do sit— Agnes!

SHE: (*Turns away. Crossing down Left.*) No, no—it's nothing. I'm all right. What do you think? That I should faint in my thirty-first year because of something so—so ordinary?

HE: Ordinary?

SHE: With two children? I didn't faint when Robert had the mumps, did I?

HE: (*Crossing down Center.*) Don't you think this is a little different?

SHE: No, Michael. This belongs to the family medicine chest.

HE: I love her!

SHE: So, not me anymore? (*HE doesn't reply.*) I don't mean as a friend, or as—as the mother of your children, but as a wife? (*HE crosses down Right.*) You may tell me honestly, really. Is that why you've been sleeping in the study?

HE: (*At window Right.*) I haven't slept a wink.

SHE: (*At Left Center.*) I see. It must be Cook who snores.

HE: (*Turns to her.*) Since when do I snore?

SHE: Not you, dear, Cook. Every night when I went down the passage.

HE: (*Goes to the door, opens it.*) Good night!

SHE: (*At Left Center.*) Sleep well.

HE: (*Crossing down Center.*) What was that?

SHE: Sleep well.

HE: Oh— (*Stops at door, then slams it shut.*) No! (*Throws clothes down on sofa at foot of bed. Down Center.*) I'll be damned, I won't stand it!

SHE: What is the matter?

HE: Cook snores! Agnes, I love somebody else! It's driving me crazy! You, the children, she, the children, you—for three weeks I have lived through hell, and all you've got to say is "Cook snores!"

SHE: (*Steps toward him.*) But darling—

HE: (*Crossing below sofa down Right.*) No, no, no, no! You are so damned sure of yourself that it makes me sick! (*SHE crosses up Center facing bed.*) I know you don't take this seriously, but believe me, I love that woman! I must have that woman or I'll go mad! (*Crosses to above sofa.*)

SHE: (*Turns to him.*) Haven't you—had her yet?

HE: (*Crosses Center to her.*) At last! Thank God, a sign of life. (*SHE sits on sofa at foot of bed.*) Why haven't you looked at me like that before? I have begged, implored, crawled to you for a little understanding and warmth, and love, and got nothing. Even my book, that was written inspired by you, longing for you—right from the beginning you have seen it as a rival. (*Crossing down Left.*) Whatever I did, whatever I tried: a carriage, servants, money, dresses, paintings, everything—you hated that book. And now? (*Crossing up Left.*) Now you have driven me into somebody else's arms. Somebody else, who understands at least one thing clearly: that she will have to share me with my work. (*Above chair down Left.*)

SHE: Does she understand that she will have to share you with other women as well?

HE: She doesn't need to. At last I found a woman who'll live with my work, and a better guarantee of my faithfulness nobody could have. (*Crosses onto dais.*)

SHE: But how does she live with it? What does she do?

HE: She listens. (*Sits on bed.*) She encourages me—with a look, a touch, a—well, an encouragement. When I cheer, she cheers with me, when I meditate, she meditates with me—

SHE: And when you throw crockery, she throws crockery with you?

HE: (*Checks himself.*) Haven't you understood one single word of what I have been saying? Won't you, can't you see that I have changed?

SHE: No.

HE: (*Rises. Crossing up Right Center.*) Then you are blind, blind, blind! That's all I can say. At any rate, *you've* changed.

SHE: I!

HE: (*Crossing Right to above sofa.*) No, don't let's start that.

SHE: Go on.

HE: No, it's senseless. No reason to torture you any longer, once I have—

SHE: Once you have tasted blood?

HE: (*Crossing around sofa.*) Agnes, I'm sorry it was necessary for me to hurt you. It couldn't very well have been done otherwise. I'm at the mercy of a feeling stronger than I. (*Sits sofa.*)

SHE: Rotten, isn't it?

HE: Horrible.

SHE: And yet—at the same time not altogether.

HE: No. On the other hand, it's delicious.

SHE: The greatest thing a human being can experience.

HE: I'm glad you understand it so well.

SHE: Understand?—why, of course. It's human, isn't it?

HE: How do you come to know that?

SHE: What?

HE: That it's—human?

SHE: Well, I'm a human being, aren't I?

HE: Agnes, I never heard you talk like this before. What's the matter with you?

SHE: Well, I might have my experience too, mightn't I? (*Rises. Crossing onto dais, picks up clock from bed-table.*) Goodnight!

HE: (*Rises. Crossing to foot of bed.*) Just a minute! I want to hear a little more about this.

SHE: But I know it now, dear.

HE: Yes, you do! But I don't! What sort of experiences are you referring to?

SHE: (*Crossing to him. Puts clock on tabouret.*) Now listen, my little friend! You have dismissed me without notice, and I haven't complained once as any other housekeeper would have done. I have accepted the facts, because I know a human being is at the mercy of this feeling, however horrible and at the same time delicious it may be.

HE: (*At up Center.*) Agnes!

SHE: (*On dais.*) I really don't understand you. I am not thwarting you in the least, and instead of your going away happily and relieved that you are not going to leave a help-less wreck behind—

HE: (*Crossing up to arch.*) You might answer just one plain question before—we finish this business. Have you—aren't you going to be alone, if I leave you?

SHE: Alone? I've got the children, haven't I?

HE: (*Crossing down Center.*) That's not at all certain.

SHE: (*After a shaky silence.*) You had better leave this room very quickly now, before you get to know a side of me that might surprise you a lot.

HE: (*Crossing to her.*) I have, I'm afraid. I demand an answer. Have you a lover?

SHE: (*Goes to door, opens it. Stands down Right of door.*) Good night.

HE: For eleven long years I have believed in you! (*Crossing to her.*) You were the purest, the noblest thing in my life!

SHE: (*Interrupting, and with him.*)—the noblest thing in my life! Good night!

HE: If you don't answer my question, you'll never see me again.

SHE: Get out of here.

HE: (*Sits sofa at foot of bed.*) No.

SHE: All right. (*Crossing onto dais.*) Then there's only one thing left to be done. (*SHE picks up wrap from bed and exists into dressing room Left.*)

HE: What? What did you want to say? (*SHE does not answer. SHE returns with second wrap and overnight case; puts them both on chair down Left and opens case.*) What's the meaning of that? (*SHE goes on, crosses onto dais, picks up nightgown and negligee. Crosses down Left, packs them in case.*) Darling, believe me, I won't blame you for anything, only tell me— (*Rises, stands Left Center.*)—where are you going?

SHE: (*Crossing up Right to dressing table and getting brushes and comb.*) Would you mind calling a cab for me?

HE: (*Turning to her.*) Agnes!

SHE: (*Crossing down Left packs brushes and comb in case.*) Please, Michael, I can't arrive there too late. It is such an embarrassing time already. Pass me my alarm clock, will you?

HE: No, I can't have been mistaken about you that much! Only yesterday you said that I had qualities—

SHE: Excuse me. (*Passes him, gets her alarm clock from the tabouret. Crosses down Left, puts clock in case.*)

HE: (*Wants to stop her when she passes, but checks himself.*) All right. It is a solution, anyhow.

SHE: (*Closes overnight case, picks it up, puts wrap over arm, crosses Left around chair to him and puts out her hand.*) Goodbye, Michael.
(*HE refuses. SHE starts Center below him. HE blocks her way.*)

EXTREMITIES

by William Mastrosimone

ACT I, SCENE 3

*Raul came into Marjorie's home in a rural area of New
Jersey and tried to rape her. He was vicious and violent,
but Marjorie managed to spray bug spray into his eyes and
tie an extension cord around his neck, subduing him. She
then blindfolded Raul and tied him up with clothesline, extension cords, and other household implements. Even in
pain, Raul continued to taunt Marjorie, telling her that
since he didn't actually rape her he will be let off and will
come back and cut her up. She poured boiling water on
him, and then chained him inside the fireplace with a bicycle chain.*

....

RAUL: Where am I? Marjorie? Where am I?

MARJORIE: How do you know my name?

RAUL: Where am I?

MARJORIE: (*Tugging his noose.*) Answer me.

RAUL: I can't talk! Marjorie!

MARJORIE: Don't you ever say my name again! How'd you
know me?

RAUL: I read it on a letter.

MARJORIE: (*Tugging his noose.*) What letter?

RAUL: Heartless bitch!

MARJORIE: What letter?

RAUL: I took some letters from your mailbox by mistake. This
guy Joe asked me to come pick up his mail.

MARJORIE: Who were the letters from?

RAUL: One from your father. One from a collection agency. A couple from guys.

MARJORIE: Who?

RAUL: Some guy Tony. He wants you come live with him in New York. He don't want you to tell Terry.

MARJORIE: Who else?

RAUL: Your brother in Marine boot camp. Says they're beatin the shit outta him down there. He thinks he's got it bad.

MARJORIE: Why me? Answer me. Why me?

RAUL: Don't know. Crazy whacko bitch! What the hell!

MARJORIE: Why me?

RAUL: I saw you around.

MARJORIE: Where?

RAUL: Around! I don't know! Please! (*She pokes him with a fireplace implement.*)

MARJORIE: Answer me!

RAUL: I don't know what to say!

MARJORIE: Try the truth!

RAUL: O, the truth! Why didn't you say so! Alright! Here it goes. The truth. This guy Joe ... (*She pokes him.*) That's the truth! I swear on my mother's grave! Whattaya nuts or what! You said the truth, I told the truth, and you go poke me! (*She stops poking.*) You wanna hear this or not?

MARJORIE: Go ahead.

RAUL: You won't poke me?

MARJORIE: I said go ahead!

RAUL: Alright. The truth. There was this guy Joe ... (*He flinches in anticipation of a poke.*) He's a pimp. Said for half a yard he'd fix me up with a knock-out pussy. Said walk right in and ask for him and you'd know what I meant but I guess he was playing a joke on me. (*She pokes him.*)

RAUL: Please! Stop! Marjorie!

MARJORIE: Don't say my name!

RAUL: You are the boss, Jack! You are the man! Whatever you say! Ok? No panic. Listen, can I ask you one little question, Marjorie?—It slipped! I swear on my grandmother's milk!—One little question. Where am I?

MARJORIE: Fireplace.

RAUL: Where?

MARJORIE: The fireplace.

RAUL: What for?

MARJORIE: Why do people put things in the fireplace?

RAUL: People put things in the fire . . . (*Pause.*) Hey, c'mon, don't joke around.

MARJORIE: (*Shaking a plastic bottle of ammonia.*) And I have some gas.

RAUL: Gas? What, for your car?

MARJORIE: No. For you.

RAUL: I don't even own a car.

MARJORIE: (*Shaking a box of wooden matches.*) And matches.

RAUL: Whoa, jack!—Listen, I been doin some deep thinkin here and now I'm ready for the truth. I mean the real truth. I'm a narco. We got a tip there was drugs in this house. Open up. I'll show you my badge. (*She douses him with ammonia.*) Hey! What the hell! Hey! I got a wife and three kids!

MARJORIE: (*Striking a match very near.*) Maybe you'll tell the truth when you're on fire! (*RAUL coughs uncontrollably. He fights for breath in the chemicalized air. MARJORIE strikes a match, holds it close to his face.*)

RAUL: Alright! This is it! The honest-to-god truth. I don't know why I didn't tell you this from the beginning because this is it. (*Pause.*) I used to work on the pothole crew. For the County. We went around patchin up potholes. One day we was patchin up potholes on the highway. In front of your driveway. Bitchin day. In the nineties. Working with hot tar. Sweatin. Thirsty. Gettin dizzy. Foreman bustin balls. Somebody says, look at this. And you come ridin down the highway on your bike in your little white shorts and everytime you pedal you could see what was tan and what wasn't and your blouse tied in a knot and the sun shinin off your hair, beautiful. And that's it.

MARJORIE: So why'd you come here?

RAUL: I just told you. You was beautiful.

MARJORIE: So what?

RAUL: You know what that does to a man. It was hot. You had on your little white shorts.

MARJORIE: You're gonna burn. (*MARJORIE flicks matches wildly.*)

RAUL: Please! We had a deal! On the milk of Mary! You

rode by in your shorts! I said How ya doin? You didn't say nothing. Looked at me like I was a dead dog. You pissed me off so I came back here to fuck you! (*MARJORIE stops flicking matches. RAUL whimpers and slumps down. MARJORIE sits. Long pause.*) You there? (*Pause.*) Whattaya gonna do wit me?

MARJORIE: (*Pause. With perfect aplomb*) Nothing.

RAUL: Nothing?

MARJORIE: Nothing.

RAUL: You mean—let me go?

MARJORIE: No. Nothing.

RAUL: I don't catch what you're talkin.

MARJORIE: (*Silence.*) You will.

RAUL: When?

MARJORIE: You'll see.

RAUL: Starve me?

MARJORIE: Good idea.

RAUL: You could get the chair for that! Why don't you just call the cops?

MARJORIE: Why should I?

RAUL: That's what they're there for! (*Pause.*)

MARJORIE: Two days. No food. No water.

RAUL: You can't do this!

MARJORIE: I am doing it.

RAUL: I really think you should call the cops.

MARJORIE: You said I have no proof, they'll let you go.

RAUL: No. Marjorie, I swear, I was just talkin. Get the cops.

MARJORIE: It's too late.

RAUL: Mother of god! I don't want to die like this! Answer me! Talk to me! Please!—What will you do wit, you know, my body?

MARJORIE: Bury it.

RAUL: Bury it?

MARJORIE: I started a graveyard near the woods for the animals that get killed up on the highway. This time I dig deeper.

RAUL: You're jerkin me off.

MARJORIE: I got a shovel.

RAUL: Don't shit around! I got a weak ticker! (*Pause.*) My wife's eight months pregnant. She won't let me touch her.

I'm goin nuts. I got to get it everyday. I need help. Honest to fuckin god. I want to go straight.

MARJORIE: You will. Straight in a fuckin hole.

RAUL: You ain't got the nuts, cunt.

MARJORIE: You say that when you're in the bottom of the hole and the first shovel of dirt hits you in the face!

RAUL: When they come home, the other chicks, they'll stop you!

MARJORIE: You think so? One helps me dig the hole, the other helps me drag you out!

RAUL: You can't do this!

MARJORIE: I want to hear you scream under the dirt, like me under the pillow. (*Exit for a shovel.*)

RAUL: Mother of god!

MARJORIE: And you suck in for air, and dirt fills your mouth and nose!

RAUL: Send me your angel, mother of god!

MARJORIE: Suck for air! Under the dirt! With possum skulls! And dog bones!

RAUL: Get the cops! I want to tell 'em everything! This is it! (*MARJORIE pretends to leave by slamming the door.*) Marjorie! Marjorie! Marjorie!—She's diggin the hole, diggin the hole, she's really diggin the hole! (*Pause.*) O mother of god, do the miracle! Break these chains! (*He tries.*) Break these bars! (*He tries.*) What's amatter? Send me an angel like before! How can you let me die like this? (*Pause. Singing.*)

Found a peanut
It was rotten
Ate it anyway just now
Then I died
Went to heaven . . .

(*Pause.*) What I do this time? What I do? I didn't do nothin. (*Pause. Singing.*)

Broke the statue
Knocked it over
Broke the Virgin just now
Got a beatin
Locked the closet
Wit the spiders just now.

(*Pause.*) You there? I know you're there, Marjorie. Please

be there. How can you just sit there after alls between us? How can you do this to me? (*He thrashes about, gags, falls down, becomes still.*)

MARJORIE: Is it too tight? You alright? (*No answer. Pause. She probes him with the shovel, nothing. MARJORIE reaches to loosen the noose. RAUL bites her hand. She screams, cries, picks up the stick, but getting a better idea, hurls it at the cage, storms the kitchen.*)

RAUL:　　Bit the big bitch!
　　　　　Bit the big bitch!
　　　　　Bit the big bitch just now!
　　　　　She was rotten!
　　　　　Rotten! rotten!
　　　　　La la la la! la la!

(*MARJORIE enters running with the plastic container of Clorox and douses him.*)

RAUL: (*Continued.*) I'm on fire! I'm good! I'm good! I'm gonna learn to tell the truth! the whole truth! nothin but the truth! I swear to fuckin god! Car! Car! Please, mother of god, let it be the cops!

MARJORIE: (*Pulling him against bars by noose.*) Talk again and I smash you like a fuckin bug!

THE DEATH OF A MINER

by Paula Cizmar

ACT II

Jack and Mary Alice are an unusual married couple in the coal mining region of Appalachia. Mary Alice is an independent woman who has become a coal miner—not a usual job for a woman—and she has become the major bread winner in the family. Jack is a carpenter who spends most of his time building an extension on to their home. He is a kind man and loves Mary Alice, but has never fully adjusted to their work situation. Like others he believes that women are not supposed to be miners, not "real" women. Sallie is Mary Alice's daughter from a previous marriage.

....

(JACK is in the unfinished part of the house, trying to fix a toaster. MARY ALICE goes to lie down on the day bed.)

JACK: Damn fool thing. Might as well just get a new one. . . . *(Shakes the toaster; nothing happens; he hears MARY ALICE coughing or sighing. Gets up to look for her and finds her asleep on the day bed.)* Mary Al—now don't she look sweet? *(JACK kneels down beside her, strokes her hair.)*

MARY ALICE: *(Stirring.)* Mmmm, Jack?

JACK: Hi sweetheart. Whatta you dreamin about?

MARY ALICE: Lord! I just sat down and before you know, I was asleep. *(Starts to get up.)*

JACK: Now don't get up, don't get up. *(Begins kissing her.)* Mmmmm that's nice.

MARY ALICE: Mmm. (*Kisses him, then abruptly.*) Oh no! Supper. . . .

JACK: Now you just lie there. . . . this is nice. (*Kisses her again.*) Better still. . . . why don't you come lie down with me in the bedroom. . . . hmmm?

MARY ALICE: (*Pecks him on the cheek and sits up.*) I've gotta get supper made.. . . .it's late. Where's Sallie?

JACK: She's around. Let's go in there first. (*Motions to offstage bedroom area.*)

MARY ALICE: Jack, not now. I gotta get supper. Gotta wash my hair. . . . have to wash out some clothes for work . . . and I'm makin—

JACK: Hell, Mary Alice!

MARY ALICE: . . . . and I'm makin curtains for Sallie's room tonight.

JACK: Sallie's room. I ain't even put the roof on it yet. Come on sweetheart. We'll go make love and be nice and snug for awhile and then I'll whip up some eggs and sausages or something. Or we can all go down to Jake's.

MARY ALICE: That's real sweet, honey, but not now. (*Gets up.*) Want some tea? Or some coffee?
(*JACK follows her and puts his arms around her, physically restraining her as he kisses her.*)

MARY ALICE: Jack. . . . let go.

JACK: (*Tightening his grip.*) Mmmm. . . . you feel good.

MARY ALICE: Jack. . . . Jack. . . . (*As he doesn't respond, she starts to almost panic.*) Jack. . . . I said let go! (*MARY ALICE starts to forcefully push him away. He suddenly releases his hold on her.*) Now just stop it!

JACK: What is the matter with you?

MARY ALICE: What's the matter with you, grabbin me like that?

JACK: I was tryin to kiss you. Oh forget it.

MARY ALICE: Honey . . . I . . . I'm just—

JACK: (*Explodes.*) Why the hell did you marry me anyway?

MARY ALICE: Jack . . .

JACK: That's what I'd like to know. Huh? Why the hell did you marry me?

MARY ALICE: Honey, I just told you—

JACK: I can't figure out why you bothered. You already got

a job, so you don't need me to support you. You already got a kid. And now you don't even need me for a little lovemakin. Go away, Jack. I'm tired, Jack. I gotta make curtains, Jack. I gotta go to a union meetin, Jack. I gotta wash some string beans, Jack. Hell! What am I supposed to be doin in this marriage anyway? Goddamnit!

(As they fight, SALLIE *arrives home from school. Hearing them argue, she sits on the porch.)*

MARY ALICE: Don't be stupid! You really are startin to sound like every other dumb hillbilly I ever met, you know that! I'm just tired! I didn't say I didn't want to be married! I didn't say I didn't need you! I'm just tired. I'm just a little edgy from work and I didn't want you to paw me like—

JACK: Paw you? Now I'm some kinda animal—

MARY ALICE: Jack, listen to me. Let's not fight. Jack, I love you. I married you cause I love you . . . cause you're different.

JACK: *(Begins to be soothed until the word* different.*)* DIFFERENT!

MARY ALICE: Oh, nothing I say is right when you get like this.

JACK: Different! Yeah. That's the problem! That's what everyone else thinks, too! Hell, I don't need to be told what's . . . *(Grabs for his jacket and looks for his keys.)*

MARY ALICE: Jack! *(Tries to calm him again.)* You're different because you understand.

JACK: I don't want to understand. I don't want to be different! I want us to be like everyone else! Hell, I'm goin where I'm appreciated for bein . . . bein . . .

MARY ALICE: *(Enraged.)* Bein what?

JACK: ME! Instead of a little cog in the big Mary Alice wheel.

MARY ALICE: SO GO! I'm sick of hearin about it! I'm sick of tryin to explain to you! I'm sick of you!

JACK: There! I KNEW IT. Hell. . . .

MARY ALICE: *(Out of control.)* GO! GO!

(JACK slams out the door.)

LATER LIFE

by A.R. Gurney

The setting is the terrace of an apartment overlooking Boston Harbor. Austin's friends have thrown a party for him to meet Ruth, a woman with whom he had a romance many years ago on the Isle of Capri when he was a young Naval officer. Austin's and Ruth's friends feel they are just what each other needs at this time in their lives. Austin is a dependable man, a banker and upright citizen who is also divorced; Ruth has been married four times, twice to the same man, who is intemperate and a gambler, and from whom she is currently separated. Austin has had a successful life, a life of good fortune, but he has always had the fear that something terrible was about to happen to him. He has told Ruth about his dread, and about taking Prozac and seeing a psychiatrist to try to calm his fears.

While Ruth went off to answer a telephone call from her husband, Austin explained to his friend Walt that while Ruth is an attractive woman, he is not the sort of man to simply jump into a relationship with someone. Ruth returns to the terrace carrying dessert and two demitasses and Walt returns to the party, leaving them alone.

....

RUTH: (*RUTH sets her plates down.*) I brought dessert.
AUSTIN: (*Settling at the table.*) Very thoughtful.
RUTH: And coffee.

AUSTIN: De-caf, I hope.

RUTH: (*Sliding him his cup.*) What else. (*They eat brownies or something.*) Mmmm.

AUSTIN: A little rich, isn't it?

RUTH: Well, we deserve it. We were so healthy with the main course.

AUSTIN: Right. In Boston, they'd say we're getting our just desserts. (*RUTH gives him a weak smile. Pause.*) Everything all right, by the way?

RUTH: With the telephone call?

AUSTIN: Judith told us who it was. (*Pause.*)

RUTH: He's at the . . . what is it? The Skyway Lounge, out at the airport.

AUSTIN: What? He's there?

RUTH: He's there.

AUSTIN: And?

RUTH: He wants me to join him.

AUSTIN: When?

RUTH: Now. Right now.

AUSTIN: But you're here.

RUTH: That's right. I'm here. Which is what I said. I said I'm having a very good time right here.

AUSTIN: What did he say to that?

RUTH: He said he could give me a better one, right there.

AUSTIN: Could he?

RUTH: He can be . . . fun.

AUSTIN: Did you tell him about me?

RUTH: No.

AUSTIN: Why not?

RUTH: He might have shown up with a baseball bat.

AUSTIN: I could have dealt with that.

RUTH: Oh yes? With your squash racquet.

AUSTIN: I would have done something.

RUTH: (*Touching him.*) I know you would have, Austin. (*She gets up.*) I just don't want you to, that's all. (*She looks out.*) He's got two tickets on tonight's red-eye back west. First class. And he wants to order a bottle of champagne to drink while we wait.

AUSTIN: Champagne? At an airport bar?

RUTH: He knows I like it. (*Pause.*) First class, too. He knows

I'm a sucker for that. (*Pause.*) And he'll charge everything to *my* credit card.

AUSTIN: Sounds like a nice guy.

RUTH: Oh he ... has his problems.

AUSTIN: Sure sounds like it.

RUTH: Of course we all do, don't we?

AUSTIN: Ouch.

RUTH: No, but I mean we do. Lord knows I do, too.

AUSTIN: Name one.

RUTH: Him.

AUSTIN: O.K.

RUTH: He's not good for me.

AUSTIN: That's an understatement.

RUTH: But he has some redeeming social virtues.

AUSTIN: Such as?

RUTH: Well ... for one thing, he loves me.

AUSTIN: Oh sure.

RUTH: He does.... He's never traded me in for some young bimbo. He's never taken me for granted. He loves me ... I walk out, I leave him, I say this is it, and what does he do? He telephones all over the country till he finds out where I am. Then he grabs a flight to Boston. Calls me here. Offers me champagne. And begs me to come back.... He loves me.

AUSTIN: How can he love you if he hits you?

RUTH: He doesn't hit me.

AUSTIN: I hear he does.

RUTH: (*More to herself.*) Judith? ... (*To* AUSTIN.) Once, maybe.

AUSTIN: Once is enough.

RUTH: By mistake.

AUSTIN: Oh Ruth.

RUTH: It was by *mistake*, Austin!

AUSTIN: Some mistake. That's a big mistake.

RUTH: Sometimes he gets ... carried away.

AUSTIN: Yes well that's not love in my book.

RUTH: Oh really?

AUSTIN: That has nothing to do with love. Rape, violence, things of that kind, I'm sorry, they elude me. They totally elude me. If that's love, then I'm afraid I know nothing about it. (*She looks at him, as if for the first time. Pause.*

Sounds of people singing around a piano come from within. They sing a lively song.) Well. How about a song at twilight?

RUTH: Maybe it's better if I just . . . (*She makes a move to go.*)

AUSTIN: (*Getting in her way.*) Ruth. (*She stops.*) Tell you what. We'll go to the Ritz Bar, you and I. It's a very pleasant, very quiet place. And *I'll* buy you champagne. And I promise you it will be a better brand than what your Marlboro Man comes up with, out at the airport. And I'll pay for it my*self.*

RUTH: Austin . . .

AUSTIN: No, and I'll tell you something else. After we've had champagne, we'll go to my place. If you'd like.

RUTH: Oh Austin . . .

AUSTIN: No, now I don't want you to feel obligated in any way. But I have a very nice apartment on Beacon Street, and we can walk there, right down Arlington Street from the Ritz. And I have a guest room, Ruth. It's a nice room. With its own bath. I keep it for the kids. You can sleep there, if you prefer. I'll even lend you a pair of decent pajamas.

RUTH: Decent pajamas . . .

AUSTIN: No, now wait. If, when we're there, you'd like to . . . to join me in my room, if you'd care to slip into my bed, naturally I'd like that very much. Very much indeed. But you wouldn't have to. Either way, you'd be most welcome. And if things worked out, why we might . . . we might make things more permanent . . . I mean, it's a thought, at least. And if they don't, well hell, you should always feel free to leave any time you want.

RUTH: Oh well . . .

AUSTIN: I mean, we obviously get along. That's obvious. We did on Capri and we do now. Hey, come to think of it, this is a second chance, isn't it? We're back where we were, but this time we're getting a second chance. (*Pause.*) So. What do you say?

RUTH: (*Kissing him.*) Oh Austin. Austin from Boston. You're such a good man. (*She starts out. Singing continues within.*)

AUSTIN: Where are you going?

RUTH: I don't want to tell you.

AUSTIN: To him?

RUTH: I think so. Yes.

AUSTIN: Why?

RUTH: Why?

AUSTIN: Why him and not me?

RUTH: Oh dear.

AUSTIN: How can you love that guy?

RUTH: If you don't know, I can't tell you.

AUSTIN: (*Turning away from her.*) You don't think I'm attractive?

RUTH: I think you're one of the most attractive men I've ever met.

AUSTIN: Then it must be my problem.

RUTH: Yes.

AUSTIN: You think it's a crock of shit!

RUTH: No! Not at all. No! I take it very seriously. I take it more seriously than you do.

AUSTIN: You think something terrible is going to happen to me?

RUTH: I think it already has.

AUSTIN: When?

RUTH: I don't know.

AUSTIN: Where?

RUTH: I don't know that either.

AUSTIN: But you think I'm damned into outer darkness?

RUTH: I do. I really do.

AUSTIN: But you won't tell me why.

RUTH: I can't.

AUSTIN: Why not?

RUTH: It's too painful, Austin.

AUSTIN: Do you think I'll ever find out?

RUTH: Oh I hope not.

AUSTIN: Why?

RUTH: Because you'll go through absolute hell.

AUSTIN: You mean I'll weep and wail and gnash my teeth?

RUTH: I don't think so, Austin. No. I think you'll clear your throat, and square your shoulders, and straighten your tie—and stand there quietly and take it. That's the hellish part. (*She looks at him feelingly.*) I've got to dash.

MONDAY AFTER THE MIRACLE

by William Gibson

ACT II

The scene is between Annie Sullivan and her husband, John Macy. But the strongest presence in the scene, although she has left the room, is Helen Keller. The play describes events seventeen years after those in the author's earlier play, The Miracle Worker, *when Annie Sullivan first became Helen Keller's teacher. Now Helen is a young woman, studying at Radcliffe and off to a promising career as a writer. Annie is still her teacher and she and Helen live together, along with Annie's husband, John.*

The scene below occurs six years after John first came to Annie and Helen's house to work as an editor for Helen. He and Annie fell in love and they married. But Annie's round-the-clock devotion to Helen left little time for companionship or tenderness. Nor has John's professional life flourished as he had hoped. He has not had the career as a writer that he sought, and he still works as an editor at Youth's Companion *magazine.*

As Helen matures into a young woman she discovers that she has all the physical and emotional needs of any woman, despite being deaf and blind. One lonely night while Annie is out, Helen and John embrace and kiss. When Annie returns she discovers that Helen, filled with guilt, is very upset. John tells her what has happened, and Annie grabs her coat and storms off in a rage, with John chasing after her. Helen becomes frantic and accidentally knocks over a lamp, starting a fire. John and Annie rush back in and put

*the fire out. After Helen is reassured that Annie will not
leave, she goes off, leaving John and Annie alone. Annie
pours herself some brandy and wipes a tear from her eye.*

....

JOHN: Kissed the girls and made them cry.

ANNIE: You haven't even the grace to be embarrassed.

JOHN: I am, very; that's when I joke.

ANNIE: It's not comic.

JOHN: It's not tragic. You should cry oftener, it's very attractive.

ANNIE: Give me a reason. Not pregnant, work fifteen hours
a day, find you kissing a younger woman, and you tell me
you're dying in this house, what have I to cry about?

JOHN: I'm not dying.

ANNIE: I didn't think so from *her* story. (*She drinks.*)

JOHN: (*Watches.*) You shouldn't drink alone. (*He reaches;
she edges away.*)

ANNIE: Get your own glass.

JOHN: (*Hand out.*) I don't want to leave you.

ANNIE: I wonder.

JOHN: Ever.

ANNIE: Why not?

JOHN: I love you, idiot.

ANNIE: Is that love?

JOHN: What else?

ANNIE: Inertia.

JOHN: All right, I'll drink out of your shoe, damnit—(*He
picks up a shoe.*)—that's a classic proof.

ANNIE: Of which?

JOHN: What's this?

ANNIE: Love me, love my foot powder.

JOHN: I'll get my own glass.

ANNIE: Here. Do you make love to others too?

JOHN: No.

ANNIE: At the office?

JOHN: No.

ANNIE: Would you tell me if you did?

JOHN: No.

ANNIE: You do.

JOHN: Yes, all day long, they line up at my desk.

ANNIE: Give me my drink.

JOHN: I don't want others; it's you I want to love. I said dying—

ANNIE: Want to?

JOHN: —because loving is the juice that keeps us alive, and I feel it—draining out of me. (*ANNIE shuts her eyes.*) And I'm frightened. Thirty-one is no longer a—Look at me, I want to be in focus.

ANNIE: (*Does.*) Go on.

JOHN: *Some*where—

ANNIE: Why draining?

JOHN: —I'm a cog here and in that office—

ANNIE: Why draining?

JOHN: Because I'm married to a pair of Siamese twins, every time I reach for you she's in the way!

ANNIE: You reached for her.

JOHN: I'm human. But I don't seduce helpless deaf-blind virgins—

ANNIE: She's not helpless.

JOHN: —and I wasn't going to.

ANNIE: If she's helpless, my whole life has been a waste—

JOHN: Whole life is right, give *me* some of that devotion—

ANNIE: (*Fierce.*) I'm trying to hold it together! I do love you, I do have her on my hands every waking hour, and I expect you to feel for me when day after day I'm yanked back and forth between the two of you.

JOHN: I do.

ANNIE: No—you feel neglected, is that what you mean by loving, I'm to spoon-feed you the way I do her? I need some looking after too—

JOHN: Can I make an appointment?

ANNIE: I have a round-the-clock duty in this house!—it was never a secret—

JOHN: I didn't marry a duty!

ANNIE: Oh yes you did!—

JOHN: Then get her mother in here!

ANNIE: —it was to see Helen with my eyes, and that's what *I* mean by loving, she's our ward, and in this house we both watch over her or I don't know what you're doing in it.

JOHN: (*Taken aback.*) Heyy—

ANNIE: Did you or did you not promise that?

JOHN: You want me out?

ANNIE: I put my life in the hands of the one man who saw me as a woman, not a doormat to Helen, and then find him in her arms—

JOHN: Now stop it—

ANNIE: —and if that's what this marriage is for I do want you out!

JOHN: Stop *ranting*!—you know you don't—

ANNIE: I don't know it!—not tonight—

JOHN: Then why didn't you leave?

ANNIE: Because I leave her to you for one minute and she's in flames!

JOHN: Sonofabitch, I—

ANNIE: You don't look after me *or* her!

JOHN: You win, you win, satisfied?

ANNIE: You look after yourself, you darling boy—

JOHN: And who else does?—all week long that office is hell by daylight, companioning youth, shrinks my brain, and what little of it's left I bring home to companion you two in a house where I don't have a wife, don't have a child—

ANNIE: Ohhh—

JOHN: —which would change everything—

ANNIE: —be careful!—

JOHN: —give us both a focus—

ANNIE: —or I'll humiliate you too, me bucko, I don't have a child you go see a doctor!

JOHN: I'll tell you one thing, the strength you've fed Helen for twenty years I find a pain in the ass as a daily diet. You're a tough morsel to digest! And if for half an hour I turn to *that* child because she needs cuddling it's the fall of the house of Usher?

ANNIE: Because it's her—can't you get that through your skull—

JOHN: She lets me feel tender! You don't. (*ANNIE sits rigid. And covers her face; now she really cries, is wracked by it. JOHN after a time touches her.*) Hey—(*She rolls away from him, and flees upstairs.*)

THE THREE SISTERS
by ANTON CHEKHOV

translated by Ann Dunnigan

ACT II

Masha and Vershinin are in love with each other, but have not spoken of it. They are both in unhappy marriages and spend as little time with their spouses as possible. Instead they seek each other out, relishing each other's company and conversation. He is an officer in the military regiment that Masha's father commanded until he died a few years before. Vershinin is philosophical and melancholy, and longs for a life filled with purpose and beauty. And he ignites in Masha a passion that she has not known before.

Masha feels trapped in her marriage and trapped in the provincial Russian town in which they live, and she yearns to return to Moscow or St. Petersburg where people are cultured and interesting. It is Carnival Week and Masha and Vershinin are returning from some evening festivities in town.

....

MASHA: I don't know. (*Pause.*) I don't know. Of course, a great deal depends on what one is accustomed to. After Father died, for instance, it took us a long time to get used to having no orderlies in the house. But even apart from habit, I have to say it in all fairness. It may not be so in other places, but in our town the most decent, the most honorable and well-bred people, are all in the army.

VERSHININ: I'm thirsty. I'd like some tea.

MASHA: (*Glancing at the clock.*) They'll bring it soon. I was married when I was eighteen, and I was afraid of my husband because he was a teacher, and I was hardly out of school. In those days he seemed to me terribly learned, clever, and important. But now, unfortunately, it is different.

VERSHININ: Yes. . . . That's how it is.

MASHA: I don't speak of my husband, I've grown used to him, but among civilians generally, there are so many coarse, impolite, ill-bred people. Coarseness upsets and offends me, I suffer when I see that a man is not fine enough, gentle enough, courteous. When I happen to be among teachers, my husband's colleagues, I am simply miserable.

VERSHININ: Yes. . . . But it seems to me that it's all the same whether they're civilians or military men, they're equally uninteresting, in this town at any rate. It's all the same! If you listen to one of the local intelligentsia, either civilian or military, he's sick and tired of everything; either he's sick and tired of his wife, or his home, his estate, or his horses. . . . A Russian is peculiarly given to an exalted way of thinking, but tell me, why is it that in life he falls so short? Why?

MASHA: Why?

VERSHININ: Why is he sick and tired of his children, sick and tired of his wife? And why are his wife and children sick and tired of him?

MASHA: You're not in a very good mood today.

VERSHININ: Perhaps not. I've had no dinner today, nothing to eat since morning. One of my daughters is not very well, and when my little girls are ill, I am seized with anxiety, my conscience torments me for having given them such a mother. Oh, if you could have seen her today! What a worthless creature! We began quarreling at seven o'clock this morning, and at nine I slammed the door and left. (*Pause.*) I never talk about this, strangely enough, I complain only to you. (*Kisses her hand.*) Don't be angry with me. Except for you I have no one—no one. . . . (*Pause.*)

MASHA: Such a noise in the stove! Just before Father died, there was a wailing in the chimney. There, just like that.

VERSHININ: Are you superstitious?

MASHA: Yes.

VERSHININ: That's strange. (*Kisses her hand.*) You are a

splendid, wonderful woman! Splendid, wonderful! It's dark here, but I can see the sparkle of your eyes.

MASHA: (*Moves to another chair.*) It's lighter here.

VERSHININ: I love you, love you, love you. . . . I love your eyes, your gestures, I dream about them. . . . Splendid, wonderful woman!

MASHA: When you talk to me like that, for some reason, I laugh, though I am frightened. Don't do it any more, I beg you. . . . (*In a low voice.*) But, say it anyway, I don't mind. . . . (*Covers her face with her hands.*) I don't mind. Someone is coming, talk about something else. . . .

HURLYBURLY

by David Rabe

ACT III, SCENE 1

Eddie lives in a house in the Hollywood Hills. He is a scriptwriter whose career hasn't been going well lately. He is angry about the course his life has taken and the state of the world. He spends a good part of his day ingesting an assortment of drugs and alcoholic beverages. Most of the time he argues with anyone he comes in contact with. Among the people he does regular battle with are his ex-wife (she has their daughter), his roommate, Mickey, his friend Phil (who is upset because his wife, who recently had a baby girl, won't take him back), and his girlfriend, Darlene. Darlene is a photojournalist, and she spends a great deal of time out of town on assignments—which Eddie interprets as a sign that she doesn't love him.

As the scene opens, Eddie tells Mickey that he's worried about Phil. Phil left some frantic messages for Eddie earlier in the day, but now he can't be found. When Mickey leaves, Eddie and Darlene are alone.

....

EDDIE: Let's just hang around a little in case he calls.

DARLENE: I'm tired anyway.

EDDIE: It's the kid thing, you know, that's the thing. He could walk in a second it wasn't for the kid.

DARLENE: He should have then.

EDDIE: Exactly. But he couldn't. (*Heading for the stairs, beginning to take off his jacket.*) So what am I talking about?

It's just a guy like Phil, for all his appearances, this is what can make him nuts. You don't ever forget about 'em if you're a guy like Phil. I mean, my little girl is a factor in every calculation I make—big or small—she's a constant. You can imagine, right?

DARLENE: Sure. I had a, you know—and that was—well, rough, so I have some sense of it, really, in a very funny way.

EDDIE: (*As he goes into his bedroom.*) What?

DARLENE: My abortion. I got pregnant. I wasn't sure exactly which guy—I wasn't going crazy or anything with a different guy every night or anything, and I knew them both very well, but I was just not emotionally involved with either one of them, seriously. (*Emerging from the bedroom, he freezes, staring down at her, his shirt half off.*) Though I liked them both. A lot. Which in a way made the whole thing even more confusing on a personal level, and you know, in terms of trying to figure out the morality of the whole thing, so I finally had this abortion completely on my own without telling anybody, not even my girlfriends. I kept thinking in my mind that it wasn't a complete baby, which it wasn't, not a fully developed person, but a fetus which it was, and that I would have what I would term a real child later, but nevertheless, I had these nightmares and totally unexpected feelings in which in my dreams I imagined the baby as this teenager, a handsome boy of real spiritual consequences, which now the world would have to do without, and he was always like a refugee, full of regret, like this treasure that had been lost in some uncalled-for way, like when a person of great potential is hit by a car. I felt I had no one to blame but myself, and I went sort of out of my mind for a while, so my parents sent me to Puerto Rico for a vacation, and I got myself back together there enough to come home with my head on my shoulders at least semistraight. I was functional, anyway. Semi-functional, anyway. But then I told everybody what had happened. I went from telling nobody to everybody.

EDDIE: This was . . .

DARLENE: What?

EDDIE: When?

DARLENE: Seven and a half years ago.

EDDIE: That's what I mean, though; those feelings.

DARLENE: I know. I understood, see, that was what you meant, which was my reason for trying to make the effort to bring it up, because I don't talk about it all that much at all anymore, but I wanted you to know that when you said that about your daughter, I, in fact, in a visceral sense, knew what you were talking about.

EDDIE: (*Moving down the stairs toward her, as it seems they agree on everything.*) I mean, everybody has this baggage, and you can't ignore it or what are you doing?

DARLENE: You're just ignoring it.

EDDIE: You're just ignoring the person then, that's all. But at the same time your own feelings are—it's overwhelming or at least it can be. You can't take it all on.

DARLENE: No.

EDDIE: (*Holding her hand, he pats her in consolation.*) There's nothing I can do about all that, you know, that happened to you.

DARLENE: No.

EDDIE: It really messed you up, though.

DARLENE: For a while. But I learned certain things from it, too, you know.

EDDIE: (*Still holding her hand.*) Sure.

DARLENE: It was painful, but I learned these things that have been a help ever since, so something came out of it good.

EDDIE: So . . . these two guys. . . . Where are they?

DARLENE: Oh, I have no idea. This was in Cincinnati.

EDDIE: Right. (*Now he rises and begins mixing drinks for them both.*)

DARLENE: I don't know what happened to them. I think one got married and I have this vague sense that—I don't know what EXACTLY—but . . . No. I can't remember. But I have this sense that SOMETHING happened to him. I don't know what. Anyway, I rarely think about it anymore. I'm a very different person.

EDDIE: Did . . . they know each other?

DARLENE: The two guys?

EDDIE: Yeah.

DARLENE: No. I mean, not that I know of. Why?

EDDIE: Just wondering.

DARLENE: What?

EDDIE: Nothing. Just . . . you know.

DARLENE: You must have been wondering something. People don't just wonder nothing.

EDDIE: No, no. I was just wondering, you know, was it a pattern? That's all.

DARLENE: No.

EDDIE: I mean, don't get irritated. You asked me.

DARLENE: You asked me. I mean, I was trying to tell you something else entirely.

EDDIE: I know that.

DARLENE: So what's the point?

EDDIE: I'm aware absolutely of what you were trying to tell me. And I heard it. But am I just supposed to totally narrow down my whole set of perceptions, just filter out everything, just censor everything that doesn't support your intention? I made an association. And it was not an unreasonable association.

DARLENE: It was totally off the wall, and hostile.

EDDIE: Hostile?

DARLENE: And you know it.

EDDIE: Give me a break! What? I'm supposed to sit still for the most arcane association I ever heard in my life, that levitation leads to dogs? But should I come up with an equally—I mean, equally, shit—when I come up with a hundred percent more logical association, I'm supposed to accept your opinion that it isn't?

DARLENE: No, no, no.

EDDIE: Well, that's all it was. An association. That's all it was.

DARLENE: Okay.

EDDIE: I mean, for everybody's good, it appeared to me a thought worth some exploration, and if I was wrong, and I misjudged, then I'm sorry.

DARLENE: It's just something I'm very, sometimes, sensitive about.

EDDIE: Sure. What? The abortion.

DARLENE: Yeah.

EDDIE: (*Handing her the drink, he pats her hand.*) Sure. Okay, though? You okay now? You feel okay?

DARLENE: I'm hungry. You hungry?

EDDIE: I mean, if we don't talk these things out, we'll just

end up with all this, you know, unspoken shit, following us
around. You wanna go out and eat? Let's go out. What are
you hungry for? How about Chinese?

DARLENE: Sure.

EDDIE: (*Grabbing up the phone and starting to dial.*) We
could go to Mr. Chou's. Treat ourselves right.

DARLENE: That's great. I love the seaweed.

EDDIE: I mean, you want Chinese?

DARLENE: I love Mr. Chou's.

EDDIE: We could go some other place. How about Ma Mai-
son?

DARLENE: Sure.

EDDIE: (*Hanging up the phone.*) You like that better than Mr.
Chou's?

DARLENE: I don't like it better, but it's great. Which one is
your preference?

EDDIE: Well, I want—you know—this should be—I'd like
this to be your choice.

DARLENE: It doesn't matter to me.

EDDIE: Which one should I call?

DARLENE: Surprise me.

EDDIE: I don't want to surprise you. I want to, you know, do
whatever you say.

DARLENE: Then just pick one. Call one. Either.

EDDIE: I mean, why should I have to guess? I don't want to
guess. Just tell me. I mean, what if I pick the wrong one?

DARLENE: You can't pick the wrong one. Honestly, Eddie, I
like them both the same. I like them both exactly the same.

EDDIE: Exactly?

DARLENE: Yes. I like them both.

EDDIE: I mean, how can you possibly think you like them
both the same? One is French and one is Chinese. They're
different. They're as different as—I mean, what is the
world, one big blur to you out there in which everything
that bears some resemblance to something else is just automatically put at the same level in your hierarchy, for chrissake, Darlene, the only thing they have in common is that
they're both restaurants!

DARLENE: Are you aware that you're yelling?

EDDIE: My voice is raised for emphasis, which is a perfectly
legitimate use of volume. Particularly when, in addition, I

evidently have to break through this goddamn cloud in which you are obviously enveloped in which everything is just this blur totally void of the most rudimentary sort of distinction.

DARLENE: Just call the restaurant, why don't you?

EDDIE: Why are you doing this?

DARLENE: I'm hungry. I'm just trying to get something to eat before I faint.

EDDIE: The fuck you are. You're up to something.

DARLENE: What do you mean, what am I up to? You're telling me I don't know if I'm hungry or not? I'm hungry!

EDDIE: Bullshit!

DARLENE: (*Leaping up from her chair, she strides across the room.*) ''Up to''? Paranoia, Eddie. Para-fucking-noia. Be alert. Your tendencies are coming out all over the place.

EDDIE: I'm fine.

DARLENE: (*Pacing near the base of the stairs.*) I mean, to stand there screeching at me about what-am-I-up-to is paranoid.

EDDIE: Not if you're up to something, it's not.

DARLENE: I'm not. Take my word for it, you're acting a little nuts.

EDDIE: I'm supposed to trust your judgment of my mental stability? I'm supposed to trust your evaluation of the nuances of my sanity? You can't even tell the difference between a French and a Chinese restaurant!

DARLENE: I like them both.

EDDIE: But they're different. One is French, and the other is Chinese. They are totally fucking different.

DARLENE: Not in my inner, subjective, emotional experience of them.

EDDIE: The tastes, the decors, the waiters, the accents. The fucking accents. The little phrases the waiters say. And they yell at each other in these whole totally different languages, does none of this make an impression on you?

DARLENE: It impresses me that I like them both.

EDDIE: Your total inner emotional subjective experience must be THIS EPIC FUCKING FOG! I mean, what are you on, some sort of dualistic trip and everything is in twos and you just can't tell which is which so you're just pulled taut between them on this goddamn high wire between people who

might like to have some kind of definitive reaction from
you in order to know!

DARLENE: Fuck you!

EDDIE: What's wrong with that?

DARLENE: Is that what this is all about? Those two guys. I
happened to mention two guys!

EDDIE: I just want to know if this is a pattern. Chinese restaurants and you can't tell the difference between people.
(*They stand, staring at each other.*)

DARLENE: Oh, Eddie. Oh, Eddie, Eddie.

EDDIE: What?

DARLENE: Oh, Eddie, Eddie. (*Moving to the couch, she
slumps down, sits there.*)

EDDIE: What?

DARLENE: I just really feel awful. This is really depressing. I
really like you. I really do.

EDDIE: I mean . . .

DARLENE: What?

EDDIE: Well, don't feel too bad, okay?

DARLENE: I do, I feel bad. I feel bad.

EDDIE: (*Moving now, he sits down on the edge of the armchair, and leans toward her.*) But, I mean, just—we have
to talk about these things, right? That's all. This is okay.

DARLENE: No, no.

EDDIE: Just don't—you know, on the basis of this, make any
sort of grand, kind of overwhelming, comprehensive, kind
of, you know, totally conclusive assessment here. That
would be absurd, you know. I mean, this is an isolated,
individual thing here, and—

DARLENE: No.

EDDIE: (*Moving to the couch, he tries to get close to her,
settles on his knees on the floor beside the couch.*) Sure. I
mean, sometimes what is it? It's stuff, other stuff; stuff under stuff, you're doing one thing you think it's something
else. I mean, it's always there, the family thing, the childhood thing, it's—sometimes it comes up. I go off. I'm not
even where I seem anymore. I'm not there.

DARLENE: Eddie, I think I should go.

EDDIE: I'm trying to explain.

DARLENE: (*Sliding away from him.*) I know all about it.

EDDIE: Whata you know all about?

DARLENE: Your fucking childhood, Eddie. You tol' me.

EDDIE: Whata you know?

DARLENE: I know all I—what is this, a test? I mean, I know: Your parents were these religious lunatics, these pious frauds, who periodically beat the shit out of you.

EDDIE: They weren't just religious, and they didn't just—

DARLENE: Your father was a minister, I know.

EDDIE: What denomination?

DARLENE: Fuck you. (*She bolts away, starts gathering up her things. She's going to leave.*)

EDDIE: You said you knew.

DARLENE: I don't think there's a lot more we ought to, with any, you know, honesty, allow ourselves in the way of bullshit about our backgrounds to exonerate what is our just plain mean behavior to one another.

EDDIE: That's not what I'm doing.

DARLENE: So, what are you doing?

EDDIE: (*Following her.*) They took me in the woods; they prayed and then they beat the shit out of me; they prayed and beat me with sticks. He talked in tongues.

DARLENE: She broke your nose and blacked your eyes, I know.

EDDIE: Because I wanted to watch *Range Rider* on TV, and she considered it a violent program. (*Phone rings.*) So she broke my nose. That's insane.

DARLENE: But I don't care, Eddie. I don't care. (*She's really ready to go now.*)

EDDIE: Whata you mean?

DARLENE: I mean, it doesn't matter. (*She steps for the door.*)

EDDIE: It doesn't matter? What are you talking about? (*Grabbing her by the arm to detain her.*)

DARLENE: It doesn't.

EDDIE: No, no, no. (*As he grabs up the phone and yells into it.*) Hold on. (*Clutching DARLENE in one hand and the phone in the other, he turns to her.*) No, no; it matters, and you care. What you mean is, it doesn't make any difference. (*Releasing her, he speaks into the phone.*) Hello.

DARLENE: I can't stand this goddamn semantic insanity anymore, Eddie—I can't be that specific about my feelings—I can't. Will you get off the phone!

EDDIE: (*Into the phone.*) What? Oh, no. No, no. Oh, no.

DARLENE: What?

EDDIE: (*Into the phone.*) Wait there. There. I'll come over. (*He hangs up and stands.*)

DARLENE: Eddie, what? You look terrible. What? (*He starts toward the front door.*) Eddie, who was that? What happened? Eddie!

EDDIE: Phil's dead.

DARLENE: What?

EDDIE: Car. Car.

DARLENE: Oh, Eddie, Eddie.

EDDIE: What?

DARLENE: I'm so sorry.

(*EDDIE gives her a look and goes.*)

BEYOND THERAPY

by Christopher Durang

SCENE 2

Bruce and Prudence are both about thirty years old and single. Will they ever find love and romance? Clearly their only chance is if they can get "beyond therapy"—if they can get out from under the influence of their totally wacky psychotherapists. Bruce's therapist urges him to find a woman by placing a personal ad in The New York Review of Books. *Prudence answers the ad, but their encounter turns out terrible for both of them. Bruce is very strange, to say the least.*

The scene that follows takes place after their encounter. Prudence is at the office of her psychotherapist, Dr. Stuart Framingham, and she has a lot to tell him about her date. As it turns out, Dr. Framingham has a lot on his mind also.

....

(Psychiatrist's office. DR. STUART FRAMINGHAM. *Very masculine, a bit of a bully, wears boots, jeans, a tweed sports jacket, open sports shirt. Maybe has a beard.)*

STUART: *(Speaking into intercom.)* You can send the next patient in now, Betty. *(Enter* PRUDENCE. *She sits. After a moment.)* So, what's on your mind this week?
PRUDENCE: Oh I don't know. I had that Catherine the Great dream again.
STUART: Yeah?

PRUDENCE: Oh I don't know. Maybe it isn't Catherine the Great. It's really more like *National Velvet*.

STUART: What do you associate to *National Velvet*?

PRUDENCE: Oh I don't know. Childhood.

STUART: Yes?

PRUDENCE: I guess I miss childhood where one could look to a horse for emotional satisfaction rather than a person. I mean, a horse never disappointed me.

STUART: You feel disappointed in people?

PRUDENCE: Well every man I try to have a relationship with turns out to be crazy. And the ones that aren't crazy are dull. But maybe it's me. Maybe I'm really looking for faults just so I won't ever have a successful relationship. Like Michael last year. Maybe he was just fine, and I made up faults that he didn't have. Maybe I do it to myself. What do you think?

STUART: What I think doesn't matter. What do you think?

PRUDENCE: But what do *you* think?

STUART: It's not my place to say.

PRUDENCE: (*Irritated.*) Oh never mind. I don't want to talk about it.

STUART: I see. (*Makes a note.*)

PRUDENCE: (*Noticing he's making notes; to make up.*) I did answer one of those ads.

STUART: Oh?

PRUDENCE: Yes.

STUART: How did it work out?

PRUDENCE: Very badly. The guy was a jerk. He talked about my breasts, he has a male lover, and he wept at the table. It was really ridiculous. I should have known better.

STUART: Well, you can always come back to me, babe. I'll light your fire for you anytime.

PRUDENCE: Stuart, I've told you you can't talk to me that way if I'm to stay in therapy with you.

STUART: You're mighty attractive when you're angry.

PRUDENCE: Stuart . . . Dr. Framingham, many women who have been seduced by their psychiatrists take them to court . . .

STUART: Yeah, but you wanted it, baby . . .

PRUDENCE: How could I have "wanted" it? One of our topics has been that I don't know what I want.

STUART: Yeah, but you wanted that, baby.

PRUDENCE: Stop calling me baby. Really, I must be out of my mind to keep seeing you. (*Pause.*) Obviously you can't be my therapist after we've had an affair.

STUART: Two lousy nights aren't an affair.

PRUDENCE: You never said they were lousy.

STUART: They were great. You were great. I was great. Wasn't I, baby? It was the fact that it was only two nights that was lousy.

PRUDENCE: Dr. Framingham, it's the common belief that it is wrong for therapists and their patients to have sex together.

STUART: Not in California.

PRUDENCE: We are not in California.

STUART: We could move there. Buy a house, get a Jacuzzi.

PRUDENCE: Stuart . . . Dr. Framingham, we're not right for one another. I feel you have masculinity problems. I hate your belt buckle. I didn't really even like you in bed.

STUART: I'm great in bed.

PRUDENCE: (*With some hesitation.*) You have problems with premature ejaculation.

STUART: Listen, honey, there's nothing premature about it. Our society is paced quickly, we all have a lot of things to do. I ejaculate quickly on purpose.

PRUDENCE: I don't believe you.

STUART: Fuck you, cunt.

PRUDENCE: (*Stands.*) Obviously I need to find a new therapist.

STUART: Okay, okay. I lost my temper. I'm sorry. But I'm human. Prudence, that's what you have to learn. People *are* human. You keep looking for perfection, you need to learn to accept imperfection. I can help you with that.

PRUDENCE: Maybe I really should sue you. I mean, I don't think you should have a license.

STUART: Prudence, you're avoiding the issue. The issue is you, not me. You're unhappy, you can't find a relationship you like, you don't like your job, you don't like the world. You *need* my help. I mean, don't get hung up on who should have a license. The issue is I can help you fit into the world. (*Very sincerely, sensitively.*) Really I can. Don't run away.

PRUDENCE: (*Sits.*) I don't think I believe you.

STUART: That's okay. We can work on that.

PRUDENCE: I don't know. I really don't think you're a good therapist. But the others are probably worse, I'm afraid.

STUART: They are. They're much worse. Really I'm very nice. I *like* women. Most men don't.

PRUDENCE: I'm getting one of my headaches again. (*Holds her forehead.*)

STUART: Do you want me to massage your neck?

PRUDENCE: Please don't touch me.

STUART: Okay, okay. (*Pause.*) Any other dreams?

PRUDENCE: No.

STUART: Perhaps we should analyze why you didn't like the man you met through the personal ad.

PRUDENCE: I . . . I . . . don't want to talk anymore today. I want to go home.

STUART: "You can never go home again."

PRUDENCE: Perhaps not. But I can return to my apartment. You're making my headache worse.

STUART: I think we should finish the session. I think it's important.

PRUDENCE: I just can't talk anymore.

STUART: We don't have to talk. But we have to stay in the room.

PRUDENCE: How much longer?

STUART: (*Looks at watch.*) Thirty minutes.

PRUDENCE: Alright. But I'm not going to talk anymore.

STUART: Okay. (*Pause. They stare at one another.*) You're very beautiful when you're upset.

PRUDENCE: Please don't you talk either. (*They stare at each other; lights dim.*)

THE SEA GULL
by ANTON CHEKHOV

translated by Ann Dunnigan

ACT IV

Treplev, though still a young man, has known many disappointments. His mother, Irina Nikolayevna Arkadina, a famous actress, has given him scant affection or attention. He has been striving as a writer to become a serious artist but has had little success. And his childhood sweetheart, Nina, ran off with Trigorin, a celebrated writer of conventional novels and his mother's lover. Treplev knows that Nina's life, too, has been filled with disappointment—that she had a child with Trigorin, which died, and that he soon left her and resumed his relationship with Arkadina; that her family cut her off, and that she has been struggling to have a career as an actress in provincial theatre companies. He also knows that Nina returned to town a few days ago and has been staying at the inn.

It has been years since the hopeful days when he wrote avant garde plays and Nina acted in them in the theatre on his mother's estate, and though he has not seen her for a long time his love for her has not diminished. His last contacts with her were the letters she used to send him which she always signed "The Sea Gull," referring to an incident in which Treplev, because of his own distress, shot a sea gull that, by chance, he happened upon. Treplev is alone in his study in the evening, writing at his desk.

···

TREPLEV: (*Preparing to write, reads through what he has already written.*) I've talked so much about new forms, and now I feel that little by little I myself am falling into a convention. (*Reads.*) "The placards on the fence proclaimed..." "A pale face framed by dark hair..." Proclaimed... framed by dark hair... That's banal. (*Scratches out what he has written.*) I'll begin where the hero is awakened by the sound of rain, and throw out all the rest. The description of the moonlight night is long and artificial. Trigorin has worked out a method, it's easy for him.... With him a broken bottleneck glitters on the dam and the mill wheel casts a black shadow—and there you have a moonlight night; but with me there's the shimmering light, the silent twinkling of the stars, the distant sounds of a piano dying away on the still, fragrant air.... It's agonizing. (*A pause.*) Yes, I'm becoming more and more convinced that it's not a question of old and new forms, but that one writes, without even thinking about forms, writes because it pours freely from the soul. (*Someone taps on the window nearest the desk.*) What's that? (*Looks out the window.*) I don't see anything. (*Opens the French windows and peers into the garden.*) Someone ran down the steps. (*Calls.*) Who's there? (*Goes out; he can be heard walking rapidly along the veranda; a moment later returns with* NINA ZARECHNAYA.) Nina! Nina!

(NINA *lays her head on his breast and quietly sobs.*)

TREPLEV: (*Moved.*) Nina! Nina! It's you... you.... It's as though I had a presentiment, all day long my soul has been in terrible torment. (*Takes off her hat and cloak.*) Oh, my precious darling, she has come at last! Don't let us cry, don't!

NINA: There's someone here.

TREPLEV: No one.

NINA: Lock the doors, someone might come in.

TREPLEV: No one will come in.

NINA: I know Irina Nikolayevna is here. Lock the doors.

TREPLEV: (*Locks the right door, goes to the door left.*) There's no lock on this one. I'll put a chair against it. (*Puts an armchair against the door.*) Don't be afraid, no one will come in.

NINA: (*Looking intently into his face.*) Let me look at you. (*Looking around.*) It's warm, cozy. . . . This used to be the drawing room. Am I very much changed?

TREPLEV: Yes. . . . You are thinner, and your eyes have grown bigger. Nina, it seems so strange to be seeing you. Why wouldn't you let me come to see you? Why didn't you come sooner? I know you've been here almost a week. . . . I went there several times every day and stood under your window like a beggar.

NINA: I was afraid you might hate me. Every night I dream that you are looking at me and don't recognize me. If you only knew! Ever since I arrived I've been walking here . . . by the lake. I came near the house many times, but I couldn't bring myself to come in. Let's sit down. (*They sit down.*) Let's sit and talk, and talk. . . . It's nice here, warm and cozy. . . . Listen—the wind! There's a passage in Turgenev: "Happy the man who on such a night has a roof over his head, who has a warm corner of his own." I am a sea gull. . . . No, that's not it. (*Rubs her forehead.*) What was I saying? Yes . . . Turgenev . . . "And may the Lord help all homeless wanderers." . . . It doesn't matter. (*Sobs.*)

TREPLEV: Nina, you're crying again—Nina!

NINA: Never mind, it does me good. . . . I haven't cried for two years. Yesterday, in the late evening, I came into the garden to see if our theater was still there. It's still standing. I began to cry, for the first time in two years, and I felt relieved, my soul felt clear. See, I'm not crying now. (*Takes his hand.*) And so you have become a writer. . . . You are a writer—and I am an actress. . . . We, too, have been drawn into the whirlpool. . . . I used to live happily, like a child— I'd wake up in the morning singing; I loved you and I dreamed of fame . . . and now? Tomorrow, early in the morning, I must go to Yelets, third class . . . traveling with peasants, and at Yelets the educated merchants will pester me with their attentions. It's a coarse life.

TREPLEV: Why to Yelets?

NINA: I've accepted an engagement for the whole winter. It's time I was going.

TREPLEV: Nina, I cursed you, I hated you, I tore up all your letters and photographs, but every minute I was conscious that my soul was bound to yours forever. I can never stop loving you. Ever since I lost you, and my work began to be published, my life has been unbearable—I am miserable. . . . All of a sudden my youth was snatched from me, and now I feel as if I had been living in this world for ninety years. I call to you, I kiss the ground you walked on; wherever I look I see your face, that tender smile that used to shine on me in the best years of my life. . . .

NINA: (*Confused.*) Why does he talk like that, why does he talk like that?

TREPLEV: I am alone, I have no one's affection to warm me, I am as cold as if I were living in a dungeon, and no matter what I write, it's dry, hard, dark. Stay here, Nina, I implore you, or let me go with you!
(*NINA quickly puts on her hat and cloak.*)

TREPLEV: Nina, why? For God's sake, Nina. . . . (*Looks at her putting on her things.*)
(*A pause.*)

NINA: My horses are waiting at the gate. Don't see me off. I'll go by myself . . . (*Through tears.*) Give me some water. . . .

TREPLEV: (*Gives her a glass of water.*) Where are you going now?

NINA: To town (*Pause.*) Is Irina Nikolayevna here?

TREPLEV: Yes. . . . On Thursday, Uncle was ill and we telegraphed her to come.

NINA: Why do you say you kissed the ground I walked on? I ought to have been killed. (*Leans on the table.*) I'm so tired! If I could rest . . . rest! (*Raising her head.*) I am a sea gull. . . . No, that's not it. . . . I'm an actress. Ah, well! (*Hears ARKADINA and TRIGORIN laughing, listens, then runs to the door on the left and looks through the keyhole.*) So, he's here, too. . . . (*Goes to TREPLEV.*) Well, it doesn't matter. . . . He didn't believe in the theater, he always laughed at my dreams, and gradually I too ceased believing and lost heart. And then there was the anxiety of love, the jealousy, the constant fears for my baby. . . . I grew petty, trivial, my acting was insipid. . . . I didn't know what to do with my hands, I didn't know how to stand on the stage, I couldn't control my voice. You can't imagine what it's like to feel that you are acting abominably. I am a sea gull. No, that's not it. . . . Do you remember, you shot a sea gull? A man came along by chance, saw it, and having nothing better to do, destroyed it. . . . A subject for a short story. . . . No, that's not it. . . . (*Rubs her forehead.*) What was I saying? . . . I was talking about the stage. . . . I'm not like that now. . . . Now I'm a real actress, I act with delight, with rapture, I'm intoxicated when I'm on the stage, and I feel that I act beautifully. And since I have been here, I've been walking, continually walking and thinking . . . and I think and feel that my soul is growing stronger with each day. . . . I know now, I understand, that in our work, Kostya—whether it's acting or writing—what's important is not fame, not glory, not the things I used to dream of, but the ability to endure. To be able to bear one's cross and have faith. I have faith, and it's not so painful now, and when I think of my vocation, I'm not afraid of life.

TREPLEV: (*Sadly.*) You have found your way, you know where you are going, but I'm still drifting in a chaos of images and dreams, without knowing why it is necessary, or for whom. . . . I have no faith, and I don't know what my vocation is.

NINA: (*Listening.*) Sh-sh! . . . I'm going. Good-bye. When I become a great actress, come and see me. Promise? And now. . . . (*Presses his hand.*) It's late. I can hardly stand on my feet. . . . I'm exhausted and hungry. . . .

TREPLEV: Stay, I'll give you supper. . . .

NINA: No, no. . . . Don't go with me, I'll go alone. . . . My horses are not far. . . . So, she brought him with her? Well, it doesn't matter. When you see Trigorin, don't say anything to him. . . . I love him. I love him even more than before. . . . A subject for a short story . . . I love him, love him passionately, desperately. . . . How good life used to be, Kostya! Do you remember? How clear, how pure, warm, and joyous, and our feelings—our feelings were like tender, delicate flowers. . . . Do you remember? (*Recites.*) "Men, lions, eagles, and partridges, horned deer, geese, spiders, silent fish that dwell in the deep, starfish, and creatures invisible to the eye—these and all living things, all, all living things, having completed their sad cycle, are no more. . . . For thousands of years the earth has borne no living creature. And now in vain this poor moon lights her lamp. Cranes no longer wake and cry in meadows, May beetles are heard no more in linden groves." . . . (*Impulsively embraces* TRE-PLEV *and runs out through the French windows.*)

ANNIE AND ARTHUR

by Michael Schulman

*As the play begins, the fading light of dusk entering through
the windows reveals a dusty living room with the furniture
covered by sheets. Outside (off stage) we hear Annie telling
Arthur, her husband, about her excitement at finally coming
home after so many years. Annie enters and as she lights
some candles and uncovers the furniture, she continues to
expound on her joy at being back together in their lovely
country home. We see that Annie is alone.*

*Soon there is loud rapping on the door and Jack enters,
gun in hand. He is the county caretaker of abandoned properties and this is one of the properties that has been on his
list for years. Annie eventually convinces Jack that she is
the rightful owner of the home and also that her husband
has gone upstairs to sleep. Soon these two lonely, mis-
matched people find themselves drawn to each other. Annie's romantic credo irritates Jack who has learned to
protect himself from people by avoiding them. Yet, against
his better judgment, he finds himself attracted by Annie's
innocence (and subtle flirtatiousness). Jack presents a danger to Annie's fantasy world, yet she desperately does not
want to be alone.*

*Annie has just convinced Jack not to kill a mouse that
was caught in a trap. She went to the cellar to get a box
to make a bed for the mouse, leaving Jack alone in the
living room.*

(ANNIE exits to the cellar. After a few seconds JACK crosses toward steps leading to the second floor landing. He quickly crosses back to his jacket hanging on the front door, removes the gun from the jacket and tucks it into his pants. He then goes back to the steps and ascends them quietly and cautiously. ANNIE re-enters.)

ANNIE: What are you doing?!

JACK: Are you sure somebody's up there?

ANNIE: Of course. My husband is up there. . . . You heard him yourself.

JACK: I don't know what I heard. He sleeps like a dead man. With all that calling and screaming you were doing, how come he didn't wake up?

ANNIE: I told you, we were both very tired and he's a very sound sleeper. Maybe he took some sleeping pills.

JACK: Very peculiar.

ANNIE: Please don't go up there. He'll be very frightened if he awakens and sees you.

JACK: Peculiar.

ANNIE: What?

JACK: You.

ANNIE: You said that before. Let's have another drink, okay? We'll toast the rescue of the mouse. You handled him very gently and I thank you.

JACK: Yeah, and he crapped in my hand.

ANNIE: He was just frightened. Here, let me wet this for you. *(She takes the dish towel, wets it, and goes to wipe his hand.)* Please put that gun away and have another drink with me.

JACK: *(Taking the towel from her.)* You said you were tired before.

ANNIE: Yes . . . no. I'm wide awake now. I'm restless now. All this excitement . . . my mind gets so crowded and restless. Sleeping was always hard for me in this old house with its creaks and its squeaks. Arthur would always have to be in bed early so he could be fresh for court in the morning, and I used to lie awake for hours listening to the night sounds . . . creaks and squeaks . . . frightening sounds—especially that last year.

JACK: Why, did the squeaks get worse? *(She doesn't answer.)* Did the squeaks get worse?

ANNIE: No . . . no, I was alone then.

JACK: Where was your husband? In the Army or something?

ANNIE: Not exactly. Just away . . . gone. The sun glaring up from the snow—

JACK: What?

ANNIE: What?

JACK: What about the sun?

ANNIE: The sun? . . . Just a memory.

JACK: Was that your first husband?

ANNIE: The cold winter sun through the trees—

JACK: I asked if that was your first husband.

ANNIE: What?

JACK: You said your husband went away.

ANNIE: Oh . . . No. There's only been one husband, one true-love husband for Annie; same husband that's probably snoring his sweet head off right now upstairs. He came back.

JACK: Oh.

ANNIE: He came back because he loved me.

JACK: Any kids?

ANNIE: No. But maybe we'll adopt some now. Kids might have made it easier during those years alone. Maybe not. Who knows? It doesn't matter now, does it? When I spake of loneliness, I tell you, I knew that of which I spake.

JACK: How long was he gone?

ANNIE: Eight years.

JACK: Eight years! Your husband came back after eight years? That's a long time between housecalls.

ANNIE: Terribly long. I couldn't believe it myself. But there he was two weeks ago.

JACK: Two weeks ago!

ANNIE: There he was—a little gray at the temples, but just as handsome . . . even more handsome—saying "Annie" . . . "Annie"—It makes me so happy to think about it I can hardly speak. He said, "Annie, I miss you. Let's go home."

JACK: Weren't you angry at all . . . his running out on you like that and then just popping up eight years later?

ANNIE: No, not one bit angry. Just so happy. I thought that during those lonely years I had turned hard as stone, had forgotten how to love or even to want love anymore. I was so sure I had surrounded my heart with a high impenetrable wall. And then, there he was, and there was no wall there at all.

JACK: I don't think I could take anybody back that left me like that. I don't think so.

ANNIE: Then you've never really been in love. You don't think about things like that, about the past. You just know that there is one person in this whole world with whom you belong and that he's asking you to come home with him. And there is nothing to think about or decide.

JACK: What about your pride?

ANNIE: You don't think about it.

JACK: I would think about it. You can't let people step on you and think that anything goes with your feelings. I couldn't love anybody who did that to me.

ANNIE: No, you're misunderstanding. He never wanted to hurt me.

JACK: I can't believe what I'm hearing.

ANNIE: Why?

JACK: Why? . . . Forget it. Like I said, it doesn't pay to mix with people, they're all crazy.

ANNIE: I'm not crazy. I know what I'm saying.

JACK: Wait a minute. I'm remembering hearing about something that's giving me a curious feeling about what you're saying. I'm remembering hearing about some couple around here, before I moved here—they said the husband caught his wife with another man. They said he came home unexpected from a business trip and he walked right in and caught them going at it in bed. They said the scandal cost him his job. Yes, that kind of thing must have been pretty big news for this little town. They said—

ANNIE: It's getting late now, Mr. Bristow; and I better put these groceries away before they spoil.

(She crosses toward kitchen.)

JACK: Hold on, I'm in the middle of an interesting recollection here. They said—and I think I'm remembering it right—they said he was a lawyer, actually an assistant district—

ANNIE: I think you better go home now, Mr. Bristow.

JACK: Well what do you know.

ANNIE: Please go home now, Mr. Bristow.

JACK: So it was you.

ANNIE: People can be cruel, Mr. Bristow, when they don't understand what they hear.

JACK: Well what do you know about that.

ANNIE: When they don't want to understand what they hear.

JACK: To think that you were giving me a sermon on true love and justice and all that crap.

ANNIE: Please, please don't be cruel to me. Not now. You don't understand.

JACK: So, it was you they were talking about. All that holier-than-thou crap, and it was you.

ANNIE: Don't, please . . .

JACK: So, it was you.

ANNIE: Yes, it was me. It was me. Why is that so hard to understand? In my sermon, as you called it, I didn't claim any exemptions for myself or to be above stumbling and falling too. What do you want me to say?

JACK: When I fell through the ice it was an accident, lady, simply an accident.

ANNIE: Yes, yes, yes, and my fall was out of my own weakness and ignorance. Yes! And I have suffered for it terribly. At least you could run back up the hill and soon it was over. Where was I to run? Where was the warmth at the top of the hill for me?

JACK: He lost his job because of you.

ANNIE: Yes! . . . No. If you want to know the whole truth, it wasn't just his job; it was his career he lost because of me.

JACK: What do you mean?

ANNIE: He just walked away from it all. He left. He disappeared. I begged him to listen to me. I tried to explain. He walked out of the house and I never saw him again. He walked out and seemed to vanish into the winter air, into the sun. The low winter sun was shining through the trees, was glaring up off the snow, was glaring into my eyes. When I got to the door I could barely see him. He was walking toward the setting sun and I could barely make out his silhouette; and then he seemed to vanish into the air like a mirage. By the time the word came that he had been fired, he was gone anyway.

JACK: Until two weeks ago.

ANNIE: Yes.

JACK: What a humiliation for him.

ANNIE: Yes. Yes. Yes. Why have you become my judge? I was young and weak, and maybe I didn't feel needed enough. Maybe I wanted him to stumble once and reach to me for help. I don't know. It's all shadows now, so hard to remember, all dimmed by the memory of that blinding sun. He was so self-contained, always so busy with his work, always traveling—away for weeks at a time on some investigation or other. I loved him, I did . . . I always did. But sometimes I couldn't bear being alone, left by myself . . . left out. That's all there ever was to it. A simple desire for companionship, that's all. Can't I ever be forgiven?

JACK: Did your husband forgive you?

ANNIE: Yes. He came back to me. He forgave me and came back.

JACK: People are fools.

ANNIE: Why? Because they make mistakes and forgive the mistakes of others?

JACK: Because they are fools, that's all!

DYLAN

by Sidney Michaels

ACT II

It is the early 1950s and Dylan Thomas, renowned Welsh poet in his late thirties, is touring America with his wife Caitlin, presenting his poetry at universities and literary clubs across the country. Dylan will die on this tour at the White Horse Tavern in New York City. He smokes much too much and drinks much too much, and when Caitlin is not around has been having affairs with some of the adoring women he has met.

As this scene begins, Dylan and Caitlin are asleep in a darkened hotel room in Texas. They are in the midst of their whirlwind tour which was organized for them by John Malcolm Brinnin, a poet and friend.

....

(The LIGHTS go up on a darkened hotel room in Texas. Asleep in the bed are DYLAN and CAITLIN. Suddenly DYLAN sits bolt upright, grabs the clock and shakes it.)

DYLAN: No! No! It can't be true! My God! (*He turns and shakes CAITLIN.*) Cat! Cat! Wake up!

CAITLIN: (*From under the covers.*) Not if we're still in Texas!

DYLAN: Wake up! The bloody alarm clock has stabbed us in the back.

CAITLIN: We forgot to set it. Jesus, Dylan!

DYLAN: Get up. We've got to get out of here and catch the damn bus to New Orleans by six.

CAITLIN: Where are we, in the name of God?

DYLAN: In Houston.

CAITLIN: No, we were in Houston last week.

DYLAN: (*Crossing the room.*) Well, then we're in Austin. They're all alike . . . shite! I stubbed my toe.

CAITLIN: I hate America!

DYLAN: Will you get out of the bed? It's Tuesday. There's four thousand people at two-fifty a head going to be at the Municipal Auditorium in New Orleans tomorrow night and you're languishing there like you thought you were the Queen of Sheba!

CAITLIN: When I go to hell they're going to make me lie forever on this mattress.

DYLAN: Holy God, my wrist watch isn't going. What does yours say?

CAITLIN: Ten past five.

DYLAN: Great!

CAITLIN: And not ticking.

DYLAN: (*With sarcasm.*) Great!

CAITLIN: (*Leaping up and running.*) Me first in the oathroom!

DYLAN: You don't have half as much to do in there as I do. Well, hell, I'll start packing and shave in here. Caitlin, why do you have to unpack and spread us out over ten drawers, every time we move into a hotel room?

CAITLIN: (*From the other room.*) I have to make a nest, don't I?

DYLAN: In Wales our nest is a sight to behold. I think you do it just to drive me out of my mind. My God, what a beard I've got!

CAITLIN: No sleep! No sleep! We never get any sleep on this bloody tour.

DYLAN: Say, this is Tuesday, isn't it?

CAITLIN: (*Comes back into room.*) Well, last night was Monday night, Dylan—it should be Tuesday.

DYLAN: Of course. Of course. It's dark out. (*He's peering out the window.*) There's a very peculiar lack of light out today. Like a tropical storm brewing.

CAITLIN: It's probably still Monday night.

DYLAN: Yes. Yes. I feel as if it were. Oh, now I see. It's dawn. We've tons of time. I can see the sun there rising in the west. Not a bad party, though, they gave us after last night's reading.

CAITLIN: If you hadn't thrown that book at me, I would never have thrown the lamp!

DYLAN: Worst of it was after we told them all to go to hell and slammed the door, having to go back to borrow the cab fare.

CAITLIN: Well, it was that or not have enough for even a bus to New Orleans.

DYLAN: And damn Brinnin. Sending us that ridiculous wire, "lest you forget," as if we couldn't get from Dallas to New Orleans without being prodded like pigs every inch of the way.

CAITLIN: And he didn't send us a penny to get there with. Dirty Brinnin.

DYLAN: Dirty Brinnin. He's kept a shamefully loose grip on this tour is all I can say. I mean he has no right to assume we've money without checking with us.

CAITLIN: You should have written him weeks ago.

DYLAN: Who's had time to write letters? I'll call him after breakfast. My God, I'm starved. I feel as if I haven't eaten in two days. Tour's nearly over and we haven't a nickel to show for it. Well, it's certainly different this time with you along! It's worse!

CAITLIN: I didn't ship two hundred dollars' worth of toys across the Atlantic Ocean!

DYLAN: No! You shipped our dirty laundry from Chicago to San Francisco for forty dollars.

CAITLIN: I'd do it again. I don't want to go to New Orleans! I want to go home to Wales!

DYLAN: Now, you listen to me a minute. Our way of life is a nuthouse. Now, I've seen another way of life in my travels and if you drive me too far, Cat, I'll have to take it. It doesn't include you.

CAITLIN: "O, Cat, you're the only girl for me," am I?

DYLAN: Love has nothing to do with it. It isn't enough to love you, Cat—I have to support you even if I have to leave you to do it. Now, New Orleans'll make it up to us. There's profit there. Then there's Washington.

CAITLIN: I'll go home without you! Who is she?

DYLAN: We don't have the fare. Don't you understand? We can't even afford to get out of the country.

CAITLIN: I've got such a headache!

DYLAN: So have I. Don't fold everything. Just throw it together. Come sit on a suitcase with me. I don't understand how the devil without so much as an added Kleenex, these bags get thicker and thicker every time we pack them up again.

CAITLIN: (*Starting to cry.*) I don't want to sit on a suitcase.

DYLAN: Cat, don't cry. Don't cry, Caitlin. I'll take care of you. I'm at a great turning point in my life. It just isn't so easy to adjust for a fool like me. But I'm trying as hard as I can.

CAITLIN: That isn't why I'm crying, Dylan.

DYLAN: Why are you crying, Cat? I'm listening, Cat.

CAITLIN: Because the sun doesn't rise in the west. (*He leaps up and looks out the window.*)

DYLAN: It's gotten darker. You're right. It's Tuesday night.

CAITLIN: It must be after six, Dylan. That means we've missed our bus. Good-bye, New Orleans!

DYLAN: Not so fast. It's about eight or eight-thirty. We'll wire Brinnin for money and we'll catch a plane. Hello, room service. What time do you have? Eight-thirty. Excellent. Hold the phone, please. I want to order dinner for two. Cat, now what would delight your sea-changed palate? Strictly American cuisine, of course. A deboned, defeathered, defrosted hot dog under glass, washed down with a jumbo-sized paper cup of fermented Coke? Or will it be Chinese food flown in from Pittsburgh?

CAITLIN: (*Softly.*) Ask room service what day it is, Dylan, while you're at it.

DYLAN: (*A long look at her and then into the phone.*) Hello, room service? This is *Tuesday* evening, of course . . . It's *Wednesday* evening? It's eight-thirty on Wednesday evening? It can't be that—I've got four thousand people sitting in the Municipal Auditorium in New Orleans waiting for me. Yes, I'd like to speak to the manager.

CAITLIN: Dylan, give up. Hang up.

DYLAN: (*On the phone.*) Never mind. (*He hangs up the phone. He crosses and sits beside her. They just sit there quietly. DYLAN lights two cigarettes and hands her one.*)

CAITLIN: Shall we call the Municipal Auditorium, Dylan?

DYLAN: And say what? "Go home. We're a thousand miles to the west of you"?

CAITLIN: Shall we call Brinnin?

DYLAN: Poor Brinnin.

CAITLIN: Poor Brinnin. Well, there's one consolation. Things can't get worse.

DYLAN: I don't know. There's still Washington, D.C.

CAITLIN: At least, we've got time to get there.

DYLAN: That's the spirit. Set your watch.

AMADEUS

by Peter Shaffer

ACT I

Wolfgang Amadeus Mozart is depicted in this play as a silly man who happens to have a gift for writing glorious music. Mozart is unaware that his career is being hampered by Salieri, a popular court composer, who is fiercely jealous of Mozart's musical genius and furious at God for giving such a gift, not to someone proper and devout like himself, but to someone so vulgar and inane. Mozart has barely been eking out a living playing concerts and wants desperately to be hired as the musical tutor of the Princess Elizabeth, a position to be awarded by Salieri.

Salieri has invited Constanze, Mozart's attractive young wife, to visit him, ostensibly to plead Mozart's case for the position. But Salieri, despite his inexperience as a seducer of women, has other things on his mind. The scene begins as Constanze enters Salieri's salon.

....

CONSTANZE: (*Curtsying.*) Excellency.

SALIERI: *Benvenuta.* (*To* VALET *in dismissal.*) *Grazie.* (*The* VALET *goes.*) Well. You have come.

CONSTANZE: I should not have done. My husband would be frantic if he knew. He's a very jealous man.

SALIERI: Are you a jealous woman?

CONSTANZE: Why do you ask?

SALIERI: It's not a passion I understand. . . . You're looking even prettier than you were last night, if I may say so.

CONSTANZE: *Ta* very much! . . . I brought you some manuscripts by Wolfgang. When you see them you'll understand how right he is for a royal appointment. Will you look at them, please, while I wait?

SALIERI: You mean now?

CONSTANZE: Yes, I have to take them back with me. He'll miss them otherwise. He doesn't make copies. These are all the originals.

SALIERI: Sit down. Let me offer you something special.

CONSTANZE: (*Sitting.*) What's that?

SALIERI: (*Producing the box.*) *Capezzoli di Venere.* Nipples of Venus. Roman chestnuts in brandied sugar.

CONSTANZE: No, thank you.

SALIERI: Do try. They were made especially for you.

CONSTANZE: Me?

SALIERI: Yes. They're quite rare.

CONSTANZE: Well then, I'd better, hadn't I? Just one. . . . *Ta* very much. (*She takes one and puts it in her mouth. The taste amazes her.*) Oh! . . . Oh! . . . Oh! . . . They're *delish!*

SALIERI: (*Lustfully watching her eat.*) Aren't they?

CONSTANZE: Mmmmm!

SALIERI: Have another.

CONSTANZE: (*Taking two more.*) I couldn't possibly. (*Carefully he moves round behind her, and seats himself on the chair next to her.*)

SALIERI: I think you're the most generous girl in the world.

CONSTANZE: Generous?

SALIERI: It's my word for you. I thought last night that Constanze is altogether too stiff a name for that girl. I shall rechristen her "Generosa." *La Generosa.* Then I'll write a glorious song for her under that title and she'll sing it, just for me.

CONSTANZE: (*Smiling.*) I am much out of practice, sir.

SALIERI: *La Generosa.* (*He leans a little toward her.*) Don't tell me it's going to prove inaccurate, my name for you.

CONSTANZE: (*Coolly.*) What name do you give your wife, Excellency?

SALIERI: (*Equally coolly.*) I'm not an Excellency, and I call my wife Signora Salieri. If I named her anything else it would be *La Statua.* She's a very upright lady.

CONSTANZE: Is she here now? I'd like to meet her.

SALIERI: Alas, no. At the moment she's visiting her mother in Verona. (*She starts very slightly out of her chair.* SALIERI *gently restrains her.*)

SALIERI: Constanze: tomorrow evening I dine with the Emperor. One word from me recommending your husband as tutor to the Princess Elizabeth, and that invaluable post is his. Believe me, when I speak to His Majesty in matters musical, no one contradicts me.

CONSTANZE: I believe you.

SALIERI: *Bene.* (*Still sitting, he takes his* mouchoir *and delicately wipes his mouth with it.*) Surely service of that sort deserves a little recompense in return?

CONSTANZE: How little? (*Slight pause.*)

SALIERI: The size of a kiss. (*Slight pause.*)

CONSTANZE: Just one? (*Slight pause.*)

SALIERI: If one seems fair to you. (*She looks at him—then kisses him lightly on the mouth.*)

SALIERI: Does it?

(*She gives him a longer kiss. He makes to touch her with his hand. She breaks off.*)

CONSTANZE: I fancy that's fairness enough. (*Pause.*)

SALIERI: (*Carefully.*) A pity. . . . It's somewhat small pay, to secure a post every musician in Vienna is hoping for.

CONSTANZE: What do you mean?

SALIERI: Is it not clear?

CONSTANZE: No. Not at all.

SALIERI: Another pity. . . . A thousand pities. (*Pause.*)

CONSTANZE: I don't believe it . . . I just don't believe it!

SALIERI: What?

CONSTANZE: What you've just said.

SALIERI: (*Hastily.*) I said nothing! What did I say? (CONSTANZE *gets up and* SALIERI *rises in panic.*)

CONSTANZE: Oh, I'm going! . . . I'm getting out of this!

SALIERI: Constanze . . .

CONSTANZE: Let me pass, please.

SALIERI: Constanze, listen to me! I'm a clumsy man. You think me sophisticated—I'm not at all. Take a true look. I've no cunning. I live on ink and sweetmeats. I never see women at all. . . . When I met you last night, I envied Mozart from the depths of my soul. Out of that envy came stupid thoughts. For one silly second I dared imagine that—out of the vast store you obviously possess—you might spare me one coin of tenderness your rich husband does not need—and inspire me also. (*Pause. She laughs.*) I amuse.

CONSTANZE: Mozart was right. You're wicked.

SALIERI: He said that?

CONSTANZE: ''All wops are performers,'' he said. ''Be very careful with that one.'' Meaning you. He was being comic, of course.

SALIERI: Yes. (*Abruptly he turns his back on her.*)

CONSTANZE: But not that comic, actually. I mean you're acting a pretty obvious role, aren't you, dear? A small-town boy, and all the time as clever as cutlets! . . . (*Mock tender.*) Ah!—you are sulking? *Are* you? . . . When Mozart sulks I smack his botty. He rather likes it. Do you want me to scold you a bit and smack your botty too? (*She hits him lightly with the portfolio. He turns in a fury.*)

SALIERI: How dare you?! . . . *You silly, common girl!* (*A dreadful silence.*)

(*Icy.*) Forgive me. Let us confine our talk to your husband. He is a brilliant keyboard player, no question. However, the Princess Elizabeth also requires a tutor in vocal music. I am not convinced he is the man for that. I would like to look at the pieces you've brought, and decide if he is mature enough. I will study them overnight—and you will study my proposal. Not to be vague: that is the price. (*He extends his hand for the portfolio, and she surrenders it.*) Good afternoon.

(*He turns from her and places it on a chair. She lingers—tries to speak—cannot—and goes out quickly.*)

FRANKIE AND JOHNNY IN THE CLAIR DE LUNE

by Terrence McNally

ACT I

*Frankie and Johnny met a few weeks ago in the restaurant
where they both work; Frankie is a waitress, Johnny is a
short-order cook. Now they are in Frankie's one-room
apartment in a tenement building in New York City where
they just had sex for the first time, great sex. And then they
talked and laughed and tried to get comfortable with each
other. Just before the following scene, Frankie offered to
make Johnny a meatloaf sandwich and Johnny, wanting to
make love again, asked her to open her robe so he could
look at her beautiful "pussy." Despite her discomfort, she
complied and somehow got into talking about her bad experience with a pet parakeet. Now she has closed her robe
and is making the sandwiches in the kitchen area. To
Johnny, this evening is as much about romance as sex. He
has fallen in love with Frankie. Frankie, having been hurt
many times before, resists his attempts to talk about feelings
and their future together.*

....

FRANKIE: You want to turn on the television.
JOHNNY: Why?
FRANKIE: We don't have to watch it. You know, just sound.
    I do it all the time. Company. It beats a parakeet.
JOHNNY: I'd rather watch you.
FRANKIE: Do you ever watch the Channel 5 Movie Club on
    Saturday night? That's right, you got a VCR. They have

this thing called the Movie Club. Talk about dumb gimmicks. You put your name and address on a postcard. If they draw it, you go on the air and tell everybody what your favorite movie is and they show it, along with intermission breaks where they tell you certain little-known facts about the movie I just as soon wouldn't have known, such as "Susan Hayward was already stricken with a fatal cancer when she made this sparkling comedy." Kind of puts a pall on things, you know?

JOHNNY: I was on that program.

FRANKIE: You were not.

JOHNNY: Sure I was.

FRANKIE: What was your favorite movie?

JOHNNY: I forget.

FRANKIE: You probably don't even have one.

(JOHNNY *has gotten up off the bed and come over to where* FRANKIE *is working.* HE *finds a place to sit very close to where* SHE *stands making the sandwiches.*)

JOHNNY: You know what I was thinking while I was looking at you over there?

FRANKIE: I should have guessed this was coming!

JOHNNY: I was thinking "There's got to be more to life than this" but at times like this I'll be goddamned if I know what it is.

FRANKIE: You don't give up, do you?

JOHNNY: I want to drown in this woman. I want to die here. So why is she talking about parakeets and meatloaf? The inequity of human relationships! I actually thought that word: "inequity." I didn't even know it was in my vocabulary. And what's the other one? Disparity! Yeah, that's it. The disparity between us at that moment. I mean, there I was, celebrating you, feasting on your loveliness, and you were talking about a fucking, pardon my French, parakeet!

FRANKIE: Maybe it's because I was ill at ease.

JOHNNY: Because of me?

FRANKIE: Maybe I don't like being looked at down there that way, how the hell should I know?

JOHNNY: Bullshit! You don't like being looked at, period.

FRANKIE: Ow!

JOHNNY: What happened?

FRANKIE: I cut myself.

JOHNNY: Let me see.

FRANKIE: It's all right.

JOHNNY: Let me see.

(*HE sucks the blood from her finger.*)

FRANKIE: Look, I don't think this is going to work out. It was very nice while it lasted but like I said . . .

JOHNNY: You'll live.

(*HE releases her hand.*)

FRANKIE: . . . I'm a BLT down sort of person and I think you're looking for someone a little more pheasant under glass. Where are you going?

JOHNNY: I'll get a bandage.

FRANKIE: That's okay.

JOHNNY: No problem.

FRANKIE: Really. What are you doing?

(*JOHNNY has gone into the bathroom. We hear him going through the medicine cabinet looking for a bandage as HE continues to speak through the open door.*)

JOHNNY: I don't remember you saying you were a BLT down sort of person.

FRANKIE: I thought I implied it when I was talking about that meatloaf.

(*JOHNNY comes out of the bathroom with a box of Band-Aids and a bottle of iodine.*)

JOHNNY: It's because I said you had a beautiful pussy, isn't it? Give me your finger.

(*FRANKIE holds out her finger while JOHNNY disinfects and dresses it.*)

FRANKIE: It's because you said a lot of things. Ow!

JOHNNY: A man compliments a woman. All right, maybe he uses street talk but it's nice street talk, affectionate. It's not one of them ugly words, like the one I'm sure we're both familiar with, the one that begins with "c." I didn't say you had a beautiful "c." I was saying something loving and you took offense.

FRANKIE: I told you I wasn't very spontaneous!

JOHNNY: Boy, if you had said to me, "Johnny, you have the most terrific dick on you" I would be so happy.

(*HE finishes with the Band-Aids.*) There you go.

FRANKIE: Thank you.

JOHNNY: You want to see scarred fingers!
(*HE holds up his hands to* FRANKIE.)

FRANKIE: (*Wincing at the sight.*) Please!

JOHNNY: They don't hurt.

FRANKIE: I don't want to look.

JOHNNY: (*Looking at them.*) It's hard to connect to them. I mean, I'm not the type who should have scarry hands.

FRANKIE: You're so good with knives. I've watched you.

JOHNNY: She admits it. The haughty waitress has cast a lustful gaze on the Knight of the Grill.

FRANKIE: "Can that new guy chop and dice," Dena tells me. "Look at him go."

JOHNNY: Now, sure! It's a breeze. I can dice an onion blindfolded. These scars were then. On my way up the culinary ladder. I knew you were looking at me.

FRANKIE: It's human curiosity. A new face in the kitchen. Male. Look, I never said I was a nun.

JOHNNY: Hey, it's okay. It was mutual. I was looking at you.

FRANKIE: Besides, there aren't that many short-order cooks who have a dictionary and a copy of Shakespeare in their locker.

JOHNNY: You'd be surprised. We're an inquiring breed. We have our own quiz shows: *Cooks Want to Know.*

AN IDEAL HUSBAND

by Oscar Wilde

ACT I

It is the turn of the century in London and Sir Robert Chiltern and his wife are throwing a party at their spacious home in Grosvenor Square. Among the splendid guests is Mrs. Cheveley, an appealing, "graceful" and mysterious woman who was brought to the party by a friend of the Chilterns. Mrs. Cheveley, recently returned from Vienna, has come to the Chilterns, not merely for the pleasure of a gracious party, but to make a demand on Sir Robert.

Wilde describes Sir Robert, who is having a brilliant and unblemished career in the Foreign Office, as a young-looking man of forty, "with a slight touch of pride" and "an almost complete separation of passion and intellect." The other guests have gone to dinner and Sir Robert and Mrs. Cheveley, who had begun a conversation a short while earlier, return to the main room (the Octagon Room). He is clearly fascinated by her and is playing the charming host. (See other scene from this play in another section for more information.)

....

SIR ROBERT CHILTERN: And are you going to any of our country houses before you leave England, Mrs. Cheveley?

MRS. CHEVELEY: Oh, no! I can't stand your English house parties. In England people actually try to be brilliant at breakfast. That is dreadful of them! Only dull people are brilliant at breakfast. And then the family skeleton is always reading family prayers. My stay in England really depends on you, Sir Robert. (*Sits down on the sofa.*)

SIR ROBERT CHILTERN: (*Taking a seat beside her.*) Seriously?

MRS. CHEVELEY: Quite seriously. I want to talk to you about a great political and financial scheme, about this Argentine Canal Company, in fact.

SIR ROBERT CHILTERN: What a tedious, practical subject for you to talk about, Mrs. Cheveley!

MRS. CHEVELEY: Oh, I like tedious, practical subjects. What I don't like are tedious, practical people. There is a wide difference. Besides, you are interested, I know, in International Canal schemes. You were Lord Radley's secretary, weren't you, when the Government bought the Suez Canal shares?

SIR ROBERT CHILTERN: Yes. But the Suez Canal was a very great and splendid undertaking. It gave us our direct route to India. It had imperial value. It was necessary that we should have control. This Argentine scheme is a commonplace Stock Exchange swindle.

MRS. CHEVELEY: A speculation, Sir Robert! A brilliant, daring speculation.

SIR ROBERT CHILTERN: Believe me, Mrs. Cheveley, it is a swindle. Let us call things by their proper names. It makes matters simpler. We have all the information about it at the Foreign Office. In fact, I sent out a special Commission to inquire into the matter privately, and they report that the works are hardly begun, and as for the money already subscribed, no one seems to know what has become of it. The whole thing is a second Panama, and with not a quarter of the chance of success that miserable affair ever had. I hope you have not invested in it. I am sure you are far too clever to have done that.

MRS. CHEVELEY: I have invested very largely in it.

SIR ROBERT CHILTERN: Who could have advised you to do such a foolish thing?

MRS. CHEVELEY: Your old friend—and mine.

SIR ROBERT CHILTERN: Who?

MRS. CHEVELEY: Baron Arnheim.

SIR ROBERT CHILTERN: (*Frowning.*) Ah! yes. I remember

hearing, at the time of his death, that he had been mixed up in the whole affair.

MRS. CHEVELEY: It was his last romance. His last but one, to do him justice.

SIR ROBERT CHILTERN: (*Rising.*) But you have not seen my Corots yet. They are in the Music-room. Corots seem to go with music, don't they? May I show them to you?

MRS. CHEVELEY: (*Shaking her head.*) I am not in a mood tonight for silver twilights, or rose-pink dawns. I want to talk business. (*Motions to him with her fan to sit down again beside her.*)

SIR ROBERT CHILTERN: I fear I have no advice to give you, Mrs. Cheveley, except to interest yourself in something less dangerous. The success of the Canal depends, of course, on the attitude of England, and I am going to lay the report of the Commissioners before the House tomorrow night.

MRS. CHEVELEY: That you must not do. In your own interests, Sir Robert, to say nothing of mine, you must not do that.

SIR ROBERT CHILTERN: (*Looking at her in wonder.*) In my own interests? My dear Mrs. Cheveley, what do you mean? (*Sits down beside her.*)

MRS. CHEVELEY: Sir Robert, I will be quite frank with you. I want you to withdraw the report that you had intended to lay before the House, on the ground that you have reasons to believe that the Commissioners have been prejudiced or misinformed, or something. Then I want you to say a few words to the effect that the Government is going to reconsider the question, and that you have reason to believe that the Canal, if completed, will be of great international value. You know the sort of things ministers say in cases of this kind. A few ordinary platitudes will do. In modern life nothing produces such an effect as a good platitude. It makes the whole world kin. Will you do that for me?

SIR ROBERT CHILTERN: Mrs. Cheveley, you cannot be serious in making me such a proposition!

MRS. CHEVELEY: I am quite serious.

SIR ROBERT CHILTERN: (*Coldly.*) Pray allow me to believe that you are not.

MRS. CHEVELEY: (*Speaking with great deliberation and em-*

phasis.) Ah! but I am. And if you do what I ask you, I . . . will pay you very handsomely!

SIR ROBERT CHILTERN: Pay me!

MRS. CHEVELEY: Yes.

SIR ROBERT CHILTERN: I am afraid I don't quite understand what you mean.

MRS. CHEVELEY: (*Leaning back on the sofa and looking at him.*) How very disappointing! And I have come all the way from Vienna in order that you should thoroughly understand me.

SIR ROBERT CHILTERN: I fear I don't.

MRS. CHEVELEY: (*In her most nonchalant manner.*) My dear Sir Robert, you are a man of the world, and you have your price, I suppose. Everybody has nowadays. The drawback is that most people are so dreadfully expensive. I know I am. I hope you will be more reasonable in your terms.

SIR ROBERT CHILTERN: (*Rises indignantly.*) If you will allow me, I will call your carriage for you. You have lived so long abroad, Mrs. Cheveley, that you seem to be unable to realise that you are talking to an English gentleman.

MRS. CHEVELEY: (*Detains him by touching his arm with her fan, and keeping it there while she is talking.*) I realize that I am talking to a man who laid the foundation of his fortune by selling to a Stock Exchange speculator a Cabinet secret.

SIR ROBERT CHILTERN: (*Biting his lip.*) What do you mean?

MRS. CHEVELEY: (*Rising and facing him.*) I mean that I know the real origin of your wealth and your career, and I have got your letter, too.

SIR ROBERT CHILTERN: What letter?

MRS. CHEVELEY: (*Contemptuously.*) The letter you wrote to Baron Arnheim, when you were Lord Radley's secretary, telling the Baron to buy Suez Canal shares—a letter written three days before the Government announced its own purchase.

SIR ROBERT CHILTERN: (*Hoarsely.*) It is not true.

MRS. CHEVELEY: You thought that letter had been destroyed. How foolish of you! It is in my possession.

SIR ROBERT CHILTERN: The affair to which you allude was no more than a speculation. The House of Commons had not yet passed the bill; it might have been rejected.

MRS. CHEVELEY: It was a swindle, Sir Robert. Let us call

things by their proper names. It makes everything simpler. And now I am going to sell you that letter, and the price I ask for it is your public support of the Argentine scheme. You made your own fortune out of one canal. You must help me and my friends to make our fortunes out of another!

SIR ROBERT CHILTERN: It is infamous, what you propose— infamous!

MRS. CHEVELEY: Oh, no! This is the game of life as we all have to play it, Sir Robert, sooner or later!

SIR ROBERT CHILTERN: I cannot do what you ask me.

MRS. CHEVELEY: You mean you cannot help doing it. You know you are standing on the edge of a precipice. And it is not for you to make terms. It is for you to accept them. Supposing you refuse—

SIR ROBERT CHILTERN: What then?

MRS. CHEVELEY: My dear Sir Robert, what then? You are ruined, that is all! Remember to what a point your Puritanism in England has brought you. In old days nobody pretended to be a bit better than his neighbours. In fact, to be a bit better than one's neighbour was considered excessively vulgar and middle class. Nowadays, with our modern mania for morality, every one has to pose as a paragon of purity, incorruptibility, and all the other seven deadly virtues—and what is the result? You all go over like ninepins—one after the other. Not a year passes in England without somebody disappearing. Scandals used to lend charm, or at least interest, to a man—now they crush him. And yours is a very nasty scandal. You couldn't survive it. If it were known that as a young man, secretary to a great and important minister, you sold a Cabinet secret for a large sum of money, and that was the origin of your wealth and career, you would be hounded out of public life, you would disappear completely. And after all, Sir Robert, why should you sacrifice your entire future rather than deal diplomatically with your enemy? For the moment I am your enemy. I admit it! And I am much stronger than you are. The big battalions are on my side. You have a splendid position, but it is your splendid position that makes you so vulnerable. You can't defend it! And I am in attack. Of course I have not talked morality to you. You must admit in fairness that I have spared you that. Years ago you did a clever, unscrupulous thing; it turned out a great success. You owe to it your fortune and position. And now you have got to pay for it. Sooner or later we all have to pay for what we do. You have to pay now. Before I leave you tonight, you have got to promise me to suppress your report, and to speak in the House in favour of this scheme.

SIR ROBERT CHILTERN: What you ask is impossible.

MRS. CHEVELEY: You must make it possible. You are going to make it possible. Sir Robert, you know what your English newspapers are like. Suppose that when I leave this house I drive down to some newspaper office, and give them this scandal and the proofs of it. Think of their loathsome joy, of the delight they would have in dragging you down, of the mud and mire they would plunge you in. Think of the hypocrite with his greasy smile penning his leading article, and arranging the foulness of the public placard.

SIR ROBERT CHILTERN: Stop! You want me to withdraw the report and to make a short speech stating that I believe there are possibilities in the scheme?

MRS. CHEVELEY: (*Sitting down on the sofa.*) Those are my terms.

SIR ROBERT CHILTERN: (*In a low voice.*) I will give you any sum of money you want.

MRS. CHEVELEY: Even you are not rich enough, Sir Robert, to buy back your past. No man is.

SIR ROBERT CHILTERN: I will not do what you ask me. I will not.

MRS. CHEVELEY: You have to. If you don't . . . (*Rises from the sofa.*)

SIR ROBERT CHILTERN: (*Bewildered and unnerved.*) Wait a moment! What did you propose? You said that you would give me back my letter, didn't you?

MRS. CHEVELEY: Yes. That is agreed. I will be in the Ladies' Gallery tomorrow night at half-past eleven. If by that time— and you will have had heaps of opportunity—you have made an announcement to the House in the terms I wish, I shall hand you back your letter with the prettiest thanks, and the best, or at any rate the most suitable, compliment I can think of. I intend to play quite fairly with you. One should always play fairly . . . when one has the winning cards. The Baron taught me that . . . amongst other things.

SIR ROBERT CHILTERN: You must let me have time to consider your proposal.

MRS. CHEVELEY: No; you must settle now!

SIR ROBERT CHILTERN: Give me a week—three days!

MRS. CHEVELEY: Impossible! I have got to telegraph to Vienna tonight.

SIR ROBERT CHILTERN: My God! what brought you into my life?

MRS. CHEVELEY: Circumstances. (*Moves towards the door.*)

SIR ROBERT CHILTERN: Don't go. I consent. The report shall be withdrawn. I will arrange for a question to be put on the subject.

MRS. CHEVELEY: Thank you. I knew we should come to an amicable agreement. I understood your nature from the first. I analyzed you, though you did not adore me. And now you can get my carriage for me, Sir Robert. I see the people coming up from supper, and Englishmen always get romantic after a meal, and that bores me dreadfully.

(*Exit SIR ROBERT CHILTERN.*)

MEASURE FOR MEASURE

by William Shakespeare

ACT III, SCENE 2

Claudio sits in a Viennese jail, having been condemned to death for having had sex with his fiancée (she is pregnant), and thus violating the law against fornication outside of marriage—a law that had not been enforced for years. But the Duke, wanting to institute moral reform, has placed Angelo, a zealous official with a reputation for piety and discipline, in charge of the affairs of state and all laws are now being enforced. Claudio's sister, Isabella, a novice who has recently entered the convent, goes to Angelo to see if anything can be done to save her brother's life. And it turns out there is something. Angelo, who is not as pure as he pretends, finds himself drawn to this innocent young woman and tells her he will release her brother if she has sex with him. When she threatens to expose his offer, he assures her that, given his reputation, no one will believe her. Shaken by Angelo's treachery, Isabella goes to the prison to tell her brother what has happened, but hesitates, fearing he will ask her to dishonor herself to save his life.

....

CLAUDIO: Now, sister, what's the comfort?

ISABELLA: Why,
    As all comforts are; most good, most good
      indeed.
    Lord Angelo, having affairs to heaven,
    Intends you for his swift ambassador,

Where you shall be an everlasting leiger:
Therefore your best appointment make with
    speed;
To-morrow you set on.

CLAUDIO: Is there no remedy?

ISABELLA: None, but such remedy as, to save a head,
To cleave a heart in twain.

CLAUDIO: But is there any?

ISABELLA: Yes, brother, you may live:
There is a devilish mercy in the judge,
If you'll implore it, that will free your life,
But fetter you till death.

CLAUDIO: Perpetual durance?

ISABELLA: Ay, just; perpetual durance, a restraint,
Though all the world's vastidity you had.
To a determined scope.

CLAUDIO: But in what nature?

ISABELLA: In such a one as, you consenting to't,
Would bark your honour from that trunk you
    bear,
And leave you naked.

CLAUDIO: Let me know the point.

ISABELLA: O, I do fear thee, Claudio; and I quake,
Lest thou a feverous life shouldst entertain,
And six or seven winters more respect
Than a perpetual honour. Darest thou die?
The sense of death is most in apprehension;
And the poor beetle, that we tread upon,
In corporal sufferance finds a pang as great
As when a giant dies.

CLAUDIO: Why give you me this shame?
Think you I can a resolution fetch
From flowery tenderness? If I must die,
I will encounter darkness as a bride,
And hug it in mine arms.

ISABELLA: There spake my brother; there my father's grave
Did utter forth a voice. Yes, thou must die:
Thou art too noble to conserve a life
In base appliances. This outward-sainted deputy,
Whose settled visage and deliberate word
Nips youth i' the head, and follies doth emmew

As falcon doth the fowl, is yet a devil;
His filth within being cast, he would appear
A pond as deep as hell.

CLAUDIO: The prenzie Angelo!

ISABELLA: O, 'tis the cunning livery of hell,
The damned'st body to invest and cover
In prenzie guards! Dost thou think, Claudio?—
If I would yield him my virginity,
Thou mightst be freed.

CLAUDIO: O heavens! it cannot be.

ISABELLA: Yes, he would give't thee, from this rank offence,
So to offend him still. This night's the time
That I should do what I abhor to name,
Or else thou diest to-morrow.

CLAUDIO: Thou shalt not do't.

ISABELLA: O, were it but my life,
I'ld throw it down for your deliverance
As frankly as a pin.

CLAUDIO: Thanks, dear Isabel.

ISABELLA: Be ready, Claudio, for your death to-morrow.

CLAUDIO: Yes. Has he affections in him,
That thus can make him bite the law by the nose,
When he would force it? Sure, it is no sin;
Or of the deadly seven it is the least.

ISABELLA: Which is the least?

CLAUDIO: If it were damnable, he being so wise,
Why would he for the momentary trick
Be perdurably fined?—O Isabel!

ISABELLA: What says my brother?

CLAUDIO: Death is a fearful thing.

ISABELLA: And shamed life a hateful.

CLAUDIO: Ay, but to die, and go we know not where;
To lie in cold obstruction and to rot;
This sensible warm motion to become
A kneaded clod; and the delighted spirit
To bathe in fiery floods, or to reside
In thrilling region of thick-ribbed ice;
To be imprison'd in the viewless winds,
And blown with restless violence round about

The pendent world; or to be worse than worst
Of those that lawless and incertain thought
Imagine howling:—'tis too horrible!
The weariest and most loathed worldly life
That age, ache, penury, and imprisonment
Can lay on nature is a paradise
To what we fear of death.

ISABELLA: Alas, alas!

CLAUDIO: Sweet sister, let me live:
What sin you do to save a brother's life,
Nature dispenses with the deed so far
That it becomes a virtue.

ISABELLA: O you beast!
O faithless coward! O dishonest wretch!
Wilt thou be made a man out of my vice?
Is't not a kind of incest, to take life
From thine own sister's shame? What should I
     think?
Heaven shield my mother play'd my father fair!
For such a warped slip of wilderness
Ne'er issued from his blood. Take my defiance!
Die, perish! Might but my bending down
Reprieve thee from thy fate, it should proceed:
I'll pray a thousand prayers for thy death,
No word to save thee.

CLAUDIO: Nay, hear me, Isabel.

ISABELLA: O, fie, fie, fie!
Thy sin's not accidental, but a trade.
Mercy to thee would prove itself a bawd:
'Tis best that thou diest quickly.

CLAUDIO: O, hear me, Isabella!

MUCH ADO ABOUT NOTHING

by William Shakespeare

ACT IV, SCENE 1

Benedick is a young lord from Padua and Beatrice is the niece of the governor of Messina. Both scorned love and marriage, and continually tried to top each other with their wit. Their friends, recognizing that their bantering is merely a way to cover up their feelings for each other, scheme to bring them together. Each "by chance" overhears conversation about how he or she is loved by the other. But now something serious has happened. Beatrice's cousin, Hero, was about to marry Benedick's close friend, Claudio. But the evil Don John, brother of the Prince, managed to mislead Claudio into believing that Hero betrayed him with another man on the eve of her wedding day. Claudio assails Hero with his terrible accusations as they stand at the altar and the innocent young woman falls into a dead faint.

After everyone leaves, Beatrice and Benedick are left alone in the church. She has been crying.

....

BENEDICK: Lady Beatrice, have you wept all this while?
BEATRICE: Yea, and I will weep a while longer.
BENEDICK: I will not desire that.
BEATRICE: You have no reason; I do it freely.
BENEDICK: Surely I do believe your fair cousin is wronged.
BEATRICE: Ah, how much might the man deserve of me that would right her!
BENEDICK: Is there any way to show such friendship?

BEATRICE: A very even way, but no such friend.

BENEDICK: May a man do it?

BEATRICE: It is a man's office, but not yours.

BENEDICK: I do love nothing in the world so well as you: is not that strange?

BEATRICE: As strange as the thing I know not. It were as possible for me to say I loved nothing so well as you: but believe me not; and yet I lie not; I confess nothing, nor I deny nothing. I am sorry for my cousin.

BENEDICK: By my sword, Beatrice, thou lovest me.

BEATRICE: Do not swear, and eat it.

BENEDICK: I will swear by it that you love me; and I will make him eat it that says I love not you.

BEATRICE: Will you not eat your word?

BENEDICK: With no sauce that can be devised to it. I protest I love thee.

BEATRICE: Why, then, God forgive me!

BENEDICK: What offence, sweet Beatrice?

BEATRICE: You have stayed me in a happy hour: I was about to protest I loved you.

BENEDICK: And do it with all thy heart.

BEATRICE: I love you with so much of my heart, that none is left to protest.

BENEDICK: Come, bid me do any thing for thee.

BEATRICE: Kill Claudio.

BENEDICK: Ha! not for the wide world.

BEATRICE: You kill me to deny it. Farewell.

BENEDICK: Tarry, sweet Beatrice.

BEATRICE: I am gone, though I am here: there is no love in you: nay, I pray you, let me go.

BENEDICK: Beatrice,—

BEATRICE: In faith, I will go.

BENEDICK: We'll be friends first.

BEATRICE: You dare easier be friends with me than fight with mine enemy.

BENEDICK: Is Claudio thine enemy?

BEATRICE: Is he not approved in the height a villain, that hath slandered, scorned, dishonoured my kinswoman? O that I were a man! What, bear her in hand until they come to take hands; and then, with public accusation, uncovered slander, unmitigated rancour,—O God, that I were a man! I would eat his heart in the market-place.

BENEDICK: Hear me, Beatrice,—

BEATRICE: Talk with a man out at a window! A proper saying!

BENEDICK: Nay, but. Beatrice—

BEATRICE: Sweet Hero! She is wronged, she is slandered, she is undone.

BENEDICK: Beat—

BEATRICE: Princes and counties! Surely, a princely testimony, a goodly count, Count Comfect; a sweet gallant, surely! O that I were a man for his sake! or that I had any friend would be a man for my sake! But manhood is melted into courtesies, valour into compliment, and men are only turned into tongue, and trim ones too: he is now as valiant as Hercules that only tells a lie, and swears it. I cannot be a man with wishing, therefore I will die a woman with grieving.

BENEDICK: Tarry, good Beatrice. By this hand, I love thee.

BEATRICE: Use it for my love some other way than swearing by it.

BENEDICK: Think you in your soul the Count Claudio hath wronged Hero?

BEATRICE: Yea, as sure as I have a thought or a soul.

BENEDICK: Enough, I am engaged; I will challenge him. I will kiss your hand, and so I leave you. By this hand, Claudio shall render me a dear account. As you hear of me, so think of me. Go, comfort your cousin: I must say she is dead: and so, farewell. (*They exit.*)

KING RICHARD III

by William Shakespeare

ACT I, SCENE 2

*The deformed Richard, Duke of Gloucester, knows his
brother, King Edward, cannot live long, and he is set on
becoming the next king of England—on becoming Richard
III. But capturing the throne requires killing off many members of his family, which Richard is more than willing to
do. He also decides he can further his cause by marrying
Lady Anne, despite the fact that he killed her husband, the
valiant Prince Edward, as well as her father-in-law, King
Henry VI.*

*Richard stops the procession that is carrying King Henry
to his grave, demands that the corpse be put down, and
proceeds to woo the grieving Lady Anne.*

....

ANNE: Foul devil, for God's sake, hence, and
                  trouble us not;
        For thou has made the happy earth thy hell,
        Fill'd it with cursing cries and deep
                  exclaims.
        If thou delight to view thy heinous deeds,
        Behold this pattern of thy butcheries.
        O, gentlemen, see, see! dead Henry's wounds
        Open their congeal'd mouths and bleed
                  afresh.
        Blush, blush, thou lump of foul deformity;
        For 'tis thy presence that exhales this blood

From cold and empty veins, where no blood
    dwells;
Thy deed, inhuman and unnatural,
Provokes this deluge most unnatural.
O God, which this blood madest, revenge his
    death!
O earth, which this blood drink'st, revenge
    his death!
Either heaven with lightning strike the
    murderer dead,
Or earth, gape open wide and eat him quick,
As thou dost swallow up this good king's
    blood,
Which his hell-govern'd arm hath butchered!

GLOUCESTER: Lady, you know no rules of charity,
Which renders good for bad, blessings for
    curses.

ANNE: Villain, thou know'st no law of God nor man:
No beast so fierce but knows some touch
    of pity.

GLOUCESTER: But I know none, and therefore am no beast.

ANNE: O wonderful, when devils tell the truth!

GLOUCESTER: More wonderful, when angels are so angry.
Vouchsafe, divine perfection of a woman,
Of these supposed evils, to give me leave,
By circumstance, but to acquit myself.

ANNE: Vouchsafe, defused infection of a man,
For these known evils, but to give me leave,
By circumstance, to curse thy cursed self.

GLOUCESTER: Fairer than tongue can name thee, let me
    have
Some patient leisure to excuse myself.

ANNE: Fouler than heart can think thee, thou canst
    make
No excuse current, but to hang thyself.

GLOUCESTER: By such despair, I should accuse myself.

ANNE: And, by despairing, shouldst thou stand
    excused
For doing worthy vengeance on thyself,
Which didst unworthy slaughter upon others.

GLOUCESTER: Say that I slew them not?

ANNE:	Why, then they are not dead: But dead they are, and, devilish slave, by thee.
GLOUCESTER:	I did not kill your husband.
ANNE:	Why, then he is alive.
GLOUCESTER:	Nay, he is dead; and slain by Edward's hand.
ANNE:	In thy foul throat thou liest: Queen Margaret saw Thy murderous falchion smoking in his blood; The which thou once didst bend against her breast, But that thy brothers beat aside the point.
GLOUCESTER:	I was provoked by her slanderous tongue, Which laid their guilt upon my guiltless shoulders.
ANNE:	Thou wast provoked by thy bloody mind, Which never dreamt on aught but butcheries: Didst thou not kill this king?
GLOUCESTER:	I grant ye.
ANNE:	Dost grant me, hedgehog? then, God grant me too Thou mayst be damned for that wicked deed! O, he was gentle, mild, and virtuous!
GLOUCESTER:	The fitter for the King of heaven, that hath him.
ANNE:	He is in heaven, where thou shalt never come.
GLOUCESTER:	Let him thank me, that holp to send him thither; For he was fitter for that place than earth.
ANNE:	And thou unfit for any place but hell.
GLOUCESTER:	Yes, one place else, if you will hear me name it.
ANNE:	Some dungeon.
GLOUCESTER:	Your bed-chamber.
ANNE:	Ill rest betide the chamber where thou liest!
GLOUCESTER:	So will it, madam, till I lie with you.
ANNE:	I hope so.
GLOUCESTER:	I know so. But, gentle Lady Anne, To leave this keen encounter of our wits,

And fall somewhat into a slower method,
Is not the causer of the timeless deaths
Of these Plantagenets, Henry and Edward,
As blameful as the executioner?

ANNE: Thou art the cause, and most accursed effect.

GLOUCESTER: Your beauty was the cause of that effect;
Your beauty, which did haunt me in my
sleep
To undertake the death of all the world,
So I might live one hour in your sweet
bosom.

ANNE: If I thought that, I tell thee, homicide,
These nails should rend that beauty from my
cheeks.

GLOUCESTER: These eyes could never endure sweet
beauty's wreck;
You should not blemish it, if I stood by:
As all the world is cheered by the sun,
So I by that; it is my day, my life.

ANNE: Black night o'ershade thy day, and death thy
life!

GLOUCESTER: Curse not thyself, fair creature; thou art both.

ANNE: I would I were, to be revenged on thee.

GLOUCESTER: It is a quarrel most unnatural,
To be revenged on him that loveth you.

ANNE: It is a quarrel just and reasonable,
To be revenged on him that slew my
husband.

GLOUCESTER: He that bereft thee, lady, of thy husband,
Did it to help thee to a better husband.

ANNE: His better doth not breathe upon the earth.

GLOUCESTER: He lives that loves you better than he could.

ANNE: Name him.

GLOUCESTER: Plantagenet.

ANNE: Why, that was he.

GLOUCESTER: The selfsame name, but one of better nature.

ANNE: Where is he?

GLOUCESTER: Here. (*She spitteth at him.*) Why dost thou
spit at me?

ANNE: Would it were mortal poison, for thy sake!

GLOUCESTER: Never came poison from so sweet a place.

ANNE: Never hung poison on a fouler toad.
Out of my sight! thou dost infect my eyes.

GLOUCESTER: Thine eyes, sweet lady, have infected mine.

ANNE: Would they were basilisks, to strike thee
dead!

GLOUCESTER: I would they were, that I might die at once;
For now they kill me with a living death.
Those eyes of thine from mine have drawn
salt tears,
Shames their aspect with store of childish
drops:
These eyes, which never shed remorseful
tear,
No, when my father York and Edward wept,
To hear the piteous moan that Rutland made
When black-faced Clifford shook his sword
at him;
Nor when thy warlike father, like a child,
Told the sad story of my father's death,
And twenty times made pause to sob and
weep,
That all the standers-by had wet their cheeks,
Like trees bedash'd with rain: in that sad
time
My manly eyes did scorn an humble tear;
And what these sorrows could not thence
exhale,
Thy beauty hath, and made them blind with
weeping.
I never sued to friend nor enemy;
My tongue could never learn sweet
smoothing words;
But, now thy beauty is proposed my fee,
My proud heart sues, and prompts my tongue
to speak. (*She looks scornfully at him.*)
Teach not thy lips such scorn, for they were
made
For kissing, lady, not for such contempt.
If thy revengeful heart cannot forgive,
Lo, here I lend thee this sharp-pointed sword;

           Which if thou please to hide in this true
                bosom,
           And let the soul forth that adoreth thee,
           I lay it naked to the deadly stroke,
           And humbly beg the death upon my knee.
           (*He lays his breast open: she offers at it with*
               his sword.)
           Nay, do not pause; for I did kill King Henry,
           But 'twas thy beauty that provoked me.
           Nay, now dispatch; 'twas I that stabb'd
                young Edward,
           But 'twas thy heavenly face that set me on.
           (*Here she lets fall the sword.*)
           Take up the sword again, or take up me.

ANNE: Arise, dissembler: though I wish thy death,
           I will not be the executioner.

GLOUCESTER: Then bid me kill myself, and I will do it.

ANNE: I have already.

GLOUCESTER: Tush, that was in thy rage:
           Speak it again, and, even with the word,
           That hand, which, for thy love, did kill thy
                love,
           Shall, for thy love, kill a far truer love;
           To both their deaths shalt thou be accessary.

ANNE: I would I knew thy heart.

GLOUCESTER: 'Tis figured in my tongue.

ANNE: I fear me both are false.

GLOUCESTER: Then never man was true.

ANNE: Well, well, put up your sword.

GLOUCESTER: Say, then, my peace is made.

ANNE: That shall you know hereafter.

GLOUCESTER: But shall I live in hope?

ANNE: All men, I hope, live so.

GLOUCESTER: Vouchsafe to wear this ring.

ANNE: To take is not to give.

GLOUCESTER: Look, how this ring encompasseth thy finger,
           Even so thy breast encloseth my poor heart;
           Wear both of them, for both of them are
                thine.
           And if thy poor devoted suppliant may
           But beg one favour at thy gracious hand,

	Thou dost confirm his happiness for ever.
ANNE:	What is it?
GLOUCESTER:	That it would please thee leave these sad designs
	To him that hath more cause to be a mourner,
	And presently repair to Crosby Place;
	Where, after I have solemnly interr'd
	At Chertsey monastery this noble king,
	And wet his grave with my repentant tears,
	I will with all expedient duty see you:
	For divers unknown reasons, I beseech you,
	Grant me this boon.
ANNE:	With all my heart; and much it joys me too,
	To see you are become so penitent.
	Tressel and Berkeley, go along with me.
GLOUCESTER:	Bid me farewell.
ANNE:	'Tis more than you deserve;
	But since you teach me how to flatter you,
	Imagine I have said farewell already.

(LADY ANNE exits.)

MACBETH

by William Shakespeare

ACT II, SCENE 2

Macbeth, prodded by his ambitious wife, has resolved to kill King Duncan as the first step down a murderous road that will bring him the throne. Duncan, who has rewarded Macbeth generously for his valor in battle, has accepted Macbeth's invitation to spend the night at his castle. It is now late at night. Duncan has gone to sleep, Lady Macbeth has drugged his guards, and Macbeth has left her waiting for him in the courtyard as he goes off to carry out the murder.

···

LADY MACBETH: That which hath made them drunk hath made me bold;
What hath quench'd them hath given me fire. Hark! Peace!
It was the owl that shriek'd, the fatal bellman,
Which gives the stern'st good-night. He is about it:
The doors are open, and the surfeited grooms
Do mock their charge with snores: I have drugg'd their possets,
That death and nature do contend about them,
Whether they live or die.

MACBETH: (*Within.*) Who's there? what, ho!

LADY MACBETH: Alack, I am afraid they have awaked
And 'tis not done: the attempt and not the deed
Confounds us. Hark! I laid their daggers ready;
He could not miss 'em. Had he not resembled
My father as he slept, I had done 't.
(*Enter MACBETH.*)
My husband!

MACBETH: I have done the deed. Didst thou not hear a noise?

LADY MACBETH: I heard the owl scream and the crickets cry.
Did not you speak?

MACBETH: When?

LADY MACBETH: Now.

MACBETH: As I descended?

LADY MACBETH: Ay.

MACBETH: Hark!
Who lies i' the second chamber?

LADY MACBETH: Donalbain.

MACBETH: This is a sorry sight.
(*Looking on his hands.*)

LADY MACBETH: A foolish thought, to say a sorry sight.

MACBETH: There's one did laugh in 's sleep, and one cried "Murder!"
That they did wake each other: I stood and heard them:
But they did say their prayers, and address'd them
Again to sleep.

LADY MACBETH: There are two lodged together.

MACBETH: One cried "God bless us!" and "Amen" the other,
As they had seen me with these hangman's hands:
Listening their fear, I could not say "Amen,"
When they did say "God bless us!"

LADY MACBETH: Consider it not so deeply.

MACBETH: But wherefore could not I pronounce
          "Amen"?
          I had most need of blessing, and "Amen"
          Stuck in my throat.

LADY MACBETH: These deeds must not be thought
          After these ways; so, it will make us mad.

MACBETH: Methought I heard a voice cry "Sleep no
          more!
          Macbeth does murder sleep"—the
          innocent sleep,
          Sleep that knits up the ravell'd sleave of
          care,
          The death of each day's life, sore labour's
          bath,
          Balm of hurt minds, great nature's second
          course,
          Chief nourisher in life's feast,—

LADY MACBETH: What do you mean?

MACBETH: Still it cried "Sleep no more!" to all the
          house:
          "Glamis hath murder'd sleep, and
          therefore Cawdor
          Shall sleep no more: Macbeth shall sleep
          no more."

LADY MACBETH: Who was it that thus cried? Why, worthy
          thane,
          You do unbend your noble strength, to
          think
          So brainsickly of things. Go get some
          water,
          And wash this filthy witness from your
          hand.
          Why did you bring these daggers from the
          place?
          They must lie there: go carry them, and
          smear
          The sleepy grooms with blood.

MACBETH: I'll go no more:
          I am afraid to think what I have done;
          Look on 't again I dare not.

LADY MACBETH: Infirm of purpose!
             Give me the daggers: the sleeping and the
                dead
             Are but as pictures: 'tis the eye of
                childhood
             That fears a painted devil. If he do bleed,
             I'll gild the faces of the grooms withal,
             For it must seem their guilt.

(Exit. Knocking within.)

MACBETH: Whence is that knocking?
             How is 't with me, when every noise
                appals me?
             What hands are here? ha! they pluck out
                mine eyes!
             Will all great Neptune's ocean wash this
                blood
             Clean from my hand? No; this my hand
                will rather
             The multitudinous seas incarnadine,
             Making the green one red.

(Re-enter LADY MACBETH.)

LADY MACBETH: My hands are of your colour, but I shame
             To wear a heart so white. *(Knocking
                within.)* I hear a knocking
             At the south entry: retire we to our
                chamber:
             A little water clears us of this deed:
             How easy is it then! Your constancy
             Hath left you unattended. *(Knocking
                within.)* Hark! more knocking:
             Get on your nightgown, lest occasion call
                us
             And show us to be watchers: be not lost
             So poorly in your thoughts.

MACBETH: To know my deed, 'twere best not know
                myself.

(Knocking within.)

             Wake Duncan with thy knocking! I would
                thou couldst! *(They exit.)*

THE TAMING OF THE SHREW

by William Shakespeare

ACT II, SCENE 1

Petruchio, having money troubles, has come from Verona to Padua to find a wealthy wife. He hears that Baptista, a rich merchant, has offered a sizable dowry to any man that can win the hand of his shrewish daughter Katharina (thus enabling his younger daughter, Bianca, to marry one of her many suitors). Everyone, including her father, is terrified of Katharina. She has a fierce temper and a sharp tongue, but Petruchio decides to take on the challenge. Baptista, elated but skeptical, asks Petruchio if he wants to have Katharina sent to him (they are in a room in Baptista's home) and Petruchio replies that he will wait for her.

....

PETRUCHIO: I pray you do; I will attend her here,
           (*BAPTISTA, GREMIO, TRANIO, and HORTENSIO exit.*)
           And woo her with some spirit when she comes.
           Say that she rail: why then I'll tell her plain
           She sings as sweetly as a nightingale:
           Say that she frown; I'll say she looks as clear
           As morning roses newly wash'd with dew:
           Say she be mute and will not speak a word;
           Then I'll commend her volubility,
           And say she uttereth piercing eloquence:
           If she do bid me pack, I'll give her thanks,

As though she bid me stay by her a week:
If she deny to wed, I'll crave the day
When I shall ask the banns, and when be
    married.
But here she comes; and now, Petruchio,
    speak.

(*Enter* KATHARINA.)

    Good morrow, Kate; for that's your name, I
        hear.

KATHARINA: Well have you heard, but something hard of
        hearing:
They call me Katharine that do talk of me.

PETRUCHIO: You lie, in faith; for you are call'd plain Kate,
And bonny Kate, and sometimes Kate the
    curst;
But Kate, the prettiest Kate in Christendom,
Kate of Kate-Hall, my super-dainty Kate,
For dainties are all Kates, and therefore, Kate,
Take this of me, Kate of my consolation;
Hearing thy mildness praised in every town,
Thy virtues spoke of, and thy beauty sounded,
Yet not so deeply as to thee belongs,
Myself am moved to woo thee for my wife.

KATHARINA: Moved! in good time: let him that moved you
        hither
Remove you hence: I knew you at the first
You were a moveable.

PETRUCHIO: Why, what's a moveable?

KATHARINA: A join'd-stool.

PETRUCHIO: Thou hast hit it: come, sit on me.

KATHARINA: Asses are made to bear, and so are you.

PETRUCHIO: Women are made to bear, and so are you.

KATHARINA: No such jade as you, if me you mean.

PETRUCHIO: Alas, good Kate, I will not burden thee!
For, knowing thee to be but young and light,—

KATHARINA: Too light for such a swain as you to catch;
And yet as heavy as my weight should be.

PETRUCHIO: Should be! should—buzz!

KATHARINA: Well ta'en, and like a buzzard.

PETRUCHIO: O slow-wing'd turtle! shall a buzzard take thee?

KATHARINA: Ay, for a turtle, as he takes a buzzard.

PETRUCHIO: Come, come, you wasp; i' faith, you are too angry.

KATHARINA: If I be waspish, best beware my sting.

PETRUCHIO: My remedy is then, to pluck it out.

KATHARINA: Ay, if the fool could find it where it lies.

PETRUCHIO: Who knows not where a wasp does wear his sting?
In his tail.

KATHARINA: In his tongue.

PETRUCHIO: Whose tongue?

KATHARINA: Yours, if you talk of tails: and so farewell.

PETRUCHIO: What, with my tongue in your tail? nay, come again,
Good Kate; I am a gentleman.

KATHARINA: That I'll try.
(*She strikes him.*)

PETRUCHIO: I swear I'll cuff you, if you strike again.

KATHARINA: So may you lose your arms:
If you strike me, you are no gentleman;
And if no gentleman, why then no arms.

PETRUCHIO: A herald, Kate? O, put me in thy books!

KATHARINA: What is your crest? a coxcomb?

PETRUCHIO: A combless cock, so Kate will be my hen.

KATHARINA: No cock of mine; you crow too like a craven.

PETRUCHIO: Nay, come, Kate, come; you must not look so sour.

KATHARINA: It is my fashion, when I see a crab.

PETRUCHIO: Why, here's no crab; and therefore look not sour.

KATHARINA: There is, there is.

PETRUCHIO: Then show it me.

KATHARINA: Had I a glass, I would.

PETRUCHIO: What, you mean my face?

KATHARINA: Well aim'd of such a young one.

PETRUCHIO: Now, by Saint George, I am too young for you.

KATHARINA: Yet you are wither'd.

PETRUCHIO: 'Tis with cares.

KATHARINA: I care not.

PETRUCHIO: Nay, hear you, Kate: in sooth you scape not
   so.

KATHARINA: I chafe you, if I tarry: let me go.

PETRUCHIO: No, not a whit: I find you passing gentle.
   'Twas told me you were rough and coy and
    sullen,
   And now I find report a very liar;
   For thou art pleasant, gamesome, passing
    courteous,
   But slow in speech, yet sweet as spring-time
    flowers:
   Thou canst not frown, thou canst not look
    askance,
   Nor bite the lip, as angry wenches will,
   Nor hast thou pleasure to be cross in talk,
   But thou with mildness entertain'st thy
    wooers,
   With gentle conference, soft and affable.
   Why does the world report that Kate doth
    limp?
   O slanderous world! Kate like the hazel-twig
   Is straight and slender, and as brown in hue
   As hazel-nuts and sweeter than the kernels.
   O, let me see thee walk: thou dost not halt.

KATHARINA: Go, fool, and whom thou keep'st command.

PETRUCHIO: Did ever Dian so become a grove
   As Kate this chamber with her princely gait?
   O, be thou Dian, and let her be Kate;
   And then let Kate be chaste and Dian sportful!

KATHARINA: Where did you study all this goodly speech?

PETRUCHIO: It is extempore, from my mother-wit.

KATHARINA: A witty mother! witless else her son.

PETRUCHIO: Am I not wise?

KATHARINA: Yes; keep you warm.

PETRUCHIO: Marry, so I mean, sweet Katharine, in thy bed:
   And therefore, setting all this chat aside,
   Thus in plain terms: your father hath
    consented
   That you shall be my wife; your dowry 'greed
    on;

And, will you, nill you, I will marry you.
Now, Kate, I am a husband for your turn;
For, by this light, whereby I see thy beauty,
Thy beauty, that doth make me like thee well,
Thou must be married to no man but me;
For I am he am born to tame you Kate,
And bring you from a wild Kate to a Kate
Conformable as other household Kates.
Here comes your father: never make denial;
I must and will have Katharine to my wife.

SCENES FOR TWO WOMEN

A TASTE OF HONEY

by Shelagh Delaney

ACT I, SCENE 2

*Jo and her mother Helen have been living in "a comfortless
flat in Manchester." Jo is 17 and Helen is described as a
"semi-whore." This is a happy day for Helen, her wedding
day. To everyone's surprise, her boyfriend Peter asked her
to marry him. With her mother and Peter about to set up
a household, Jo is uncertain about what her life will be
like. And there is another reason for her uncertainty. She
has just given up her virginity to her boyfriend, a young,
"colored" boy who is in the Navy. He has gone to sea but
gave her a ring before leaving (which she wears on a cord
around her neck) and promised he would come back and
marry her. But Jo has her doubts about his sincerity. She
also has a cold.*

....

(Music. Wedding bells. HELEN'S *music. She dances on
with an assortment of fancy boxes, containing her
wedding clothes.)*

HELEN: Jo! Jo! Come on. Be sharp now.

(JO comes on in her pyjamas. She has a heavy cold.)

For God's sake give me a hand. I'll never be ready. What
time is it? Have a look at the church clock.

JO: A quarter past eleven, and the sun's coming out.

HELEN: Oh! Well, happy the bride the sun shines on.

JO: Yeah, and happy the corpse the rain rains on. You're not getting married in a church, are you?

HELEN: Why, are you coming to throw bricks at us? Of course not. Do I look all right? Pass me my fur. Oh! My fur! Do you like it?

JO: I bet somebody's missing their cat.

HELEN: It's a wedding present from that young man of mine. He spends his money like water, you know, penny wise, pound foolish. Oh! I am excited. I feel twenty-one all over again. Oh! You would have to catch a cold on my wedding day. I was going to ask you to be my bridesmaid too.

JO: Don't talk daft.

HELEN: Where did you put my shoes? Did you clean 'em? Oh! They're on my feet. Don't stand there sniffing, Jo. Use a handkerchief.

JO: I haven't got one.

HELEN: Use this, then. What's the matter with you? What are you trying to hide?

JO: Nothing.

HELEN: Don't try to kid me. What is it? Come on, let's see.

JO: It's nothing. Let go of me. You're hurting.

HELEN: What's this?

JO: A ring.

HELEN: I can see it's a ring. Who give it to you?

JO: A friend of mine.

HELEN: Who? Come on. Tell me.

JO: You're hurting me.

(HELEN breaks the cord and gets the ring.)

HELEN: You should have sewn some buttons on your pyjamas if you didn't want me to see. Who give it you?

JO: My boyfriend. He asked me to marry him.

HELEN: Well, you silly little bitch. You mean that lad you've been knocking about with while we've been away?

JO: Yes.

HELEN: I could choke you.

JO: You've already had a damn good try.

HELEN: You haven't known him five minutes. Has he really asked you to marry him?

JO: Yes.

HELEN: Well, thank God for the divorce courts! I suppose just because I'm getting married you think you should.

JO: Have you got the monopoly?

HELEN: You stupid little devil! What sort of a wife do you think you'd make? You're useless. It takes you all your time to look after yourself. I suppose you think you're in love. Anybody can fall in love, do you know that? But what do you know about the rest of it?

JO: Ask yourself.

HELEN: You know where that ring should be? In the ashcan with everything else. Oh! I could kill her, I could really.

JO: You don't half knock me about. I hope you suffer for it.

HELEN: I've done my share of suffering if I never do any more. Oh Jo, you're only a kid. Why don't you learn from my mistakes? It takes half your life to learn from your own.

JO: You leave me alone. Can I have my ring back, please?

HELEN: What a thing to happen just when I'm going to enjoy myself for a change.

JO: Nobody's stopping you.

HELEN: Yes, and as soon as my back's turned you'll be off with this sailor boy and ruin yourself for good.

JO: I'm already ruined.

HELEN: Yes, it's just the sort of thing you'd do. You make me sick.

JO: You've no need to worry, Helen. He's gone away. He may be back in six months, but there again, he may . . .

HELEN: Look, you're only young. Enjoy your life. Don't get trapped. Marriage can be hell for a kid.

JO: Can I have your hanky back?

HELEN: Where did you put it?

JO: This is your fault too.

HELEN: Everything's my fault. Show me your tongue.

JO: Breathing your flu bugs all over me.

HELEN: Yes, and your neck's red where I pulled that string.

JO: Will you get me a drink of water, Helen?

HELEN: No, have a dose of this (*Offering whisky.*) It'll do you more good. I might as well have one myself while I'm at it, mightn't I?

JO: You've emptied more bottles down your throat in the last few weeks than I would have thought possible. If you don't watch it, you'll end up an old down-and-out boozer knocking back the meths.

HELEN: It'll never come to that. The devil looks after his own, they say.

JO: He certainly takes good care of you. You look marvellous, considering.

HELEN: Considering what?

JO: The wear and tear on your soul.

HELEN: Oh well, that'll have increased its market value, won't it?

JO: Old Nick'll get you in the end.

HELEN: Thank God for that! Heaven must be the hell of a place. Nothing but repentant sinners up there, isn't it? All the pimps, prostitutes and politicians in creation trying to cash in on eternity and their little tin god. Where's my hat?

JO: Where's your husband?

HELEN: Probably drunk with his pals somewhere. He was going down to the house this morning to let some air in. Have you seen a picture of the house? Yes, you have. Do you like it? (*She peers and primps into mirror.*)

JO: It's all right if you like that sort of thing, and I don't.

HELEN: I'll like it in a few years, when it isn't so new and clean. At the moment it's like my face, unblemished! Oh look at that, every line tells a dirty story, hey?

JO: Will you tell me something before you go?

HELEN: Oh! You can read all about that in books.

JO: What was my father like?

(*HELEN turns away.*)

HELEN: Who?

JO: You heard! My father! What was he like?

HELEN: Oh! Him.

JO: Well, was he so horrible that you can't even tell me about him?

HELEN: He wasn't horrible. He was just a bit stupid, you know. Not very bright.

JO: Be serious, Helen.

HELEN: I am serious.

JO: Are you trying to tell me he was an idiot?

HELEN: He wasn't an idiot, he was just a bit—retarded.

JO: You liar!

HELEN: All right, I'm a liar.

JO: Look at me.

HELEN: Well, am I?

JO: No.

HELEN: Well, now you know.

JO: How could you give me a father like that?

HELEN: I didn't do it on purpose. How was I to know you'd materialize out of a little love affair that lasted five minutes?

JO: You never think. That's your trouble.

HELEN: I know.

JO: Was he like a . . . a real idiot?

HELEN: I've told you once. He was nice though, you know, a nice little feller!

JO: Where is he now, locked up?

HELEN: No, he's dead.

JO: Why?

HELEN: Why? Well, I mean, death's something that comes to us all, and when it does come you haven't usually got time to ask why.

JO: It's hereditary, isn't it?

HELEN: What?

JO: Madness.

HELEN: Sometimes.

JO: Am I mad?

HELEN: Decide for yourself. Oh, Jo, don't be silly. Of course you're not daft. Not more so than anybody else.

JO: Why did you have to tell me that story? Couldn't you have made something up?

HELEN: You asked for the truth and you got it for once. Now be satisfied.

JO: How could you go with a half-wit?

HELEN: He had strange eyes. You've got 'em. Everybody used to laugh at him. Go on, I'll tell you some other time.

JO: Tell me now!

HELEN: Mind my scent!

JO: Please tell me. I want to understand.

HELEN: Do you think I understand? For one night, actually it was the afternoon, I loved him. It was the first time I'd ever really been with a man . . .

JO: You were married.

HELEN: I was married to a Puritan—do you know what I mean?

JO: I think so.

HELEN: And when I met your father I was as pure and unsullied as I fondly, and perhaps mistakenly, imagine you to be. It was the first time and though you can enjoy the second, the third, even the fourth time, there's no time like the first, it's always there. I'm off now. I've got to go and find my husband. Now don't sit here sulking all day.

JO: I was thinking.

HELEN: Well, don't think. It doesn't do you any good. I'll see you when the honeymoon's over. Come on, give us a kiss. You may as well. It's a long time since you kissed me.

JO: Keep it for him.

HELEN: I don't suppose you're sorry to see me go.

JO: I'm not sorry and I'm not glad.

HELEN: You don't know what you do want.

JO: Yes, I do. I've always known what I want.

HELEN: And when it comes your way will you recognize it?

JO: Good luck, Helen.

HELEN: I'll be seeing you. Hey! If he doesn't show up I'll be back.

JO: Good luck, Helen.

(Exit HELEN. "Here Comes the Bride" on the cornet.)

THE MISS FIRECRACKER CONTEST

by Beth Henley

ACT I, SCENE 1

Carnelle Scott, age 24, wants desperately to win the Miss Firecracker Beauty Contest, which is a very important event every Fourth of July in the small town of Brookhaven, Mississippi. Carnelle has been trying to redeem her reputation as the town tramp, and winning the contest would be, as she calls it, "an honor." She has dyed her hair bright red, hired a seamstress to make her a costume, and has been practicing the tap routine she will perform to "The Star Spangled Banner" (with Roman candles shooting out over the heads of the audience).

She is visited in the house she inherited from her Aunt Ronnelle by her cousin Elain who has arrived with her luggage and a cosmetic case a few days before she was expected. Elain is 32, beautiful, elegantly dressed, but "somewhat wilted in the summer heat." Carnelle admires Elain because when Elain was 17 she won the Miss Firecracker contest.

Elain has just given the seamstress, Popeye, some earrings as a gift and Popeye has exited.

....

CARNELLE: Bye, bye. (*Turning and coming back to ELAIN.*) Oh, Elain! That was so sweet what you did—giving Popeye those earrings. It meant so much to her. You're so generous!

ELAIN: (*Meaning it.*) Don't talk about it, please. It was nothing. Oh, mind if I have a glass of this delicious looking ice tea? I'm about ready to drop dead from the heat.

CARNELLE: Oh, of course! Please! Here, I'll run get you a fresh glass out from the kitchen. (*CARNELLE picks up the tray and exits. ELAIN takes off her hat and fans herself. She looks sadly around the room. CARNELLE returns with a glass with a small umbrella in it.*) Here, now—

ELAIN: Bless you.

CARNELLE: There you are.

ELAIN: Why, Carnation, you're saving my life. This is heaven. Sheer heaven!

CARNELLE: (*Running to ELAIN'S clothes bag.*) Oh, Elain, did you bring that dress along with you that I asked about on the phone? You know, the beautiful red antebellum dress that you wore at the Natchez Pilgrimage the first year you got married. See, it's gonna be perfect for me to wear in the contest. I'm trying to make crimson red my thematic color. (*Opening the bag: she discovers the dress is not there.*)

ELAIN: I see—but I thought you said you weren't gonna be needing a formal dress for the audition this Saturday.

CARNELLE: I know, that's true. We'll just need them in the actual contest for the opening Parade of Firecrackers.

ELAIN: So, why don't we just wait till after the audition and see if you make it to the pageant.

CARNELLE: Why? Don't you think I'll make it?

ELAIN: Well, I hope so, Carnelle, but they only pick five girls.

CARNELLE: Well . . . I've thought about it, and I, frankly, can't think of five other girls in town that are prettier than me. I'm speaking honestly now. Course I know there's Caroline Jeffers, but she has those yellow teeth—

ELAIN: (*Not wanting to get into it.*) My this mint is delicious! Did you grow it yourself?

CARNELLE: Aunt Ronelle planted it before she died.

ELAIN: Well, it's quite refreshing.

CARNELLE: I know why you're worried. You think I've ruined my chances, 'cause—'cause of my reputation.

ELAIN: I don't know what you mean—you're perfectly sweet.

CARNELLE: Well, everyone knew I used to go out with lots of men and all that. Different ones. It's been a constant thing with me since I was young and—

ELAIN: Let's not discuss it in all a this heat.

CARNELLE: I just mention it 'cause it's different now, since Aunt Ronelle died and since—I got that disease.

ELAIN: Please, Carnelle, nobody's profiting by this information!

CARNELLE: Anyway, I go to church now and I'm signed up to where I take an orphan home to dinner once a week or to a movie; and—and I work on the cancer drive here just like you do in Natchez.

ELAIN: That's all very admirable, I'm sure.

CARNELLE: My life has meaning. People aren't calling me Miss Hot Tamale anymore like they used to. Everything's changed. And being in that contest—it would be such an honor to me . . . I can't explain the half of it.

ELAIN: Well, if you don't make it to the finals, just try to remember that Mama was at her most noblest when she was least attractive.

CARNELLE: I wish you had about a drop a faith in me. I'm not all that ugly.

ELAIN: And I wish you would stop fishing for compliments—'cause I'm sick and worn out with giving people compliments about themselves!

CARNELLE: (*Overlapping.*) I'm sorry. I'm so, so sorry, I make such stupid blunders. I know you don't think I'm ugly.

ELAIN: (*Overlapping.*) I'm not myself—I'm just not myself. (*She begins brushing her hair. The phone rings. ELAIN freezes. CARNELLE goes to answer it.*) If it's for me—say—say, I'm resting.

CARNELLE: Hello. . . . Oh, hello, Franklin. . . . Yes, she's here. . . . Well, I think she decided not to stop by there. . . . No, she's asleep now. She's gone on to sleep. . . . Well, wait just a minute, I'll go see. (*She puts her hand over the phone.*) He wants me to go wake you up.

ELAIN: (*In a whisper.*) He what! Oh, how inconsiderate can he be! Why, I've been driving all day long in this blazing heat and he doesn't even care if I get my rest. You tell him I'm out dead with exhaustion and you absolutely can not wake me.

CARNELLE: (*She waits a few beats and then says breathlessly into the phone.*) Franklin . . . I absolutely can not wake her. She's out dead with exhaustion. . . . Alright, I'll tell her. Bye, bye. (*She hangs up the phone.*) He says for you to please call him when you wake up.

ELAIN: Oh, he does, does he? Well, he can just sit and wait, 'cause I'm not calling him—not ever.

CARNELLE: Why not?

ELAIN: Listen Carnation, I think you should know something—I'm not just here on a visit.

CARNELLE: You're not?

ELAIN: No. (*Then after a moment.*) I've left Franklin.

CARNELLE: What?!

ELAIN: Now, remember, it's a sworn secret and not a living soul is to find it out.

CARNELLE: I won't say a word to anyone. I swear.

ELAIN: You see, I haven't told Franklin yet and he actually still believes everything is—bearable between us.

CARNELLE: I just can't believe all this. You were so in love. It seemed like Franklin loved you so much. I thought I wanted a man to love me that much.

ELAIN: Yes; he did love me. But it just caused him to follow me around asking, "Do you love me? How much do you love me? Tell me how you love me," till I could shake him till he rattled.

CARNELLE: Then you don't love him anymore?

ELAIN: (*Taking off her jewelry.*) No. He makes me ill.

CARNELLE: How awful.

ELAIN: Yes.

CARNELLE: But what about your two little boys? They need a mother.

ELAIN: Oh, children manage in this world. Don't ask me about them.

CARNELLE: Gosh, Aunt Ronelle said you had it all up there in Natchez; everything—just like a queen in a castle.

ELAIN: I know. I did. I only hope I can stand to give it all up. (*Deeply moved.*) We had such beautiful clocks. I must have a bath. (*She rises.*)

CARNELLE: Elain. (*ELAIN stops.*) What was it like—when you had it all?

ELAIN: Ah, Carnation! The abundance of treasures merely serves to underline the desperate futility of life. (*She exits upstairs to the bedrooms.*)

CARNELLE: Oh—Tell me more—Please! Tell me more! (*She picks up all of the bags and follows ELAIN out of the room.*)

ALL THE WAY HOME

by Tad Mosel

ACT III

This play is based on James Agee's novel, A Death in the Family. *It is a May morning in 1915 in Knoxville, Tennessee, and Jay Follet is to be buried today. The family is waiting for his wife Mary to come down from her room so they can proceed to the cemetery. Jay was a free spirit who loved his wife and son but needed to go off on his own occasionally, sometimes for days, to be with friends and drink and watch Charlie Chaplin movies. Mary loved Jay but was often angry at him, angry that he needed to seek pleasures outside the family, angry for his rejection of religion, and angry for the distance that somehow always remained between them.*

Jay died in an automobile accident on his way home from one of his trips and Mary is finding her anger at Jay persisting and intruding into her terrible grief. She asked his brother Ralph whether Jay was driving drunk but Ralph refused to tell her. The family is getting impatient and Aunt Hannah, a wise and loving woman, has come up to Mary's room to get her.

(To use as a two-person scene, omit the exchanges between Hannah and Andrew.)

....

HANNAH: Mary, the service is due to start in a very few minutes.

MARY: I'm going to stay here in this room.

HANNAH: Shall I send Father Jackson up to you?

MARY: No.

ANDREW: (*He has come up the stairs.*) Is she coming?

HANNAH: The rest of you get in the cars. We'll come when we can.

(ANDREW *goes back downstairs, and during the following, all but* CATHERINE *and* RUFUS *file out.*)

MARY: Why don't they all leave? You too, Hannah. For I'm not going.

HANNAH: (*Touching her shoulder.*) I'm staying here.

MARY: If you are, please don't touch me. (*In a sudden rage.*) That miserable Ralph! Damn him! You were right, Hannah, God is coming harder to me now. And Jay, too! I can't seem to find either one of them. (HANNAH *stands back quietly.* MARY *gets a necktie from the bureau and scrutinizes the label.*) This necktie was bought in Chattanooga some place. When, do you suppose? Sometimes when he went off like that, he was said to be seen as far as Clairborne County. But Chattanooga—Whatever made Jay do it, *ever*! The night we moved into this house, where did he *go*! And when he first went to work in Papa's office—! (*Stopping, remembering, more softly.*) Not when Rufus was born, though. He was very dearly close to me then, very. But other times, he'd feel himself being closed in, watched by superintendents, he'd say, and—There was always a special quietness about him afterwards, when he came home, as if he were very far away from where he'd been, but very far away from me, too, keeping his distance, but working his way back.

HANNAH: Let the man rest, Mary.

MARY: I want him to rest.

HANNAH: (*Angrily.*) Aren't you even going to attend the funeral!

MARY: Do you think he'll rest simply by lowering him into the ground? I won't watch it. How *can* he when he was *lost* on the very day he died!

HANNAH: You don't know that he was *lost*, or drunk, or *what* he was.

MARY: (*After a moment.*) No. That's just what I don't know.

HANNAH: And *that's* what you can't bear.

MARY: (*After an even longer moment.*) I never knew. Not for sure. There were times we *all* knew about, of course, but there were other times when it wasn't always the whiskey. He'd be gone for a night, or a day, or even two, and I'd know he hadn't touched a drop. And it wasn't any of the other things that come to a woman's mind, either, in case you're thinking that.

HANNAH: I wasn't thinking that.

MARY: Those are easy enemies. It was Market Square. And talking to country people about country secrets that go way on back through the mountains. And any one who'd sing his old songs with him. Or all-night lunch rooms. What's an all-night lunch room for, he'd say, except to sit in all night. And drink coffee so strong it would burn your ribs. And it was locomotives, I suppose, and railroad people, and going fast, and even Charlie Chaplin. What's wrong with Charlie, he'd ask me, not because he didn't know what I'd say, but to make me say it. He's so nasty, I'd say, so vulgar, with his nasty little cane, looking up skirts. And Jay would laugh and go off to see Charlie Chaplin and not come home. Where he went, I can't even imagine, for he'd never tell me. It was always easier to put everything down to whiskey.

HANNAH: To put it down to an enemy.

MARY: Why couldn't I let him have those things, whatever they were, if they meant something to him? Why can't I let him have them now? The dear. He always worked his way back.

ANDREW: (*He runs in, to the foot of the stairs. In a loud whisper.*) Aunt Hannah, we can't wait any longer.

HANNAH: (*At the top.*) All *right*, Andrew. (ANDREW *goes off again.*)

MARY: They must be suffocating in those cars. (*She smooths the bed for a moment, then straightens up.*) I'm glad Ralph didn't tell me. I must just accept not knowing, mustn't I? I must let Jay *have* what I don't know. (*She picks up her hat and veil and looks at them.*) What if he was drunk? What in the world if he was? Did I honestly think *that* was a gulf? *This* is a gulf! (*She tears a rent in the veil.*) If he was drunk, Hannah, just *if* he was, I hope he loved being. Speeding along in the night—singing at the top of his lungs—racing because he loved to go fast—racing to us because he loved us. And for the time, enjoying—revelling in a freedom that was his, that no place or person, that nothing in this world could ever give him or take away from him. Let's hope that's how it was, Hannah, how he looked death itself in the face. In his strength. (*She puts on the hat and pulls the veil over her face, goes down the stairs. HANNAH follows her into the yard.*) That's what we'll put on the gravestone, Hannah. In his strength. (*They go off Left.*)

ISN'T IT ROMANTIC

by Wendy Wasserstein

ACT II, SCENE 5

*The scene takes place in Harriet Cornwall's apartment.
Janie Blumberg, her closest friend, has just learned that
Harriet is going to marry a man she has been dating for
only two weeks—and Janie is puzzled and upset. Both
women are in their late twenties. They were friends at Har-
vard and decided together to come back to New York
(where they grew up) in the hopes of building successful
careers and finding exciting love lives. Harriet, beautiful
and poised, has been doing very well in the career category. She's rising up the ranks as an executive at Colgate-
Palmolive. But her love life hasn't worked out well. She
had a disappointing affair with a married man (Paul Stuart), a vice-president at her company, and she often spends
her evenings with her mother, Lillian, watching* The Rockford Files *reruns.*

*Janie, more of an oddball than Harriet (and plumper),
hasn't been very successful in either category. Earlier in
the week she turned down marrying Marty, a "nice Jewish
doctor" who her mother, Tasha, thought would bring her
lots of* naches *(the Jewish word for happiness). She turned
him down because he needed a traditional wife, that is, one
who lets him make all the decisions. But Janie has been
trying to feel good about herself as a capable and independent woman, and wants a relationship in which she is
an equal partner.*

Janie's career as a writer hasn't been working out very

well either, although she just had some hopeful news: Sesame Street hired her part-time to work on the letter "B."

As the scene begins, Lillian, who is fond of quoting the latest wisdom from the popular women's magazines, has just left.

....

JANIE: She's in a good mood.

HARRIET: She's been reading *Redbook*. So, what do you think?

JANIE: It's wonderful. Mazel tov.

HARRIET: (*Exiting to kitchen.*) I didn't mean to surprise you like this. I wanted to have you and Marty to dinner. Are things O.K. with Marty?

JANIE: Yeah. Fine.

HARRIET: (*From kitchen.*) You O.K.?

JANIE: Harriet, have you thought maybe you should live with Joe first? Better yet, maybe you should have dinner with him first?

HARRIET: I want to marry him. Janie, he's the only person who's even cared about me in a long time. He listens to me. (HARRIET *re-enters with flowers in a vase.*) Tasha's right. You and I deserve a little nachos.

JANIE: *Naches.*

HARRIET: Joe makes me feel like I have a family. I never had a family. I had you and Lillian, but I never felt I could have what other women just assumed they would get.

JANIE: I want to know one thing. I want to know why when I asked you about my living with Marty, you told me you didn't respect women who didn't learn to live alone and pay their own rent? And then, the first chance you have to change your life, you grasp it.

HARRIET: What? Marrying Joe is just a chance that came along.

JANIE: I see. You've been waiting for some man to come along and change your life. And all the things you told me about learning to live alone and women and friendship, that was so much social nonsense. I feel like an idiot! I made choices based on an idea that doesn't exist anymore.

HARRIET: What choices?

JANIE: Never mind.

HARRIET: Janie, when I told you that, I didn't know what it would be like when Paul Stuart would leave at ten and go home to Cathy and I would have to pretend I wasn't hurt. I didn't know what it would be like to have lunch with Lillian and think I'm on my way to watching *Rockford File* reruns. Of course you should learn to live alone and pay your own rent, but I didn't realize what it would feel like for me when I became too good at it. Janie, I know how to come home, put on the news, have a glass of wine, read a book, call you. What I don't know is what to do when there's someone who loves me in the house.

(Pause.)

JANIE: I could throw this table at you.

HARRIET: Why? Janie, we're too good friends for you to be jealous.

JANIE: I'm not jealous.

HARRIET: Don't blame me for your doubts about Marty.

JANIE: Harriet, I don't blame you for anything. I'm sorry. Right now I just don't like you very much.

HARRIET: Why? Because I'm leaving you? Because I'm getting married?

JANIE: Because our friendship didn't mean very much to you. You bring me the sugar, the bread, and the salt, and then you stand there and tell me you never had a family. Harriet, you never really listened to me and you never really told me about yourself. And that's sad.

HARRIET: Janie, I love you. But you want us to stay girls together. I'm not a girl anymore. I'm almost thirty and I'm alone.

JANIE: You lied to me.

HARRIET: I never lied to you. I lied to myself. It doesn't take any strength to be alone, Janie. It's much harder to be with someone else. I want to have children and get on with my life.

JANIE: What do you do? Fall in with every current the tide pulls in? Women should live alone and find out what they can do, put off marriage, establish a vertical career track, so you do that for a while. Then you almost turn thirty and *Time* magazine announces, ''Guess what, girls, it's time to have it all.'' Jaclyn Smith is married and pregnant and playing Jacqueline Kennedy. Every other person who was analyzing stocks last year is analyzing layettes this year. So you do that. What are you doing, Harriet? Who the hell are you? Can't you conceive of some plan, some time-management scheme that you made up for yourself? Can't you take a chance?

HARRIET: I am taking a chance. I hardly know this man.

JANIE: You don't have to force yourself into a situation—a marriage because it's time.

HARRIET: You're just frightened of being with someone, Janie. You're just frightened of making a choice and taking responsibility for it.

JANIE: That sounds romantic.

HARRIET: That's life.

JANIE: Harriet, you're getting married to someone you've been dating for two weeks. I am much more scared of being alone than you are. But I'm not going to turn someone into the answer for me.

HARRIET: Then you'll be alone.

JANIE: Then I'll be alone. (*Pause.*) I better go. I have to get up early with the letter ''B.'' If they like this, they'll hire me full time. In charge of consonants.

HARRIET: Give my love to Marty.

JANIE: I can't. I told him I won't move with him to Brooklyn.

HARRIET: So you'll get an apartment in Manhattan.

JANIE: (*She cries.*) We broke up. I decided not to see him anymore.

HARRIET: Won't you miss him?

JANIE: I missed him today when I saw someone who looks sweet like him walking down the street, and I'll miss him late tonight.

HARRIET: Maybe you should call him.

JANIE: No.

HARRIET: Life is a negotiation.

JANIE: I don't believe I have to believe that.

HARRIET: Janie, it's too painful not to grow up.

JANIE: That's not how I want to grow up. (*She kisses* HARRIET *and starts to go.*)

HARRIET: You don't have to separate from me. I'm not leaving you.

JANIE: (*Picking up the trash.*) Want me to throw this out for you?

HARRIET: Sure.

JANIE: Do you really think anyone has ever met someone throwing out the garbage?

(They shake their heads no. JANIE exits.)

PLAYING FOR TIME

by Arthur Miller

It is Fania's singing voice that is keeping her from the gas chamber. A short while ago she was a popular French night club singer, but now, because she is half Jewish, she is in a Nazi concentration camp and alive only because she has managed to join the camp orchestra which was set up to entertain the German officers. The orchestra is made up of prisoners (some of whom are not very good musicians) and the conductor is Alma Rosé, an imperious German Jew from an illustrious musical family. Alma drives her musicians mercilessly, in part because of her high musical standards and in part because of her fear that a disappointing performance will earn them all a death sentence.

Fania has had trouble adjusting to the fact that the brutal officers and guards that oversee the camp, particularly the infamous Dr. Mengele, are moved, sometimes to tears, by her singing. Just before the scene below, Alma has hit Etalina, a young, not very responsible member of the orchestra, for playing the wrong note during a rehearsal. Alma then walked out and Fania followed her into her room.

....

(Cut to ALMA's *room.* FANIA *is massaging* ALMA's *shoulders and neck as she sits in a chair by the window.* ALMA *moves* FANIA's *fingers to her temples, which she lightly massages. After a moment she has* FANIA *massage her hands, and* FANIA *sits before her doing this.)*

ALMA: Talk to me, Fania. (FANIA *keeps silent, wary of expressing herself.*) There must be strict discipline. As it is,

Dr. Mengele can just bear to listen to us. If we fall below a certain level anything is possible. . . . He's a violently changeable man. (*FANIA does not respond, only massages.*) The truth is, if it weren't for my name they'd have burned them up long ago; my father was first violin with the Berlin Opera, his string quartet played all over the world. . . .

FANIA: I know, Madame.

ALMA: That I, a Rosé, am conducting here is a . . .

FANIA: I realize that, Madame.

ALMA: Why do you resent me? You are a professional, you know what discipline is required; a conductor must be respected.

FANIA: But I think she can be loved, too.

ALMA: You cannot love what you do not respect. In Germany it is a perfectly traditional thing, when a musician is repeatedly wrong . . .

FANIA: To slap?

ALMA: Yes, of course! Furtwängler did so frequently, and his orchestra idolized him. (*FANIA keeping her silence, simply nods very slightly.*) I need your support, Fania. I see that they look up to you. You must back up my demands on them. We will have to constantly raise the level of our playing or I . . . I really don't know how long they will tolerate us. Will you? Will you help me?

FANIA: I . . . I will tell you the truth, Madame—I really don't know how long I can bear this. (*She sees resentment in ALMA's eyes.*) I am trying my best, Madame, and I'll go on trying. But I feel sometimes that pieces of myself are falling away. And believe me, I recognize that your strength is probably what our lives depend on. . . .

ALMA: Then why do you resent me?

FANIA: I don't know! I suppose . . . maybe it's simply that . . . one wants to keep *something* in reserve; we can't . . . we can't really and truly wish to please them. I realize how silly it is to say that, but . . .

ALMA: But you *must* wish to please them, and with all your heart. You are an artist, Fania—you can't purposely do less than your best.

FANIA: But when one looks out the window . . .

ALMA: That is why I have told you *not* to! You have me

wrong, Fania—you seem to think that I fail to see. But I *refuse* to see. Yes. And *you* must refuse!

FANIA: (*Nearly an outcry.*) But what . . . (*She fears it will sound accusatory.*) . . . what will be left of me, Madame!

ALMA: Why . . . yourself, the artist will be left. And this is not new, is it?—what did it ever matter, the opinions of your audience?—or whether you approved of their characters? You sang because it was in you to do! And more so now, when your life depends on it! Have you ever married?

FANIA: No, Madame.

ALMA: I was sure you hadn't—you married your art. I did marry . . . (*ALMA breaks off. She moves, finds herself glancing out the window, but quickly turns away.*) Twice. The first time to that . . . (*She gestures ironically toward her violin case lying on her cot.*) The second time to a man, a violinist, who only wanted my father's name to open the doors for him. But it was my fault—I married him because I pitied myself; I had never had a lover, not even a close friend. There is more than a violin locked in that case, there is a life.

FANIA: I couldn't do that, Madame, I need the friendship of a man.

ALMA: (*Slight pause.*) I understand that, Fania. (*She is moved by an impulse to open up.*) Once I very nearly loved a man. We met in Amsterdam. The three good months of my life. He warmed me . . . like a coat. I think . . . I could have loved him.

FANIA: Why didn't you?

ALMA: They arrested me . . . as a Jew. It still astonishes me.

FANIA: Because you are so German?

ALMA: Yes. I am. (*Slight pause.*) In this place, Fania, you will have to be an artist and only an artist. You will have to concentrate on one thing only—to create all the beauty you are capable of. . . .

FANIA: (*Unable to listen further.*) Excuse me, Madame . . . (*Exits.*)

ANTON CHEKHOV'S "THE DUEL"

adapted by Michael Schulman and Eva Mekler
from the translation by Ann Dunnigan

ACT II, SCENE 2

Nadyezhda Fyordorovna left her husband in St. Petersburg and ran away with her lover, Ivan Andreich Layevsky, to a village in the Caucasus on the Black Sea. She quickly became bored with her new life (as did Layevsky), but she was trapped without money or family to help her return home. She longs desperately for the excitement of city life— the balls, the flirtations, the impassioned conversations. Now Nadyezhda has received word that her husband has died, but at this point in time neither she nor Layevsky are thinking about marriage. They still care for each other, but Layevsky finds himself irritated at almost everything she does, and she has had an affair with a local official.

The scene below takes place in the kitchen of Nadyezhda and Layevsky's cottage. There are soiled dishes and glasses on a table. Marya, a local townswoman who is married to a village official, has come to pay a condolence call. She hands Nadyezhda a basket of fruit and flowers.

(For more information, see other scenes from this play in other sections of this book. To use as a two-person scene, Layevsky's line may be omitted.)

MARYA: My dear, I'm so distressed and shocked! This morning our dear, sweet doctor told my Nikodim Aleksandrych that he heard your husband had passed away. Tell me, my dear . . . tell me, is it true?

NADYEZHDA: Yes, it's true, he's dead. Thank you for these.

MARYA: That's dreadful, dreadful, my dear! But there's not evil without good. Your husband was, no doubt, a wonderful, noble, saintly man, and such men are more needed in heaven than on earth . . . Yes, and so you are free, my dear. Yes, now you can hold up your head and look people boldly in the eye. From now on God and man will bless your union with Ivan Andreich. I'm so excited for you that I'm trembling with joy. My dear, we'll give you away . . . It will give us such pleasure. Nikodim Aleksandrych and I are so fond of you. You will allow us to give our blessing to your pure lawful union? When, when do you intend to be married?

NADYEZHDA: I haven't even thought about it.

MARYA: That is not possible, dear. You have thought about it, you must have!

NADYEZHDA: No, I really haven't. Why should we get married? It wouldn't make things any better. On the contrary, it would make them worse . . . We should lose our freedom.

MARYA: My dear, my dear . . . what are you saying? Come to your senses. You must settle down!

NADYEZHDA: What do you mean, "settle down"? I haven't even lived yet and you tell me to settle down. Do you realize that as soon as I completed my studies at the institute I married a man I did not love and then I ran away with Layevsky and have been living the whole time with him on this dull, desolate shore? Always in the expectation of something better. Is that life? No! It is not life when from morning to night one has no idea how to spend the useless hours. I'm wasting my youth!

MARYA: (*Taking back her basket.*) Good-bye, my dear. Forgive me for having troubled you. Although it is not easy for me, I am obliged to tell you that from this day on, all is over between us, and in spite of my profound respect for Ivan Andreich, my door is closed to you! (*She begins to walk off.*)

NADYEZHDA: Ivan Andreich did not even come home to me last night!

(MARYA returns and puts down basket. There are tears in her eyes. She holds out her hands to NADYEZHDA. NADYEZHDA rushes to her, they embrace, and both begin to weep. They sit, continue to weep, and while weeping MARYA begins.)

MARYA: Oh, my dear, my dear child. I wish I could spare you, but I must tell you some hard truths. Trust me, my dear, as you would a mother or older sister. Remember, of all the ladies here, I was the only one to receive you in my home. I was scandalized by you from the first day, but I didn't have the heart to treat you with contempt, as everyone else did. I grieved for dear, good Ivan Andreich as if he were my own son—a young man in a strange place, inexperienced, weak, without a mother . . . But I was uneasy about you . . . I have a daughter, a son . . . You understand . . . the tender mind, the pure heart of a child . . . "Whoso offendeth one of these little ones . . ." I received you, but I trembled for my little ones. And everyone was surprised at my receiving you—you will forgive me—like a respectable woman.

NADYEZHDA: But why? Why? What harm have I done anyone?

MARYA: You are a dreadful sinner. You broke the vow you made to your husband at the altar. You seduced a fine young man. You have ruined his future. Don't speak, don't speak, my dear! I will not believe that it's the man who is to blame for our sins. It is always the woman's fault. Men are frivolous in these matters; they are guided by their hearts, not by their heads. Oh, my dear, if women were more foolish than men, or weaker, God never would have entrusted them with the upbringing of little boys and girls. Any other woman in your position would have hidden herself away, would have been seen only in church. But you flaunted yourself and lived openly, waywardly. And watching you I trembled fearing that a thunderbolt from heaven would strike our home when you visited us. Don't speak, don't speak, my dear! Listen to me . . . God marks the great sinner and you have been marked. It's not by accident that your style of dress has always been appalling.

NADYEZHDA: I thought I dressed very well.

MARYA: No, appalling. Anyone could judge your behavior from the showiness and gaudiness of your attire. And I grieved, grieved . . . And forgive me, my dear, but you are not clean in your person. When we meet in the bathhouse, you make me shudder. Your outer clothing is passable, but your petticoat, your chemise . . . My dear, I blush. And your house—it's simply dreadful, dreadful. No one else in the whole town has flies, but you are plagued by them, your plates and saucers are black with them. Just look at your windows . . . and the table-tops—they are covered with dust, dead flies, soiled glasses . . . And one is embarrassed to go into your bedroom; underclothes flung about everywhere, and your various rubber things hanging on the wall, basins standing about . . . My dear! A husband ought to know nothing of these things, and a wife ought to appear before him as immaculate as a little angel.

NADYEZHDA: All this is not worth bothering about. If only I were happy, but I'm so unhappy!

MARYA: Yes, yes, you're unhappy, and terrible grief awaits you in the future. A solitary old age, illness, and then you will have to answer at the Last Judgment . . . Dreadful! . . . Dreadful! Now fate itself holds out a helping hand and you foolishly thrust it aside. Get married . . . get married quickly!

NADYEZHDA: But it's impossible.

MARYA: Why?

NADYEZHDA: I can't. I'm going away. Ivan Andreich may remain here, but I'm going away.

MARYA: Where?

NADYEZHDA: To Russia.

MARYA: But how will you live there? Why, you have nothing!

NADYEZHDA: I'll do translations or . . . or open a book-shop . . .

MARYA: These are childish fantasies, my dear. You need money for a bookshop.

NADYEZHDA: I can't live this kind of life . . . I'm not worthy of him.

LAYEVSKY: (*He calls from off-stage.*) Nadyezhda.

MARYA: Well, I'll leave you now.

NADYEZHDA: I must do something, what can I do?

MARYA: You calm yourself and think things over and tomorrow come and see me in a gay mood. That will be lovely. Well, good-bye, my little angel. Let me kiss you.

COME BACK TO THE 5 AND DIME, JIMMY DEAN, JIMMY DEAN

by Ed Graczyk

ACT II

It is a hot, dry September 30th in McCarthy, Texas, in the year 1975, and the H. L. Kressmont five-and-dime store is decorated for a most unusual celebration. As the sign on the wall says, it is "The 20th Anniversary Reunion of the Disciples of James Dean." Twenty years have passed since James Dean died, and the Disciples—now women in their late thirties—are gathered to reminisce about their teenage fan club and their deceased idol. Mona was and is the most devoted of the Disciples. She has always claimed that her son was fathered by James Dean during the time he was filming Giant *in a nearby town.*

Unlike the other women, Mona has never left McCarthy. She works in the five-and-dime. Her son, whose name is Jimmy Dean, is now twenty years old, and, without saying a word to his mother, has driven off in a car belonging to one of the women. His mother is beside herself with worry. She tells the women that the boy is retarded and alerts the state police about his disappearance.

This scene follows a series of revelations by the women about how their lives have evolved. Sissy, who returned to live in McCarthy a few years ago, has revealed that her enormous breasts—always her most prominent feature— are now rubber replacements for those removed in a cancer operation. As the scene below opens, Sissy has been mocking Mona's self-righteousness.

(To use as a two-person scene, the reference to Joanne can be ignored.)

....

MONA: *(Goes to the phone.)* I just don't understand what is takin' them so long. Maybe the phone is out of order, along with everythin' else.

SISSY: *(Goes after her.)* There's nothin' wrong with the Goddamn phone. *(Grabs it from her.)* He's gone!

MONA: *(Innocently.)* Well, I know that he's gone, Heavens, I'm not blind am I?

SISSY: Then why do you think everybody else is?

MONA: I don't understand your point.

SISSY: Stop all the crap, Mona . . . He's run away . . . Flew the coop . . . Gone!

MONA: *(Small laugh.)* He couldn't run away . . . he doesn't even know what it means . . . He doesn't know how to do anythin' without me to help him. *(Moves away.)* He's only a child . . . a poor helpless . . .

SISSY: That's what you are, for Chrissake, not him! He's all grown up, Mona . . . Open your damn eyes an' see it.

MONA: His mind isn't . . . his mind is like a . . .

SISSY: The only thing wrong with his mind is that he couldn't make it up soon enough to get the hell outta here . . . away from you an' your crazy ideas about him. He finally made it up, Mona . . . He's gone!

MONA: No, he couldn't decide somethin' like that by himself.

SISSY: I helped him!

MONA: You?!

SISSY: Yes, me, Mona . . . an' I gave him every damn redcent I had . . . *(Gestures.)* there in my purse to get him started . . . someplace else . . . away from you!

MONA: *(Charging at her.)* You are a disgustin', deceitful . . . *(Slapping at SISSY. A crazed woman.)* Hypocrite . . . claiming all these years to be my friend. He was none of your Goddamn business. *(JOANNE tries to pull her off SISSY.)* . . . putting crazy ideas like that into the head of a helpless moron.

SISSY: He is not a moron, Goddammit!

MONA: *(Simply to JOANNE.)* Take your hands off me. *(To SISSY.)* You should be arrested an' locked up.

SISSY: Mona, dammit . . . there is nothin' wrong with that boy.

MONA: *(Covers her ears.)* Lies! . . . lies, nothin' but lies! All those doctors . . . those doctors said he was a . . .

SISSY: *(Prying her hands away from her ears.)* You never took him to no doctors . . . he told me so!

MONA: He's lyin' . . . He doesn't know the truth.

SISSY: And neither do you anymore, Mona. Where the hell did you get the idea anyhow? . . . Did you see it in some movie, or did it jump out at you from the pages of some damn novel-of-the-month?

MONA: I am his mother and I know what he is! I don't believe one word you have just said . . . This is a trick isn't it? *(Gestures to JOANNE.)* The two of you got together, didn't you? . . . Got together to trick me into sayin' . . . sayin' . . .

SISSY: Sayin' what, Mona? . . . That he isn't the son of James Dean? . . . Hell, we've all known that for years . . . everybody's known it, an' accepted it, but you.

MONA: He needs me!

SISSY: Not anymore, he doesn't. You tried to make him helpless an' dependent on you to keep him to yourself . . . to keep James Dean alive . . . *(Pleading.)* Let him go, for Chrissake.

MONA: *(Reaching for breath.)* I knew it would come to this in time. I could feel it inside me . . . I had a premonition.

SISSY: You had gas.

MONA: *(A cornered child.)* I don't know why you have done this. We were friends . . . I gave up a formal college education just to come back here . . . *(Starts to wheeze.)* so we could . . . be together . . . my pills, Sissy, get me my . . .

SISSY: That asthma of yours is as phony as my rubber tits an' you know it.

ABSENT FRIENDS

by Alan Ayckbourn

ACT I

Diana and Paul are having old friends over for a Saturday afternoon tea. Paul, who is a good provider but not a very attentive husband, has not yet returned from playing squash. So far only Evelyn (who doesn't say much) and Marge have arrived. After Evelyn goes to the "lavatory," Diana tells Marge of her suspicions that Paul is having an affair with Evelyn. Marge has come from a shopping spree with bags aplenty and excited to show Diana her new shoes (described by Ayckbourn as "very unsuitable"). Evelyn has left her baby in the room sleeping in a pram and Marge has trouble remembering the child's name. (See other scene from this play in another section for more information.)

⋯⋯⋯

DIANA: Am I glad to see you.

MARGE: Why's that?

DIANA: She's been here for ages.

MARGE: Who do you mean—oh, yes. Miss Chatterbox.

DIANA: I know she's been up to something. I don't trust her. I never did.

MARGE: I must show you my shoes. (*Starts to unpack them.*) How do you mean?

DIANA: I know that girl's been up to something.

MARGE: Oh, you mean with . . . ?

DIANA: She and Paul. I know they have.

MARGE: Well . . . (*Producing a pair of very unsuitable shoes.*) There, you see. Aren't they nice?

DIANA: Lovely.

MARGE: They had them in blue which was nicer, actually. But then I had nothing else that would have gone with them.

DIANA: He didn't want them to come round here today. That's how I know they're up to something.

MARGE: Who?

DIANA: Evelyn and John. He didn't want them round.

MARGE: Who? Paul didn't?

DIANA: No.

MARGE: (*Parading around in her shoes.*) Look, you see . . . these tights aren't right with them but . . .

DIANA: I mean, why should he suddenly not want them round? They've been round here enough in the past and then all of a sudden he doesn't want to see them.

MARGE: Odd. There was another sort, you know, with the strap but I found they cut me across here.

DIANA: They suit you.

MARGE: Yes, I'm very pleased.

DIANA: I tried to get her to say something.

MARGE: Evelyn?

DIANA: Just now.

MARGE: Oh. Did she?

DIANA: No. She's not saying anything. Why should she? I know Paul, you see. I know he's with someone. I'm sure it's her. He came home, went straight upstairs and washed his shirt through the other night. I said, what's got into you? He said, well, what's wrong with me washing my shirt? I said, you've never washed anything in your life. He said, well, we all have to start some time. I said, lovely, but why do you want to start doing it in the middle of the night. And he had no answer to that at all. Nothing. He just stood there with it dripping all over the floor.

MARGE: Well . . .

DIANA: After twelve years, you get to know someone.

MARGE: I wonder if these will go with that other coat.

DIANA: What's she doing up there?

MARGE: Well, she's . . .

DIANA: I bet she's having a really good snoop around.

MARGE: Oh, Di . . .

DIANA: I bet that's what she's up to. I've never trusted her an inch. She's got one of those really mean little faces, hasn't she?

MARGE: Well . . .

DIANA: I bet it was her that went off with my scarf, you know.

MARGE: I shouldn't think so. Why don't you talk it over with Paul?

DIANA: Paul? We haven't talked for years. Not really. Now he's had his own way and sent the children off to school, there's even less to talk about. I don't know why he wanted them at boarding school. They're neither of them happy. I know they're not. You should see the letters they write.

MARGE: I don't know what to say . . . (*To pram.*) Poogy, poogy. Hallo, Walter.

DIANA: Wayne.

MARGE: Hallo.

DIANA: Don't for God's sake wake him up. He's been bawling his head off half the afternoon. I don't think she feeds him properly.

MARGE: He looks nice and chubby.

DIANA: It doesn't look all there to me.

MARGE: Di!

DIANA: No, truthfully, you look at its eyes.

MARGE: He's asleep.

DIANA: Well, you look at them when it wakes up. Don't tell me that's normal. I mean, our Mark's were never like that. Nor were Julie's. And she's had to wear glasses.

MARGE: She looks lovely in her little glasses.

DIANA: Paul doesn't think so. He won't let her wear them when she's at home.

MARGE: Well, I think he's a lovely baby. I was on at Gordon again the other day about adopting one.

DIANA: What did he say?

MARGE: Still no. He won't hear of it. He's frightened of it, I think. He keeps saying to me, it's not like a dog, Marge. We can't get rid of it if we don't like it and I say, we will like it, we'll grow to like it and then he says, well what happens if we adopt one and then it grows up to be a murderer? Then what do we do? They'll blame us.

DIANA: It's not very likely.

MARGE: Try convincing him. No, he's just going to keep on going with his tests ... till the cows come home. That reminds me, I must ring him up. I said I would as soon as I got here. See if he's coping. Do you mind?

DIANA: No, go ahead.

MARGE: He's got the phone by his bed.

(MARGE starts to dial.)

SYLVIA

by A.R. Gurney

ACT I

In "Sylvia" an actress gets the rare opportunity to play a dog, a large, friendly dog named Sylvia, who is described as "pert and sexy," but also "scruffy" with "messy" hair. She also gets the funniest lines. Greg found Sylvia in the park this afternoon (her collar had her name on it) at just the right time in his life. His children are grown, his wife, Kate, is deeply involved in her career as a public school English teacher, and he no longer finds fulfillment in his job as a financial trader. Feeling despondent, Greg left work early today and wandered into the park where he met Sylvia and promptly fell in love with her, knowing instantly that she would satisfy some vague "need" in him. So, of course, he brought her home to his Manhattan apartment, where before long she was introduced to Kate.

Kate knew just as instantly that Sylvia must go—out of her home, off of her furniture, and away from her meticulously managed, orderly life. Kate is a busy teacher with definite ideas about what is good for her and Greg at this time in their lives, and Sylvia doesn't fit into her scheme. Just before the scene below, Greg's boss telephoned and Greg went into another room to talk to him, leaving Kate and Sylvia alone for the first time. Kate has been working at her desk, ignoring Sylvia.

SYLVIA: (*Finally.*) Hi. (*KATE sits at her desk, takes books and a notebook out of her bag, begins to work.*) I said Hi.

KATE: (*Working.*) I'm busy, Sylvia. (*SYLVIA goes to her, nudges her.*)

SYLVIA: Hello, Kate.

KATE: Go away, Sylvia.

SYLVIA: I'm just trying to make friends.

KATE: Don't bother me, please. I'm trying to prepare my fall curriculum.

SYLVIA: You don't like me, do you?

KATE: (*Working.*) It's not a question of that.

SYLVIA: You don't like dogs.

KATE: I like them when they belong to other people.

SYLVIA: You're prejudiced.

KATE: Not at all.

SYLVIA: I think you're prejudiced against dogs!

KATE: (*Putting down her work.*) I am not prejudiced, Sylvia. When I was a girl, I read the Albert Payson Terhune dog books cover to cover. I watched *Lassie* on television. I'm a huge fan of *One Hundred and One Dalmatians*. When we lived in the suburbs, when the children were around, we had several dogs, and guess who ended up feeding the damn things. But I don't want a dog *now*, Sylvia. That is the point. Our last child has gone off to college, and we have moved into town, and the dog phase of my life is definitely over. I've gotten my master's degree, Sylvia, and I have a very challenging teaching job, and frankly I don't want to worry about animals. So if you'll excuse me, I will return to the daunting task of planning how to teach Shakespeare in the inner city junior high school. (*She returns to her work.*)

SYLVIA: O.K. Fine. No problem. (*She goes to the couch.*) I'll just stay out of your hair. (*She steps onto the couch, turns around once or twice, then settles on it.*)

KATE: (*Looking up.*) Off, Sylvia!

SYLVIA: You speaking to me?

KATE: I said off that couch! Right now!

SYLVIA: I'm just relaxing. Can't I even relax? (*KATE leaves her desk, pulls SYLVIA off the couch.*)

KATE: Now off! And stay off!

SYLVIA: Easy! Take it easy! . . . Jesus!

KATE: I'm sorry, but you've got to learn. (*She returns to her work. Pause.*)

SYLVIA: (*Sitting grumpily on the floor.*) I've sat on couches before, you know.

KATE: (*Working.*) What?

SYLVIA: I said I've sat on couches before. I've sat on plenty of couches.

KATE: Well you can't sit on this one.

SYLVIA: Hoity-toity to you.

KATE: Quiet. I'm working.

SYLVIA: (*Getting up; easing onto the chair.*) Can I at least sit on a chair?

KATE: No, Sylvia. Off!

SYLVIA: (*Slumping again onto the floor.*) Shit. Piss. Fuck.

KATE: (*Putting down her pencil.*) This is not going to work, Sylvia.

SYLVIA: What do you mean?

KATE: I'm afraid you'll have to go to the pound.

SYLVIA: Hey, I'm sitting, aren't I? I'm sitting on the floor. Look how quickly I sat.

KATE: Still, you've got to go.

SYLVIA: O.K. I get the picture. I'll avoid the furniture. I'm not dumb.

KATE: No, I'm sorry, Sylvia. You're going to the pound. I'm sure someone will come along and give you a nice home.

SYLVIA: I've got a nice home right here.

KATE: No, now listen, Sylvia. It doesn't make sense. Nobody's around all day long. You'd be bored out of your mind, stuck in this apartment.

SYLVIA: I don't mind. I'll sleep. I'll chew things.

KATE: That's just the trouble.

SYLVIA: All right. I *won't* chew things. Just show me the rules and I'll follow them, I swear.

KATE: We go out a lot, Sylvia. We visit friends in the country on weekends. We see the kids at college.

SYLVIA: I'll come, too!

KATE: (*Crossing to her.*) No, I don't want that. I want my freedom, Sylvia. I want freedom from dogs. Now you'll be much happier somewhere else.

SYLVIA: In the *pound*?

KATE: Well not the *pound*, really, Sylvia. I shouldn't have

said the pound. We'll give you to . . . what is it? The Animal
Rescue League. Or the Humane Society.

SYLVIA: They suck.

KATE: Now, now.

SYLVIA: They *suck*! You have no idea what they do.

KATE: Well I'm sure they make every effort to—

SYLVIA: Have you ever been there? Have you ever bothered
to check them out?

KATE: No, but—

SYLVIA: The rows of cages. The shitty food.

KATE: Oh now.

SYLVIA: The time limit.

KATE: The time limit?

SYLVIA: They all have time limits. They don't broadcast it,
but they do. If someone doesn't bail you out, normally
within five working days, then they put you to sleep.

KATE: Sylvia . . .

SYLVIA: They do! They kill you! Listen. It's a tough world
out there, lady. I know. I've been there. (*Nuzzling her.*)
That's why I want to be here.

KATE: Well you can't, Sylvia. I'm terribly sorry but I really
have to put my foot down. (*GREG comes back in.*)

STEEL MAGNOLIAS

by Robert Harling

ACT I, SCENE 1

The play is set in Truvy's beauty shop in a small Louisiana town. Annelle, fresh out of beauty school, is nervously demonstrating her technique on Truvy, hoping to be hired. Truvy's is the place to go for the best hairdos in town, and the best gossip. And if you need advice for almost any problem, you can count on Truvy for some good common sense. As the scene begins, Annelle is putting the final touches on Truvy's hair, using "more hairspray than necessary." Annelle is tense and she is also very confused about her life (for example, she is not sure whether or not she is still married). During the scene there are sounds of gunshots and a dog barking.

....

ANNELLE: Oops! I see a hole.

TRUVY: I was hoping you'd catch that.

ANNELLE: It's a little poofier than I would normally do, but I'm nervous.

TRUVY: I'm not real concerned about that. When I go to bed I wrap my entire head with toilet tissue so it usually gets a little smushed down anyway in that process.

ANNELLE: In my class at the trade school, I was number one when it came to frosting and streaking. I did my own.

TRUVY: Really? I wouldn't have known. And I can spot a bottle job at twenty paces. (*Studying her hairdo.*) Well . . .

your technique is good, and your form and content will improve with experience. So, you're hired.

ANNELLE: (*Overcome.*) Oh!!

TRUVY: And not a moment too soon! This morning we're going to be as busy as a one-armed paper hanger.

ANNELLE: Thank you, Miss Truvy! Thank you . . .

TRUVY: No time. Now. You know where the coffee stuff is. Everything else is on a tray next to the stove. (*TRUVY removes her smock.*)

ANNELLE: Here. Let me help you. (*Dusts her off.*) You've got little tiny hairs and fuzzies all over you.

TRUVY: Honey, there's so much static electricity in here I pick up everything except boys and money. (*Points ANNELLE toward the kitchen.*) Be a treasure. (*ANNELLE exits into the kitchen. TRUVY immediately starts redoing her hairdo.*) Annelle? This is the most successful shop in town. Wanna know why?

ANNELLE: (*Offstage.*) Why?

TRUVY: Because I have a strict philosophy that I have stuck to for fifteen years . . . "There is no such thing as natural beauty." That's why I've never lost a client to the Kut and Kurl or the Beauty Box. And remember! My ladies get only the best. Do not scrimp on anything. Feel free to use as much hair spray as you want. (*ANNELLE returns with the tray. The sound of a gunshot makes her jump, but she recovers.*) Just shove that stuff to one side, it goes right there. (*Pointing out the room.*) Manicure station here . . .

ANNELLE: There's no such thing as natural beauty . . .

TRUVY: Remember that, or we're all out of a job. Just look at me, Annelle. It takes some effort to look like this.

ANNELLE: I can see that. How many ladies do we have this morning?

TRUVY: I restrict myself to the ladies of the neighborhood on Saturday mornings. Normally that would be just three, but today we've got Shelby Eatenton. She's not a regular, she's the daughter of a regular. I have to do something special with her hair. She's getting married this afternoon. Now. How long have you been here in town?

ANNELLE: A few weeks . . .

TRUVY: New in town! It must be exciting being in a new place. I wouldn't know. I've lived here all my life.

ANNELLE: It's a little scary.

TRUVY: I can imagine. Well . . . tell me things about yourself.

ANNELLE: There's nothing to tell. I live here. I've got a job now. That's it. Could I borrow a few of these back issues of *Southern Hair*?

TRUVY: Uh . . . sure. It's essential to keep abreast of the latest styles. I'm glad to see your interest. I get *McCall's*, *Family Circle*, *Glamour*, *Mademoiselle*, *Ladies' Home Journal*, every magazine known to man. You must live close by. Within walking distance, I mean. I didn't see a car.

ANNELLE: My car's . . . I don't have a car. I've been staying across the river at Robeline's Boarding House.

TRUVY: That's quite a walk. Ruth Robeline . . . now there's a story. She's a twisted, troubled soul. Her life has been an experiment in terror. Husband killed in World War II. Her son was killed in Vietnam. I have to tell you, when it comes to suffering, she's right up there with Elizabeth Taylor.

ANNELLE: I had no idea. (*There is a loud gunshot and barking.*) Is that a gunshot?

TRUVY: Yes, dear. I believe it is. Plug in the hotplate, please.

ANNELLE: But why is someone firing a gun in a nice neighborhood like this?

TRUVY: It's a long story. It has to do with Shelby's wedding and her father. (*More gunfire and barking.*) You'll be happier if you just ignore it like the rest of the neighborhood.

PIAF

by Pam Gems

ACT I, SCENE 1

*The play tells the story of Edith Piaf, the French singer—
of her rise from an impoverished street life to international
stardom. Her audiences were thrilled by her voice and her
honest, emotional singing style, and they were titillated by
reports of her tempestuous love affairs, her bouts of drinking and drug use, her breakdowns and her comebacks.*

*As the play opens we see Piaf, already a star, staggering
during a song and having to be helped off the stage. The
scene then changes to an earlier time and we are outside
a posh Paris nightclub, the Cluny Club. The young Piaf is
singing in the streets for money. The owner of the club
hears her, hires her on the spot, and hands her some
money. Then we are in Piaf's apartment a short while later.
Her friend, Toine, enters, "throws down her large Thirties'
clutch bag, and sits heavily, taking off her shoes and massaging her feet, wincing." Toine is a prostitute—as is Piaf.*

....

PIAF: Toine—here—guess what!

TOINE: Fuck off.

PIAF: Wassa matter with you?

TOINE: Fucking pimp's had me on that corner, I thought my
bleeding toes would burst. I haven't seen more than a couple
of fellers all night . . . he's gotta change my shift.

PIAF: Here, listen—

TOINE: Him with his bloody favorites, think I don't know?

PIAF: Listen! You're never going—

TOINE: That fat Hélène, sits in the fucking caff half the time, I'm not going to stand for it—

PIAF: This bloke . . . !

TOINE: (*Irritable.*) What?

PIAF: Me big chance!—you know, like on the movies.

TOINE: (*Baffled.*) Eh?

PIAF: This bloke comes up to me—hey! Remember what the fortune teller told us—!

TOINE: Hang on . . .

PIAF: *You* remember! I was standing outside the Cluny Club, singing—

TOINE: Singing?

PIAF: Yeah, you know . . . for a lark . . . I'm just getting going when up he comes . . . real swell . . . top hat, silk scarf, silver cane, the lot. Next thing I know he asks me inside.

TOINE: Iyiy!

PIAF: Toine, you've never seen nothing like it—white tablecloths, little velvet chairs with gold tassels, anything I wanted to drink—

TOINE: Hah, I get it—another fucking funny, Christ he must be hard up . . . here, can you see any crabs?

PIAF: (*Looks perfunctorily.*) No, listen! He says to me, he says "You've got a good voice, kid . . ."

TOINE: Hah!

PIAF: Shut up . . . "I want you . . ." (*She fixes* TOINE *with a magnetic stare.*) . . . "I want you to star in my club!" Whatcha think of that!

TOINE: Oh Christ, she's away.

PIAF: It's true!

TOINE: Ede—

PIAF: Look, I'm not saying he's young or good looking or anything—

TOINE: Ede, have you gone off your head or something?

PIAF: I keep trying to *tell* you! (*Her rage subsides as she concedes the unlikeliness of the tale.*) He wants me to sing . . . in his show . . . Cluny Club.

TOINE: Where all the swells go? Get away.

(*But* PIAF *is counting the money.*)

Listen . . . where did you get that?

PIAF: He *gave* it me . . . honest. For nothing!

(They both look at the money. TOINE *shakes her head slowly.)*

TOINE: Nah.

(PIAF waits patiently for the verdict.)

Nah . . . sounds funny to me. Look, kid, I wouldn't have nothing to do wiv it. He's got a little business going, he's short of girls—*(She laughs.)* haha, hahaha . . . he must be!

PIAF: Speak for your bloody self!

TOINE: *(Threatening.)* Get off.

(PIAF backs away prudently.

Hiatus.

She scuffs moodily . . . picks up the dress TOINE *has taken off.)*

TOINE: *(Without raising her eyes from her magazine.)* It's too big for yuh.

(PIAF hums moodily, ruining TOINE'S *efforts to read. She puts down her book with a martyred sigh.)*

Oh all right. You can have this. *(She proffers her long, thin, dark-purple Thirties-style scarf.)*

PIAF: Thanks! *(She arranges it around her neck.)* Here, don't laugh. He told me to have a bath . . . wash me hair.

(They laugh, jeering.)

TOINE: Tell you what, though. *(She finds a comb in her bag . . . tidies* PIAF'S *hair, arranges a spitcurl on her forehead.)* That's better—we-ell, you wanna look decent.

PIAF: Thanks. *(She makes to go . . . pauses.)*

TOINE: *(Without looking up from her book.)* OK, what is it now?

PIAF: Can I have a lend of your handbag?

TOINE: No.

(But PIAF knows the value of fidgeting.

TOINE *grinds her teeth, hurls the bag at her.)*

PIAF: Thanks! *(She tucks the unsuitably large poche under her arm and struts off proudly, causing* TOINE *to grin.)*

TOINE: Take it easy, squirt. *(To the audience, tired.)* Well, can't be for the fucking singing, can it—he can hear that for nothing in the street. Be Tangier for you, I shouldn't doubt. *(She picks up her things and goes.)*

TWELFTH NIGHT; OR, WHAT YOU WILL

by William Shakespeare

ACT I, SCENE 5

Viola was shipwrecked and, fearing that she would be harmed as an unprotected young woman in a strange land, she disguised herself as a man and managed to gain employment in the service of the handsome Duke Orsino, with whom she immediately fell in love. But Orsino loves the beautiful Countess Olivia, who has refused all his overtures. Orsino sends Viola (whom he knows as Cesario) to win Olivia for him, but instead Olivia becomes smitten with the clever, beautiful youth before her; she falls madly in love with Viola. As the scene begins, Viola is finally allowed in to speak with Olivia who has covered her face with a veil and asked her gentlewoman, Maria, to join them.

....

OLIVIA: Give me my veil: come, throw it o'er my face. We'll once more hear Orsino's embassy.
(Enter VIOLA and ATTENDANTS.)

VIOLA: The honourable lady of the house, which is she?

OLIVIA: Speak to me; I shall answer for her. Your will?

VIOLA: Most radiant, exquisite and unmatchable beauty,—I pray you, tell me if this be the lady of the house, for I never saw her: I would be loath to cast away my speech, for besides that it is excellently well penned, I have taken great pains to con it. Good beauties, let me sustain no scorn; I am very comptible, even to the least sinister usage.

OLIVIA: Whence came you, sir?

VIOLA: I can say little more than I have studied, and that question's out of my part. Good gentle one, give me modest assurance if you be the lady of the house, that I may proceed in my speech.

OLIVIA: Are you a comedian?

VIOLA: No, my profound heart: and yet, by the very fangs of malice I swear, I am not that I play. Are you the lady of the house?

OLIVIA: If I do not usurp myself, I am.

VIOLA: Most certain, if you are she, you do usurp yourself; for what is yours to bestow is not yours to reserve. But this is from my commission: I will on with my speech in your praise, and then show you the heart of my message.

OLIVIA: Come to what is important in 't: I forgive you the praise.

VIOLA: Alas, I took great pains to study it, and 'tis poetical.

OLIVIA: It is the more like to be feigned: I pray you, keep it in. I heard you were saucy at my gates, and allowed your approach rather to wonder at you than to hear you. If you be not mad, be gone; if you have reason, be brief: 'tis not that time of moon with me to make one in so skipping a dialogue.

MARIA: Will you hoist sail, sir? here lies your way.

VIOLA: No, good swabber; I am to hull here a little longer. Some mollification for your giant, sweet lady. Tell me your mind: I am a messenger.

OLIVIA: Sure, you have some hideous matter to deliver, when the courtesy of it is so fearful. Speak your office.

VIOLA: It alone concerns your ear. I bring no overture of war, no taxation of homage: I hold the olive in my hand; my words are as full of peace as matter.

OLIVIA: Yet you began rudely. What are you? what would you?

VIOLA: The rudeness that hath appeared in me have I learned from my entertainment. What I am, and what I would, are as secret as maidenhead; to your ears, divinity, to any other's, profanation.

OLIVIA: Give us the place alone: we will hear this divinity. (*Exit MARIA and ATTENDANTS.*) Now, sir, what is your text?

VIOLA: Most sweet lady,—

OLIVIA: A comfortable doctrine, and much may be said of it.
Where lies your text?

VIOLA: In Orsino's bosom.

OLIVIA: In his bosom! In what chapter of his bosom?

VIOLA: To answer by the method, in the first of his heart.

OLIVIA: O, I have read it: it is heresy. Have you no more to
say?

VIOLA: Good madam, let me see your face.

OLIVIA: Have you any commission from your lord to nego-
tiate with my face? You are now out of your text: but we
will draw the curtain and show you the picture. Look you,
sir, such a one I was this present. Is't not well done?
(Unveiling.)

VIOLA: Excellently done, if God did all.

OLIVIA 'Tis in grain, sir; 'twill endure wind and weather.

VIOLA: 'Tis beauty truly blent, whose red and white Nature's
own sweet and cunning hand laid on: Lady, you are the
cruell'st she alive,
If you will lead these graces to the grave
And leave the world no copy.

OLIVIA: O, sir, I will not be so hard-hearted; I will give out
divers schedules of my beauty: it shall be inventoried, and
every particle and utensil labelled to my will: as, item, two
lips, indifferent red; item, two grey eyes, with lids to them;
item, one neck, one chin, and so forth. Were you sent hither
to praise me?

VIOLA: I see what you are, you are too proud;
But, if you were the devil, you are fair.
My lord and master loves you: O, such love
Could be but recompensed, though you were
crown'd
The nonpareil of beauty!

OLIVIA: How does he love me?

VIOLA: With adorations, fertile tears,
With groans that thunder love, with sighs of fire.

OLIVIA: Your lord does know my mind; I cannot love him:
Yet I suppose him virtuous, know him noble,
Of great estate, of fresh and stainless youth;
In voices well divulged, free, learn'd and valiant;
And in dimension and the shape of nature
A gracious person: but yet I cannot love him;

He might have took his answer long ago.

VIOLA: If I did love you in my master's flame,
With such a suffering, such a deadly life,
In your denial I would find no sense;
I would not understand it.

OLIVIA: Why, what would you?

VIOLA: Make me a willow cabin at your gate,
And call upon my soul within the house;
Write loyal cantons of contemned love
And sing them loud even in the dead of night;
Halloo your name to the reverberate hills,
And make the babbling gossip of the air
Cry out "Olivia!" O, you should not rest
Between the elements of air and earth,
But you should pity me!

OLIVIA: What is your parentage? You might do much.

VIOLA: Above my fortunes, yet my state is well: I am a
gentleman.

OLIVIA: Get you to your lord;
I cannot love him: let him send no more;
Unless, perchance, you come to me again,
To tell me how he takes it. Fare you well:
I thank you for your pains: spend this for me.

VIOLA: I am no fee'd post, lady; keep your purse:
My master, not myself, lacks recompense.
Love make his heart of flint that you shall love;
And let your fervour, like my master's, be
Placed in contempt! Farewell, fair cruelty

(*VIOLA Exits.*)

OLIVIA: "What is your parentage?"
"Above my fortunes, yet my state is well:
I am a gentleman." I'll be sworn thou art;
Thy tongue, thy face, thy limbs, actions, and spirit,
Do give thee five-fold blazon: not too fast: soft,
soft!
Unless the master were the man. How now!
Even so quickly may one catch the plague?
Methinks I feel this youth's perfections
With an invisible and subtle stealth
To creep in at mine eyes. Well, let it be.
What ho, Malvolio!

SCENES FOR TWO MEN

SPEED-THE-PLOW

by David Mamet

SCENE 1

Bobby Gould and Charlie Fox have worked for a Holly-wood movie studio for years, starting together in the mail room. Gould has moved up the ranks, becoming Head of Production with access to the top executives of the studio and the power to decide which movies (within a certain budget) get made. Both men want nothing more than to be rich and powerful, and this morning Fox has brought Gould great news: A big-money star, Douggie Brown, liked a "Buddy Picture" script that Fox showed him and has agreed to make the movie for the studio.

This is a dream come true for these two men who have spent careers sucking up to those above them in the studio hierarchy (with Fox having, at times, to suck up to Gould). As they describe themselves, they are "Two Whores" in a business that produces "garbage"—and they love it. As the scene begins, Karen, the attractive temp secretary, has just left Gould's office with instructions to cancel all appointments for the day and to make a reservation at the Coventry restaurant where the men are going to celebrate their good fortune.

....

FOX: Lunch at the Coventry.
GOULD: That's right.
FOX: Thy will be done.

GOULD: You see, all that you got to do is eat my doo doo for eleven years, and eventually the wheel comes round.

FOX: Pay back time.

GOULD: You brought me the Doug Brown script.

FOX: Glad I could do it.

GOULD: You son of a *bitch* . . .

FOX: Hey.

GOULD: Charl, I just hope.

FOX: What?

GOULD: The shoe was on the other foot, I'd act in such a . . .

FOX: . . . hey . . .

GOULD: Really, princely way toward you.

FOX: I *know* you would, Bob, because lemme tell you: experiences like this, *films* like this . . . these are the films . . .

GOULD: . . . Yes . . .

FOX: *These* are the films, that whaddayacallit . . . (*Long pause.*) that make it all worthwhile.

GOULD: . . . I think you're going to find a *lot* of things now, make it all worthwhile. I think *conservatively*, you and me, we build ourselves in to split, minimally, ten percent. (*Pause.*)

FOX: Of the net.

GOULD: Char, Charlie: permit me to tell you: two things I've learned, twenty-five years in the entertainment industry.

FOX: What?

GOULD: The two things which are always true.

FOX: One:

GOULD: The first one is: there is no net.

FOX: Yeah . . . ? (*Pause.*)

GOULD: And I forgot the second one. Okay, I'm gonna meet you at the Coventry in half an hour. We'll talk about boys and clothes.

FOX: Whaddaya gonna do the interim?

GOULD: I'm gonna *Work* . . . (*Indicating his figures on the pad.*)

FOX: Work . . . ? You never did a day's work in your life.

GOULD: Oooh, Oooh, . . . the Bitching Lamp is Lit.

FOX: You never did a fuckin' day's work in your life.

GOULD: That true?

FOX: Eleven years I've known you, you're either scheming or you're ziggin' and zaggin', hey, I *know* you, Bob.

GOULD: Oh yes, the scorn of the impotent . . .

FOX: I know you, Bob. I know you from the *back*. I know what you're staying for.

GOULD: You do?

FOX: Yes.

GOULD: What?

FOX: You're staying to Hide the Afikomen.

GOULD: Yeah?

FOX: You're staying to put those moves on your new secretary.

GOULD: I am?

FOX: Yeah, and it *will* not work.

GOULD: It will not work, what are you saying . . . ?

FOX: No, I was just saying that she . . .

GOULD: . . . she wouldn't go for me.

FOX: That she won't go for you.

GOULD: (*Pause.*) Why?

FOX: Why? (*Pause.*) I don't know.

GOULD: What do you see . . . ?

FOX: I think . . . I think . . . you serious?

GOULD: Yes.

FOX: I don't want to pee on your parade.

GOULD: No . . .

FOX: I mean, I'm sorry that I took the edge off it.

GOULD: I wasn't *going* to hit on her.

FOX: Hmmm.

GOULD: I was gonna . . .

FOX: You were gonna work.

GOULD: Yes.

FOX: Oh.

GOULD: (*Pause.*) But tell me what you see.

FOX: What I see, what I *saw*, just an observation . . .

GOULD: . . . yes . . .

FOX: It's not important.

GOULD: Tell me what you see. Really.

FOX: I just thought, I just thought she falls between two stools.

GOULD: And what would those stools be?

FOX: That she is not, just some, you know, a "floozy" . . .

GOULD: A "floozy" . . .

FOX: . . . on the other hand, I think I'd have to say, I don't think she is so *ambitious* she would schtup you just to get ahead. (*Pause.*) That's all. (*Pause.*)

GOULD: What if she just "liked" me? (*Pause.*)

FOX: If she just "liked" you?

GOULD: Yes.

FOX: Ummm. (*Pause.*)

GOULD: Yes.

FOX: You're saying, if she just . . . *liked* you . . . (*Pause.*)

GOULD: You mean nobody loves me for myself.

FOX: No.

GOULD: No?

FOX: Not in *this* office . . .

GOULD: And she's neither, what, vacant nor ambitious enough to go . . .

FOX: . . . I'm not saying you don't *deserve* it, you do deserve it. Hey, . . . I think you're worth it.

GOULD: Thank you. You're saying that she's neither, what, dumb, nor ambitious enough, she would go to bed with me.

FOX: . . . she's too, she's too . . .

GOULD: She's too . . . High-line . . . ?

FOX: No, she's, she's too . . .

GOULD: She's too . . .

FOX: . . . yes.

GOULD: Then what's she doing in this office?

FOX: She's a *Temporary* Worker.

GOULD: You're full of it, Chuck.

FOX: Maybe. And I didn't mean to take the *shine* off our . . .

GOULD: Hey, hey, he sends the cross, he sends the strength to bear it. Go to, go to lunch, I'll meet you at . . .

FOX: I didn't mean to imply . . .

GOULD: Imply. Naaa. Nobody Loves Me. Nobody loves me for myself. Hey, Big Deal, don't go mopin' on me here. We'll go and celebrate. A Douglas Brown Film. Fox and Gould . . .

FOX: . . . you're very kind . . .

GOULD: . . . you brought the guy in. Fox and Gould Present:

FOX: I'll see you at lunch . . . (*Starts to exit.*)

GOULD: But I bet she would go, I bet she *would* go out with me.

FOX: I bet she would, too.

GOULD: No, No. I'm saying, I think that she "likes" me.

FOX: Yeah. I'm sure she does.

GOULD: No, joking apart, Babe. My *perceptions* . . . Say I'm nuts, I don't *think* so—she likes me, and she'd go out with me.

FOX: How much?

GOULD: How much? Seriously . . . ? (*Pause.*)

FOX: Yeah.

GOULD: . . . that she would . . . ?

FOX: Yeah. That she would *anything*. (*Pause.*) That she would anything. (*Pause.*) That she would deal with you in any other than a professional way. (*Pause.*)

GOULD: Well, my, my, my, my, my.

FOX: What can I tell you, "*Bob*."

GOULD: That I can get her on a date, that I can get her to my house, that I can screw her.

FOX: I don't think so.

GOULD: How much? (*Pause.*)

FOX: A hundred bucks.

GOULD: That's enough?

FOX: Five hundred bucks that you can't.

GOULD: Five hundred? That's enough?

FOX: A gentleman's bet.

GOULD: Done. Now get out of here, and let me work . . . the Coventry at One. I need . . .

FOX: The script, the budget, chain of ownership . . .

GOULD: Good.

FOX: I'll swing by my, I'll bring it to lunch.

GOULD: Good. Char . . . (*Pause.*)

FOX: What?

GOULD: Thank you.

FOX: Hey. Fuck you. (*Exits.*)

SUBURBIA

by Eric Bogosian

ACT II, SCENE 1

Tim, Jeff, and their friends, all in their early twenties, hang out at night in the parking lot of a convenience store (such as a 7-Eleven) in the suburbs. Jeff has had some college, has a philosophical bent, finds life confusing and scary, and dreams of doing something with his life. Tim is the macho member of the group. He has been in the Air Force and is an alcoholic. Tonight an old high school classmate, "Pony," has returned to town for a visit and come by the parking lot (in his limo and with his publicist, Erica). Pony has had modest success with a band.

    Just before this scene, Jeff's adventurous girlfriend Sooze went off with Pony, and Jeff, though upset, did little to try to stop her. In the scene, Tim's story about what he did to Erica is a lie. Unable to get an erection, he embarrassed himself with her and she went off with another friend, Buff.

....

TIM: A toast to womanhood. (*TIM drinks and passes the bottle to JEFF. JEFF takes a long hit.*) Without suffering, Jeff, you will never have knowledge.

JEFF: I'm not suffering, because I'm not jealous of Pony.

TIM: That's because you're a coward.

JEFF: No. I don't want her, not who she is now. (*TIM goes into overdrive, finally throwing Chinese food at him as he hounds JEFF.*)

TIM: You're a coward. It's lying there right in front of you, but you have to think about it.

JEFF: No.

TIM: You're a paralyzed baby. You wouldn't last two minutes in a prison, in a concentration camp. The ones who survive don't think, they just act.

JEFF: It's good to think.

TIM: You say "think," you mean "fear." It's like a black rubber bag over your head. That's all it is. All your philosophy's just there to cover the obvious.

JEFF: No. I understand something now. It's no big deal.

TIM: No, it's no big deal. The guy probably has his arm around her right now. Holding her close, nudging her tit with his finger. He's probably talking about "the revolution" and she's looking up at him with her big eyes. (*JEFF ponders the image. Stunned, he stands.*)

JEFF: No.

TIM: In a few minutes they'll be in his suite. They'll talk for a while. Maybe they'll talk for hours. About life, about their "work." They'll feel close and warm with each other. She'll start to trust him. They'll decide to sleep with each other but "not do anything." By six AM, I bet they're making the beast with two backs. (*JEFF is lost. He wanders, sees the Chinese food on himself.*)

JEFF: Fuck!

TIM: It's human nature, Jeff. She can't help herself and he can't help himself.

JEFF: But Tim, what should I do?

TIM: I'll lend you my .45. Blow his brains out.

JEFF: (*Nauseous.*) Seriously.

TIM: I'm serious. Kill him or kill her.

JEFF: Kill me.

TIM: You don't have the guts.

JEFF: I don't feel so good. (*TIM grabs him by the face and pulls him to him, making him listen.*)

TIM: Because you don't want to admit what you *are*. Drink the last beer, go home, have a piss, jerk off and pass out. And you will have completed your mission on earth for one more day. It's the way it is, pal, it's the way it is. (*TIM starts to leave.*)

JEFF: Tim? (*TIM stops.*) What happened to you and Erica?

TIM: Nothing.

JEFF: Nothing? Really? (*Pause.*)

TIM: I'll tell you if you keep it to yourself.

JEFF: What happened?

TIM: I had her around back in the van, and it's going hot and heavy. She's this animal.

JEFF: Yeah?

TIM: And I looked down at her and suddenly I was filled with disgust.

JEFF: Disgust? (*TIM gets up, pacing.*)

TIM: I got up, and she started hanging on me. She's crying: "Tim, Tim! Come back, I love you. What's wrong?" She wouldn't let go. And I looked down at her stupid face. Her stupid eyes. Her stupid mouth. (*Pause.*)

JEFF: Yeah?

TIM: And I hit her. (*Pause.*) She wouldn't let go.

JEFF: You hit her. (*TIM is facing away from JEFF.*)

TIM: I guess. I was drunk.

JEFF: You don't know? How many times did you hit her? (*TIM turns and looks at JEFF.*)

TIM: She wasn't moving. I hit her until she wasn't moving. She's still back there. (*Pause.*) Go take a look. (*JEFF is frozen, looking at TIM.*)

JEFF: She's unconscious? (*TIM doesn't answer.*)

TIM: I'm going home. I have a hard day of drinking tomorrow.

JEFF: Wait, Tim, what are you saying? Why isn't she moving?

TIM: Take a look. See for yourself if you don't believe me.

JEFF: Tim? You didn't . . . ?

TIM: Go look. Do you have the guts to take a look? (*TIM leaves. JEFF starts to move toward the back, then stops. He's stuck. He views the mess lying all around him and half-heartedly starts to pick up the Chinese food containers and throws them in the garbage can. But suddenly he stops and walks back behind the store, toward the van.*)

OTHER PEOPLE'S MONEY

by Jerry Sterner

ACT I

William Coles, the president of New England Wire and Cable Company, is in trouble. Lawrence Garfinkle, a "take-over artist" from New York, has just bought a substantial share of the company's stock. Coles, Jorgenson (the long-term Chairman of the Board), and the many workers who have been with the company for years are in the business of making a worthwhile product: wire and cable. Garfinkle is in the business of making a quick profit by gaining control of undervalued companies, selling their assets, and then liquidating the company (which means throwing all the workers out of their jobs).

Coles has come to Garfinkle's office in New York to convince him to give him time to make the company more profitable.

....

COLES: That's an impressive office you have out there.

GARFINKLE: No big deal. Only lawyers. What can I do for you?

COLES: Thanks for seeing me on such short notice. I'm not really here on business. My wife and I came down to spend the evening with Bill, Jr. He's attending Columbia. Got two more after him. Both girls. Claire's out shopping now. It's always a treat to come to this city.

GARFINKLE: Great.

COLES: We're from small towns in Florida. Met at Florida State.

GARFINKLE: What'd you come here for—to give me your biography?

COLES: I didn't know I was boring you.

GARFINKLE: Now you know.

COLES: ...I'll get to the point. I see by the latest 13-D you hold just over four hundred thousand shares. That's ten per cent.

GARFINKLE: Four hundred and twenty-five thousand. Bought some this morning.

COLES: The filing says they were purchased for "investment purposes only."

GARFINKLE: I never read filings.

COLES: What does "investment purposes only" mean?

GARFINKLE: Means I bought them to make money.

COLES: How much more do you intend on buying?

GARFINKLE: That's none of your business.

COLES: Can we speak frankly?

GARFINKLE: No. Lie to me. Tell me how thrilled you are to know me. Tell me how gorgeous I am.

COLES: You don't want to speak frankly?

GARFINKLE: I always speak frankly. I don't like people who say "Can we speak frankly?" Means they're bullshitting me the rest of the time.

COLES: I'm sorry. I won't use that phrase anymore.

GARFINKLE: What do you want?

COLES: Two years. I want two years.

GARFINKLE: For what?

COLES: Jorgenson is sixty-eight. In two years he'll be seventy. He steps down at seventy.

GARFINKLE: Says who?

COLES: It's an agreement he has with the Board. His employment contract expires at seventy.

GARFINKLE: The Board are his cronies. He is the Board. What he wants done gets done.

COLES: He gave me his word. He's a man of his word.

GARFINKLE: Stop playing with yourself.

COLES: Twelve years ago he told me if I did the job it'd be my company to run when he steps down. That's why I came to that Godforsaken place. It's the same reason I'm here. I don't want the rug pulled out from under me so close to the finish line.

GARFINKLE: You're wasting your time. I don't have two years.

COLES: Listen, Mr. Garfinkle. I said we could grow our other businesses by fifteen per cent. I was being conservative. We'll grow them in excess of twenty. I can manage. I can manage the hell out of a company. In two years we'll be worth considerably more.

GARFINKLE: Billy boy, look at me. I weigh a ton. I smoke three packs a day. I walk from here to there I'm out of breath. I can't even steal life insurance. Two years for me is forever. Do what you have to do now. I'm not a long term player.

COLES: I can't do it now. I can't do it till he leaves. If I try I'm out on my ear.

GARFINKLE: (*Handing COLES his briefcase.*) That's the problem with working for a living.

COLES: Two years is not a long time. I have waited a lifetime for the opportunity.

GARFINKLE: Hey—you got stock, don't you?

COLES: Yes.

GARFINKLE: Fifty, seventy-five thousand, right?

COLES: Sixty.

GARFINKLE: Well, shit, look—want to feel better? (*GARFINKLE taps out stock on his quote machine.*) Before you heard my name your stock was ten. Now it's fourteen and a half. In two months I made you a quarter of a million dollars. Billy boy, the least you can do is smile. Ozzie at the bank, he's sending me flowers. All I'm asking from you is a smile.

GLENGARRY GLEN ROSS

by David Mamet

SCENE 2

Moss and Aaronow are real-estate salesmen and both are having a hard time making sales. They have just finished their meal at a Chinese restaurant and are venting their frustrations about their business.

(For more information see other scenes from this play in the "Monologues for Men" section of this book.)

....

MOSS: Polacks and deadbeats.

AARONOW: ... Polacks ...

MOSS: Deadbeats *all*.

AARONOW: ... they hold on to their money ...

MOSS: All of 'em. They, *hey*: it happens to us all.

AARONOW: Where am I going to work?

MOSS: You have to cheer up, George, you aren't out yet.

AARONOW: I'm not?

MOSS: You missed a fucking sale. Big deal. A deadbeat Polack. Big deal. How you going to sell 'em in the *first* place . . . ? Your mistake, you shoun'a took the lead.

AARONOW: I had to.

MOSS: You had to, yeah. Why?

AARONOW: To get on the . . .

MOSS: To get on the board. Yeah. How you goan'a get on the board sell'n a Polack? And I'll tell you, I'll tell you what *else.* You listening? I'll tell you what else: don't ever try to sell an Indian.

AARONOW: I'd never try to sell an Indian.

MOSS: You get those names come up, you ever get 'em, "Patel"?

AARONOW: Mmm . . .

MOSS: You ever get 'em?

AARONOW: Well, I think I had one once.

MOSS: You did?

AARONOW: I . . . I don't know.

MOSS: You had one you'd know it. *Patel.* They keep coming up. I don't know. They like to talk to salesmen. (*Pause.*) They're *lonely,* something. (*Pause.*) They like to feel *superior,* I don't know. Never bought a fucking thing. You're sitting down "The Rio Rancho *this,* the blah blah blah," "The Mountain View—" "Oh yes. My brother told me that. . . ." They got a grapevine. Fuckin' Indians, George. Not my cup of tea. Speaking of which I want to tell you something: (*Pause.*) I never got a cup of tea with them. You see them in the restaurants. A supercilious race. What is this *look* on their face all the time? I don't know. (*Pause.*) I don't know. Their broads all look like they just got fucked with a dead *cat,* I don't know. (*Pause.*) I don't know. I don't like it. Christ . . .

AARONOW: What?

MOSS: The whole fuckin' thing . . . The pressure's just too great. You're ab . . . you're absolu . . . they're too important. All of them. You go in the door. I . . . "I got to *close* this fucker, or I don't eat lunch," "or I don't win the *Cadillac* . . ." We fuckin' work too hard. You work too hard. We all, I remember when we were at Platt . . . huh? Glen Ross Farms . . . *didn't* we sell a bunch of that . . . ?

AARONOW: They came in and they, you know . . .

MOSS: Well, they fucked it up.

AARONOW: They did.

MOSS: They killed the goose.

AARONOW: They did.

MOSS: And now . . .

AARONOW: We're stuck with *this* . . .

MOSS: We're stuck with *this* fucking shit . . .

AARONOW: . . . *this* shit . . .

MOSS: It's too . . .

AARONOW: It is.

MOSS: Eh?

AARONOW: It's too . . .

MOSS: You get a bad month, all of a . . .

AARONOW: You're on this . . .

MOSS: All of, they got you on this "board . . ."

AARONOW: I, I . . . I . . .

MOSS: Some *contest* board . . .

AARONOW: I . . .

MOSS: It's not right.

AARONOW: It's not.

MOSS: No. (*Pause.*)

AARONOW: And it's not right to the *customers*.

MOSS: I know it's not. I'll tell you, you got, you know, you got . . . what did I learn as a kid on Western? Don't sell a guy one car. Sell him *five* cars over fifteen years.

AARONOW: That's right?

MOSS: Eh . . . ?

AARONOW: That's right?

MOSS: Goddamn right, that's right. Guys come on: "Oh, the blah blah blah, *I* know what I'll do: I'll go in and rob everyone blind and go to Argentina 'cause nobody ever *thought* of this before."

AARONOW: . . . that's right . . .

MOSS: Eh?

AARONOW: No. That's absolutely right.

MOSS: And so they kill the goose. I, I, I'll . . . and a fuckin' *man*, worked all his *life* has got to . . .

AARONOW: . . . that's right . . .

MOSS: . . . cower in his boots . . .

AARONOW: (*Simultaneously with "boots."*) Shoes, boots, yes . . .

MOSS: For some fuckin' "Sell ten thousand and you win the steak knives . . ."

AARONOW: for some *sales* pro . . .

MOSS: . . . sales promotion, "You *lose*, then we fire your . . ." No. It's *medieval* . . . it's wrong. "Or we're going to fire your ass." It's wrong.

AARONOW: Yes.

MOSS: Yes, it is. And you know who's responsible?

AARONOW: Who?

MOSS: You know who it is. It's Mitch. And Murray. 'Cause it doesn't have to be this way.

AARONOW: No.

MOSS: Look at Jerry Graff. He's *clean*, he's doing business for *himself*, he's got his, that *list* of his with the *nurses* ... see? You see? That's *thinking*. Why take ten percent? A ten percent comm ... why are we giving the rest away? What are we giving ninety per ... for *nothing*. For some jerk sit in the office tell you "Get out there and close." "Go win the Cadillac." Graff. He goes out and *buys*. He pays top dollar for the ... you see?

AARONOW: Yes.

MOSS: That's *thinking*. Now, he's got the leads, he goes in business for *himself*. He's ... that's what I ... that's *thinking*! "Who? Who's got a steady *job*, a couple bucks nobody's touched, who?"

AARONOW: Nurses.

MOSS: So Graff buys a fucking list of nurses, one grand—if he paid two I'll eat my hat—four, five thousand nurses, and he's going *wild* ...

AARONOW: He is?

MOSS: He's doing *very* well.

AARONOW: I heard that they were running cold.

MOSS: The nurses?

AARONOW: Yes.

MOSS: You hear a *lot* of things. ... He's doing very well. He's doing *very* well.

AARONOW: With River Oaks?

MOSS: River Oaks, Brook Farms. *All* of that shit. Somebody told me, you know what he's clearing *himself*? Fourteen, fifteen grand a *week*.

AARONOW: Himself?

MOSS: That's what I'm *saying*. Why? The *leads*. He's got the good leads ... what are we, we're sitting in the shit here. Why? We have to go to *them* to *get* them. Huh. Ninety percent our sale, we're *paying* to the *office* for the *leads*.

AARONOW: The leads, the overhead, the telephones, there's *lots* of things.

MOSS: What do you need? A *telephone*, some broad to say "Good morning," nothing ... nothing ...

AARONOW: No, it's not that simple, Dave . . .

MOSS: *Yes*. It *is*. It *is* simple, and you know what the hard part is?

AARONOW: What?

MOSS: Starting up.

AARONOW: What hard part?

MOSS: Of doing the thing. The dif . . . the difference. Between me and Jerry Graff. Going to business for yourself. The hard part is . . . you know what it is?

AARONOW: What?

MOSS: Just the *act*.

AARONOW: What act?

MOSS: To say "I'm going on my own." 'Cause what you do, George, let me tell you what you do: you find yourself in *thrall* to someone else. And we *enslave* ourselves. To *please*. To win some fucking *toaster* . . . to . . . to . . . and the guy who got there first made *up* those . . .

AARONOW: That's right . . .

MOSS: He made *up* those rules, and we're working for *him*.

AARONOW: That's the truth . . .

MOSS: That's the *God's* truth. And it gets me depressed. I *swear* that it does. At MY AGE. To see a goddamn: "Somebody wins the Cadillac this month. P.S. Two guys get fucked."

AARONOW: *Huh.*

MOSS: You don't *ax* your sales force.

AARONOW: No.

MOSS: You . . .

AARONOW: You . . .

MOSS: You *build* it!

AARONOW: That's what I . . .

MOSS: You fucking *build* it! Men come . . .

AARONOW: Men come *work* for you . . .

MOSS: . . . you're absolutely right.

AARONOW: They . . .

MOSS: They have . . .

AARONOW: When they . . .

MOSS: Look look look look, when they *build* your business, then you can't fucking turn around, *enslave* them, treat them like *children*, fuck them up the ass, leave them to fend for themselves . . . no. (*Pause.*) No. (*Pause.*) You're absolutely right, and I want to tell you something.

AARONOW: What?

MOSS: I want to tell you what somebody should do.

AARONOW: What?

MOSS: Someone should stand up and strike *back*.

AARONOW: What do you mean?

MOSS: *Somebody* . . .

AARONOW: Yes . . . ?

MOSS: Should do something to *them*.

AARONOW: What?

MOSS: Something. To pay them back. (*Pause.*) Someone, someone should hurt them. Murray and Mitch.

AARONOW: Someone should hurt them.

MOSS: Yes.

AARONOW: (*Pause.*) How?

MOSS: How? Do something to hurt them. Where they live.

AARONOW: What? (*Pause.*)

MOSS: Someone should rob the office.

AARONOW: Huh.

MOSS: That's what I'm *saying*. We were, if we were that kind of guys, to knock it off, and *trash* the joint, it looks like robbery, and *take* the fuckin' leads out of the files . . . go to Jerry Graff. (*Long pause.*)

AARONOW: What could somebody get for them?

MOSS: What could we *get* for them? I don't know. Buck a *throw* . . . buck-a-half a throw . . . I don't know. . . . Hey, who knows what they're worth, what do they *pay* for them? All told . . . must be, I'd . . . three bucks a throw . . . I don't know.

AARONOW: How many leads have we got?

MOSS: The *Glengarry* . . . the premium leads . . . ? I'd say we got five thousand. Five. Five thousand leads.

AARONOW: And you're saying a fella could take and sell these leads to Jerry Graff.

MOSS: Yes.

AARONOW: How do you know he'd buy them?

MOSS: Graff? Because I worked for him.

AARONOW: You haven't talked to him.

MOSS: No. What do you mean? Have I talked to him about *this*? (*Pause.*)

AARONOW: Yes. I mean are you actually *talking* about this, or are we just . . .

MOSS: No, we're just . . .

AARONOW: We're just "*talking*" about it.

MOSS: We're just *speaking* about it. (*Pause.*) As an *idea*.

AARONOW: As an idea.

MOSS: Yes.

AARONOW: We're not actually *talking* about it.

MOSS: No.

AARONOW: Talking about it as a . . .

MOSS: *No.*

AARONOW: As a *robbery*.

MOSS: As a "robbery"?! No.

AARONOW: *Well*. Well . . .

MOSS: *Hey*. (*Pause.*)

AARONOW: So all this, um, you didn't, actually, you didn't actually go talk to Graff.

MOSS: Not actually, no. (*Pause.*)

AARONOW: You didn't?

MOSS: No. Not actually.

AARONOW: Did you?

MOSS: What did I say?

AARONOW: What did you say?

MOSS: Yes. (*Pause.*) I said, "Not actually." The fuck *you* care, George? We're just *talking* . . .

AARONOW: We are?

MOSS: Yes. (*Pause.*)

AARONOW: Because, because, you know, it's a *crime*.

MOSS: That's right. It's a crime. It is a crime. It's also very safe.

AARONOW: You're actually *talking* about this?

MOSS: That's right. (*Pause.*)

AARONOW: You're going to steal the leads?

MOSS: Have I said that? (*Pause.*)

AARONOW: Are you? (*Pause.*)

MOSS: Did I say that?

AARONOW: Did you talk to Graff?

MOSS: Is that what I said?

AARONOW: What did he say?

MOSS: What did he say? He'd *buy* them. (*Pause.*)

AARONOW: You're going to steal the leads and sell the leads to him? (*Pause.*)

MOSS: Yes.

AARONOW: What will he pay?

MOSS: A buck a shot.

AARONOW: For five thousand?

MOSS: However they are, that's the deal. A buck a throw. Five thousand dollars. Split it half and half.

AARONOW: You're saying "me."

MOSS: Yes. (*Pause.*) Twenty-five hundred apiece. One night's work, and the job with Graff. Working the premium leads. (*Pause.*)

AARONOW: A job with Graff.

MOSS: Is that what I said?

AARONOW: He'd give me a job.

MOSS: He would take you on. Yes. (*Pause.*)

AARONOW: Is that the truth?

MOSS: Yes. It is, George. (*Pause.*) Yes. It's a big decision. (*Pause.*) And it's a big reward. (*Pause.*) It's a big reward. For one night's work. (*Pause.*) But it's got to be tonight.

AARONOW: What?

MOSS: What? What? The *leads*.

AARONOW: You have to steal the leads tonight?

MOSS: That's *right*, the guys are moving them downtown. After the thirtieth. Murray and Mitch. After the contest.

AARONOW: You're, you're saying so you have to go in there tonight and . . .

MOSS: *You* . . .

AARONOW: I'm sorry?

MOSS: *You.* (*Pause.*)

AARONOW: Me?

MOSS: *You* have to go in. (*Pause.*) *You* have to get the leads. (*Pause.*)

AARONOW: I do?

MOSS: Yes.

AARONOW: I . . .

MOSS: It's not something for nothing, George, I took you in on this, you have to go. That's your thing. I've made the deal with Graff. I can't go. I can't go in, I've spoken on this too much. I've got a big mouth. (*Pause.*) "The fucking leads'' et cetera, blah blah blah ''. . . the fucking tight ass company . . .''

AARONOW: They'll know when you go over to Graff . . .

MOSS: What will they know? That I stole the leads? I *didn't* steal the leads, I'm going to the *movies* tonight with a friend, and then I'm going to the Como Inn. Why did I go to Graff? I got a better deal. *Period.* Let 'em prove something. They can't prove anything that's not the case. (*Pause.*)

AARONOW: *Dave.*

MOSS: Yes.

AARONOW: You want me to break into the office tonight and steal the leads?

MOSS: Yes. (*Pause.*)

AARONOW: No.

MOSS: Oh, yes, George.

AARONOW: What does that mean?

MOSS: Listen to this. I have an alibi, I'm going to the Como Inn, why? Why? The place gets robbed, they're going to come looking for *me*. Why? Because I probably did it. Are you going to turn me in? (*Pause.*) George? Are you going to turn me in?

AARONOW: What if you don't get caught?

MOSS: They come to you, you going to turn me in?

AARONOW: Why would they come to me?

MOSS: They're going to come to *everyone*.

AARONOW: Why would I *do* it?

MOSS: You wouldn't, George, that's why I'm talking to you. Answer me. They come to you. You going to turn me in?

AARONOW: No.

MOSS: Are you sure?

AARONOW: Yes. I'm sure.

MOSS: Then listen to this: I have to get those leads tonight. That's something I have to do. If I'm not at the *movies* . . . if I'm not eating over at the inn . . . If you don't do this, then *I* have to come in here . . .

AARONOW: . . . you don't have to come in . . .

MOSS: . . . and *rob* the place . . .

AARONOW: . . . I thought that we were only talking . . .

MOSS: . . . they *take* me, then. They're going to ask me who were my accomplices.

AARONOW: *Me?*

MOSS: Absolutely.

AARONOW: That's ridiculous.

MOSS: Well, to the law, you're an accessory. Before the fact.

AARONOW: I didn't ask to be.

MOSS: Then tough luck, George, because you are.

AARONOW: Why? *Why*, because you only *told* me about it?

MOSS: That's right.

AARONOW: Why are you doing this to me, Dave. Why are you talking this way to me? I don't understand. Why are you doing this at *all* . . . ?

MOSS: That's none of your fucking business . . .

AARONOW: Well, well, well, *talk* to me, we sat down to eat dinner, and here I'm a *criminal* . . .

MOSS: You went for it.

AARONOW: In the abstract . . .

MOSS: So I'm making it concrete.

AARONOW: Why?

MOSS: Why? Why *you* going to give me five grand?

AARONOW: Do you need five grand?

MOSS: Is that what I just said?

AARONOW: You need money? Is that the . . .

MOSS: Hey, hey, let's just keep it simple, what I need is not the . . . what do *you* need . . . ?

AARONOW: What is the five grand? (*Pause.*) What is the, you said that we were going to split five . . .

MOSS: I lied. (*Pause.*) Alright? My end is *my* business. Your end's twenty-five. In or out. You tell me, you're out you take the consequences.

AARONOW: I do?

MOSS: Yes. (*Pause.*)

AARONOW: And why is that?

MOSS: Because you listened.

COVER

by Jeffrey Sweet (with Stephen Johnson and Sandra Hastie)

This three-character, one-act play opens with Frank working at his desk in his new office (with a great view of New Jersey). His friend Marty enters, a little early for their appointment to go to the movies (with Marty's wife Diane who is expected to arrive very shortly). As the scene unfolds we learn that Frank and Marty are old friends and that Marty wants to draw on their friendship to persuade Frank to tell Diane—who is very jealous and very neurotic—a "little" lie for him. He wants Frank to tell her that the two men were together on the previous evening. But Frank is Diane's friend too and is disinclined to lie to her.

....

MARTY: Work, work, work.

FRANK: Oh, Marty.

MARTY: I'm early.

FRANK: You're early.

MARTY: If I'm interrupting . . .

FRANK: No, this is nothing. Just odds and ends.

MARTY: Nice office.

FRANK: Oh, that's right—you've never been up here, have you?

MARTY: No, this is the first time.

FRANK: Well, you've got to take a look out this window. I've got a view that will knock your eyes out. My big status symbol.

MARTY: You've got to be good, they give you a window like this. They've got to like you.

FRANK: See Jersey over there?

MARTY: I'll be damned, Jersey.

FRANK: What's great is to watch thunderstorms come over the Hudson. Hell of a show. Lightning and huge gothic clouds.

MARTY: Always said that was the best thing that could happen to New Jersey.

FRANK: Well, OK.

MARTY: No, I'm impressed. I really am. This is very nice.

FRANK: Yes, I'm very . . .

MARTY: So, you all set and ready to go?

FRANK: Just let me put this stuff away.

MARTY: Take your time.

FRANK: Where's Diane?

MARTY: Oh, she'll be along in a few minutes. I told her to meet me here. She had an appointment crosstown, so I figured . . .

FRANK: Sure.

MARTY: Actually, I'm glad I got here a little earlier. There's a favor I want to ask of you.

FRANK: Ask away.

MARTY: OK. Well, see, as a topic of conversation, it may come up during the evening where I was last night. And it would make it a lot easier if we could decide between us that I was with you.

FRANK: To say that?

MARTY: Not to say necessarily, but to sort of give the impression that we were together. It would make things a lot simpler for me. I mean, if it comes up.

FRANK: You want me to say . . .

MARTY: Just to say . . .

FRANK: That you and I . . .

MARTY: That we were . . .

FRANK: Together . . .

MARTY: Together . . .

FRANK: Last night.

MARTY: Yeah.

FRANK: You want me to lie.

MARTY: Well . . .

FRANK: Not ''well.'' You want me to lie.

MARTY: Well . . .

FRANK: That's what you're asking.

MARTY: I wouldn't put it . . .

FRANK: Is that what you're asking?

MARTY: Well, yes.

FRANK: To lie?

MARTY: A little bit. Just to give the impression so that Diane won't worry. To avoid confusion and upset for her.

FRANK: I see. You want me to do a favor for you for her.

MARTY: I couldn't have said it better myself.

FRANK: Where were you last night? I mean, I have to know.

MARTY: It doesn't matter.

FRANK: Well, yes, it does. I have to know whether you're wanting me to tell a white lie or a black lie.

MARTY: It's a white lie.

FRANK: How white? I mean, where were you?

MARTY: I was out.

FRANK: Alone? With someone?

MARTY: With someone.

FRANK: Yeah?

MARTY: Diane wouldn't understand.

FRANK: A woman?

MARTY: She'd take it the wrong way.

FRANK: You were out with another woman.

MARTY: Yes, I was out with another woman.

FRANK: I see. And that's a white lie?

MARTY: It's no big deal.

FRANK: I'm sorry, I can't do it.

MARTY: Hey, really, it's no big deal.

FRANK: No, I wouldn't feel good about it.

MARTY: Why not? It's just a little favor.

FRANK: It's not a little . . . You're asking me to lie to her. You don't understand. She's my friend.

MARTY: Aren't I your friend?

FRANK: You're my friend and she's my friend. But she's not my friend because you're my friend. I mean, it's not that you and I have a primary friendship and she's a secondary friend by extension. You're both primary friends.

MARTY: I understand that.

FRANK: You don't break that trust.

MARTY: I'm not asking you to break that trust. I'm asking you to spare her confusion and upset.

FRANK: You're asking me to lie to her.

MARTY: To give a different impression of the truth.

FRANK: A false impression, which is a lie.

MARTY: You've never told a lie in your life?

FRANK: That's not the issue.

MARTY: Of course it's the issue. You're saying you don't tell lies.

FRANK: I'm saying I will not tell *this* lie.

MARTY: How do you decide when you will or will not tell a lie?

FRANK: I try not to lie.

MARTY: But what makes you decide if you'll tell a given lie? Say that an opportunity for a lie presents itself—how do you decide if you'll tell it?

FRANK: This is not the issue.

MARTY: You have told lies, haven't you? You've told lies in the past.

FRANK: I have, but that has nothing to do with this.

MARTY: You just won't tell a lie for me.

FRANK: I don't want to tell an active lie, no.

MARTY: Well, are you going to tell her that I was out with another woman last night?

FRANK: No, of course not.

MARTY: Then isn't that creating a false impression? Isn't that, in fact, a lie?

FRANK: That's a passive lie, my not telling something.

MARTY: Ah, that's different.

FRANK: It is.

MARTY: A difference in kind, right? Active versus passive.

FRANK: There *is* a difference, whether you see it or not.

MARTY: Would you care to elaborate?

FRANK: What do you mean?

MARTY: On the distinction. Active, passive.

FRANK: What does this have to do with . . . ?

MARTY: If we correlate an active lie as being a lie you won't tell and a passive lie as a lie you will, then perhaps we can find that point in the grey area between where we can come to an understanding.

FRANK: Look, I don't want to lie to her.

MARTY: I'm not asking you to *want* to.

FRANK: You're just asking me to do it.

MARTY: Yes, as a favor to a friend.

FRANK: No, I don't want to.

MARTY: You do lots of things you don't want to do. Everybody does.

FRANK: The things that I sometimes do that I don't want to do are things that I have to do. I don't have to do this. I don't have to break that trust.

MARTY: No, and we don't have to be friends, either.

FRANK: Oh, come on. Are you saying if I won't lie for you we won't be friends any more?

MARTY: Of course not. I'm just asking you for a favor.

FRANK: I can't do it.

MARTY: Can't means won't.

FRANK: Can't means can't.

MARTY: Can't means won't.

FRANK: Can't means can't.

MARTY: No, you could.

FRANK: I couldn't.

MARTY: You *could*.

FRANK: I couldn't.

MARTY: Your mouth could say the words. Physically, your mouth could say the words.

FRANK: I couldn't do it.

MARTY: Of course you could.

FRANK: No, I couldn't.

MARTY: You could, but what you're saying is you won't.

FRANK: I'm saying I can't.

MARTY: You're saying you won't.

FRANK: I'm saying ... OK, I'm saying I won't because I can't.

MARTY: But you *could*.

FRANK: I wouldn't if I could, but I can't so I won't. Anyway, you don't want me to lie for you.

MARTY: Yes, I do.

FRANK: I'm a terrible liar. She'd see right through me.

MARTY: How do you know until you try?

FRANK: Look, I'm not going to tell her where you were. I mean, I couldn't because I don't know.

MARTY: I was at Marvin Gardens. That's on the West Side.

FRANK: I don't want to know. Don't tell me any more.

MARTY: Barbara Schaeffer.

FRANK: I don't want to know who.

MARTY: Barbara Schaeffer.

FRANK: Barbara Schaeffer?

MARTY: See, now you know.

FRANK: I wish you hadn't told me.

MARTY: But you know, and if you don't tell Diane that means you've already lied. Passive-shmassive, it's a lie, and if you've gone that far, why not go a little farther for a friend?

FRANK: Look, you can argue rings around me, but I'm not going to.

MARTY: OK, sorry I asked.

FRANK: I wish you'd understand.

MARTY: It really is a hell of a nice office. You should be very proud. (*A beat. DIANE enters.*)

SIGHT UNSEEN

by Donald Margulies

ACT I, SCENE 1

Nick (an Englishman) and Patricia (an American) are married and living in a cold farmhouse in rural England, working together as archeologists. This evening they get a surprise visit from Jonathan Waxman, Patricia's lover from years earlier, who has become a celebrated and wealthy painter and is in England for his first showing in Europe. Jonathan, who walked out on Patricia, now seeks her out to try to recapture some sense of the innocent, passionate days before his commercial success. And while Patricia has never forgiven him for leaving her, he has remained in her thoughts and conversation, filling Nick with jealousy over this man he has never met. Compounding Nick's discomfort, Patricia has hung over the mantle a portrait that Jonathan painted of her. It is a troubling time in Jonathan's life, with confusions over his relationship to art, to his wife, and to his Jewish roots.

Patricia, who has just told Jonathan that although she can't forgive him, he can stay the night, has gone to the garden to pick vegetables for dinner, leaving Jonathan alone in the room. He "soon gravitates toward the painting and looks at it for a while." Nick enters, holding a "depleted bottle of Scotch in his hand." When Jonathan first arrived, Nick was home alone and seemed almost tongue-tied, barely saying anything, and he went off shortly after Patricia came home from the grocery. Now Nick's demeanor has loosened considerably.

....

NICK: Oops.

(*JONATHAN sees him. A beat.*)

You've spotted your painting.

JONATHAN: Yes.

NICK: I can't tell you how many nights I've stared at the fire and imagined that painting in the flames.

JONATHAN: Excuse me?

NICK: Oh, I wouldn't dream of damaging it. It's a work of art. And I am a preservationist by nature. (*A beat.*) It makes Patricia happy to have a piece of you on the wall. Did I say *a piece of you*? I meant a piece *from* you. Or perhaps I *meant* a piece *of* you. A piece of *yours*, at any rate. She gazes at it sometimes, when we're sitting by the fire. It doesn't move me in the same way. No, the eye of the beholder and all that. Drink?

JONATHAN: No. I painted it a long time ago. When Patty and I were at school. It's strange seeing something I did like twenty years ago and see all these things I couldn't possibly have seen when I painted it.

NICK: You're rich now, aren't you?

JONATHAN: What?

NICK: Patricia tells me you're rich.

JONATHAN: Oh, God.

NICK: Read it in some magazine.

JONATHAN: Well, we talked about that. Actually, I . . .

NICK: (*Over "Actually, I."*) She said you're rich. You're successful.

JONATHAN: Those are two different things, really.

NICK: Are they?

JONATHAN: Yes, I think—

NICK: How much do you make in a year?

JONATHAN: Well, I don't—

NICK: Am I out of line?

JONATHAN: Well, maybe.

NICK: How much then?

JONATHAN: It's difficult to say. I've had years in which I've made almost nothing. It's only in the last couple of years—

NICK: *(Over "couple of years.")* How much would you get for something like that, for instance? *(Meaning the painting on the wall.)*

JONATHAN: A student painting? I have no idea.

NICK: Guess.

JONATHAN: I really don't know.

NICK: Come on. A pivotal work. You said so yourself. A seminal work. How much would a seminal work, given your current currency, if you will, your current notoriety, how much would an old, young Waxman bring?

JONATHAN: I really have no idea.

NICK: Come on, guess.

JONATHAN: In the thousands, certainly. I don't know.

NICK: *(Over "I don't know.")* Oh, I would think more than that.

JONATHAN: Look, I really don't pay much attention to this stuff.

NICK: Don't pay attention to money? Surely you must.

JONATHAN: No, I let my gallery worry about it.

NICK: Art for art's sake, eh? Well, even I, even I who know, or for that matter, *care* very little about contemporary values in art, or, even, the value *of* contemporary art, even I would guess you're being awfully stingy on yourself. Considerably more than in the thousands, I would say. More like in the *tens* of thousands, wouldn't you agree?

JONATHAN: Maybe. I really don't know.

NICK: Oh, I would think. A pivotal, precocious painting like this? A seminal masterpiece?

JONATHAN: I don't know. What do you want to hear? Whatever you want to hear.

NICK: You.

JONATHAN: What.

NICK: I feel as though I've known you all along.

JONATHAN: Oh, yeah?

NICK: Your picture. She has this snapshot.

JONATHAN: What snapshot?

NICK: A Polaroid. The two of you. Patricia the co-ed. The party girl. Lithe and sunny. Her tongue in your ear. You, squirming like a boy caught in a prank. With gums showing.

You don't look at all handsome. She assured me you were. A costume party of some kind.

JONATHAN: A costume party?

NICK: Mm. Patricia in a swimsuit dressed as Miss America. You're dressed like a jester. A clown. A clown or a pimp.

JONATHAN: A what?

NICK: Loud clashing plaids, a camera 'round your neck. Sunglasses.

JONATHAN: Oh. Halloween. I was a tourist.

NICK: Hm?

JONATHAN: A tourist. I went dressed as a tourist.

NICK: A tourist.

JONATHAN: A visitor, a stranger. An observer. The camera, the Hawaiian shirt.

NICK: It doesn't read.

(JONATHAN shrugs.)

You look like a pimp.

JONATHAN: The idea was a tourist.

NICK: Hm?

JONATHAN: Never mind.

NICK: Patricia had forgotten what you'd dressed up *as*. She thought a pimp.

JONATHAN: No.

NICK: Mm. (*A beat.*) What was the idea?

JONATHAN: The idea?

NICK: What did it mean? Was there some symbolic value? Dressing as a tourist?

JONATHAN: I don't know . . .

NICK: Symbolic of your perception of yourself at that time, perhaps? A transient person? Dislocated?

JONATHAN: That's interesting. I wonder if—

NICK: Rubbish. Now, that picture, that photo. Was all I had to go on. For years. Until that *New York Times* article. That one Polaroid she keeps in a box with letters. (*Confidentially.*) I've snooped. There's a postal card from you in that box. One picture postal card. No letters.

JONATHAN: I didn't write much.

NICK: Hm?

JONATHAN: There was no need to write. We were in school together. We saw each other all the time.

NICK: No, I imagine there *were* letters. Painful collegiate prose. Heartsick poems. Declarations of lust.

JONATHAN: Sorry.

NICK: I imagine there *were* letters, but she burned them. Like Hedda Gabler or somebody. Watched with glee while the missives went up in flames.

JONATHAN: No.

NICK: I think there *were*. I prefer to think there *were*. And all that remains is an innocuous postal card. From Miami Beach, Florida or someplace.

JONATHAN: Yes. A visit to my grandparents. Fort Lauderdale.

NICK: Then there are the stories. Tales of Waxman. The Jonathan Stories. Faraway sounding, exotic. Like from the Old Testament, if you will. Patricia's voice becomes especially animated while telling a Jonathan story. She achieves a new range in a different key. A new tune, a new music entirely. Fascinating. I watch her face. The dimples that sprout! The knowing smiles! Remarkable behavioural findings. (*A beat. He drags his chair closer.*) I've become a Waxmanologist, you see. A Waxmanophile. No, a Waxmanologist. It's my nature. Beneath this reticent exterior lies a probing, tireless investigator. A detective. An historian. And I'm good at my work. I'm compulsive. I'm meticulous. I study the past in order to make sense of the present.

JONATHAN: I understand.

NICK: You're smaller in person than I imagined. I held out for a giant. A giant among men. Instead, what's *this*? You're medium-sized. Compact. Razor burn on your neck. Pimple on your cheek. She said you were handsome; you're alright. Perhaps your appeal lies below the belt, but I doubt I'd be surprised.

JONATHAN: Look, I think I'll—(*Pointing to the door.*)

NICK: Circumcision isn't common practice in the U.K., you know.

(*JONATHAN stops.*)

Jews still do it the world over, don't they. On religious grounds. Here the risk is too great. Too many accidents. Too many boy sopranos. Here we hold on to our overcoats. (*PATRICIA returns . . .*)

I HATE HAMLET

by Paul Rudnick

ACT I, SCENE 1

Andrew, handsome, charming, and a successful television actor, is about to encounter some complications in his life. His series (in which he played Dr. Jim Corman) has been cancelled and against his better judgment he has agreed to star in a Shakespeare-in-the-Park production of Hamlet, *knowing he won't be good in it. What's more, he has rented an apartment in New York City that was once lived in by John Barrymore, who was considered the greatest Hamlet of his era. Unfortunately for Andrew, Barrymore's ghost still inhabits the apartment.*

His friend Gary shows up to convince Andrew to cancel Hamlet *and come back to Los Angeles to begin working with him on a new series. Gary is described as "an extremely happy, overgrown child" who "personifies LA shaggy-chic," wearing extremely expensive, casual clothing.*

(To do as a two person scene, omit Barrymore's lines and make adjustments in Gary's and Andrew's lines.)

....

GARY: Andy, Andy boy, Andy my love—we got it. Green light. The go-ahead. Network approval! A pilot and five episodes!

ANDREW: A pilot and five episodes—of what?

GARY: Of the show! Of *our* show!

ANDREW: What are you talking about?

GARY: Okay, I didn't tell you. Because I didn't want you to be disappointed, and blame me, if it didn't go. But it went! I used your name to tip it through the hoop. I told the network it was your all-time favorite project, that you were ready to roll. And after Jim Corman, you're network candy, they're crawling.

ANDREW: Really?

GARY: America cries out! Your commitment was just the push!

BARRYMORE: But he's not committed. He's playing Hamlet.

ANDREW: Well . . .

GARY: Wait a second—which network?

BARRYMORE: In the park. This summer.

GARY: What, it's like for some special? Hallmark Hall Of Fame?

BARRYMORE: It's not for anything. It's . . . theater.

GARY: Wait, let me get this. It's Shakespeare, right, it's like algebra on stage. And it's in Central Park, which probably seats, what, 500 tops. And the only merchandising involves, say, Gielgud cassettes and Mostly Mozart tote-bags. And on top of this, it's free. So Andy, tell me, who the hell is representing you nowadays?

ANDREW: Lillian is all for it.

GARY: Lillian! Jesus, of course. Andy, I love her, but she's a war criminal. I'm not kidding. She's a ten hour documentary waiting to happen. Okay Andy, fine, do your little show in the park. Is it a deduction? I mean, it's not even dinner theater. What, they sell whole wheat brownies and little bags of nuts and raisins. It's snack theater. It's Shakespeare for squirrels. Wait, just answer me one question, one simple thing: why? Why are you doing this? Are you broke?

ANDREW: No. I have savings.

GARY: Is there a bet involved?

ANDREW: No!

GARY: Andy—are you in some sort of trouble?

ANDREW: Yes, Gary, that's it, you finally hit it. Joe Papp has my parents.

GARY: *Hamlet*. Andy, I have to say this, 'cause we're buds, and I cherish that budship—but think reputation. Word on the street. When folks—let's call 'em Hollywood—when they hear that you're doing the greatest play in the English-speaking world, they're gonna know you're washed up!

ANDREW: Gary . . .

GARY: I'm serious. You haven't had offers? Nothing? What about the commercials? That Trailburst crap?

ANDREW: Gary, have you ever seen those ads? Have you seen what I have to work with?

BARRYMORE: What?

GARY: A puppet. A furry little chipmunk. It's cute.

ANDREW: It's a *hand puppet*. (*To* BARRYMORE.) Have you ever worked with a puppet? There's some guy, kneeling down near your crotch, working the puppet. And he's doing a chipmunk voice, into a microphone. And the guy, the chipmunk operator, he says, (*In a high-pitched, cutesy chipmunk voice.*) "Oh Andy, can I have a Trailburst Nugget?" And I say no, they're for people, not chipmunks. And he starts . . . to cry. And I . . .

(ANDREW *can't quite continue.*)

BARRYMORE: You what?

ANDREW: (*Mortified.*) I . . . kiss him. On the top of his little chipmunk head.

GARY: It's great!

ANDREW: It's disgusting! It's humiliating! I didn't spend four years in college and two in drama school to end up comforting someone's fist! It's not even a decent product. Trailburst Nuggets are like sawdust dipped in chocolate, and they have more calories than lard.

GARY: And that's why you're doing *Hamlet*?

ANDREW: Gary, you don't understand, about the theater. About why people do Shakespeare.

BARRYMORE: They do it because—it's art.

GARY: (*After a beat.*) Andy. Andy my honey, Andy my multi-talented prime-time delight. You don't do art. You buy it. You do TV, or a flick, you make a bundle and you nail a Monet. I was at this producer's place in Brentwood on the weekend. Incredible. Picassos. Van Gogh. A Rembrandt. And all from his TV shows.

ANDREW: But Gary, I don't want to just buy art. I mean, which would you rather do, paint a Picasso or own one?

GARY: Are you kidding? I'd like to sell one. At auction. Cash-flow. See, that's what I like—balls in the air. Activity. You're my Rembrandt.

ANDREW: I am?

GARY: How much are you gonna clear from this Shakespeare deal? Zip, right? Actually, you're paying them, because your time is valuable. A pilot and five episodes, high six figures. And if it hits, you get participation.

ANDREW: (*Impressed.*) Participation? In syndication?

GARY: Yup. You'll get paid every time it airs, first run, rerun, four AM in Singapore in the year 3000. Basically, you'll be able to afford to buy England, dig up Shakespeare, and get him to write the Christmas show!

BARRYMORE: This television program you're promoting, this goldmine—what is it exactly?

GARY: Okay—the pitch. Gather ye round. It's not cops, it's not young doctors, none of that TV crap.

ANDREW: Great.

GARY: You're a teacher. Mike Sullivan. You're young, idealistic, new to the system. Inner city high school. Rough. Dope. M-1's. Teen sex.

ANDREW: Wow...

GARY: No one cares. All the other teachers are burn-outs. Not you.

BARRYMORE: Why not?

GARY: Because... you care. You grew up in the neighborhood. You want to give something back.

ANDREW: (*Sincerely.*) You know, that sounds sort of... okay. It's almost realistic. I mean, you could deal with real problems. I could be vulnerable. I could mess up sometimes.

GARY: And at night, after the sun goes down, you have superpowers.

BARRYMORE: Superpowers?

GARY: Sure. I mean, who wants to watch that caring-feeling-unwed mothers bullshit? It's over. But, after sundown, you're invincible. Modified x-ray vision. You can fly, but only about ten feet up. See, we're keeping it real. Gritty. And so, after dark, you help the community, you help the kids, with your powers.

ANDREW: Do they know it's me? When I have superpowers?

GARY: No. You're in leather, denim, they just think it's some great dude. Great title, killer title—*Night School*. Dolls. Posters. The clothes. You could get an album, easy.

ANDREW: But . . . I can't sing.

GARY: Someone can. You can keep the Trailburst gig, there's no conflict—they'll probably extend, 'cause now you're a teacher! So think about it. What's to think, you've got a network commitment. Just forget this *Hamlet* crap—I mean, who are you kidding?

ANDREW: What do you mean?

GARY: Andy, I know you. I gave you your break. You're no actor.

ANDREW: What?

GARY: You're better than that. An actor, what, that's just some English guy who can't get a series. Look, I'm in town, I'm at the Ritz. I'll talk to Lillian, get things rolling. (*GARY hugs ANDREW.*)

ANTON CHEKHOV'S "THE DUEL"

adapted by Michael Schulman and Eva Mekler
from the translation by Ann Dunnigan

ACT I, SCENE 1

*The play takes place in the 1880s in a small sea town on
the fringe of the Russian Empire in the Caucasus by the
Black Sea. It is early morning in the parlor of Aleksandre
Davidych Samoilenko, a middle-aged army physician.
Alone in the parlor is Ivan Andreich Layevsky, a young
man in his late twenties.*

*Layevsky comes from a wealthy St. Petersburg family.
He ran away to the Caucasus two years ago with his mis-
tress (a married woman), seeking a meaningful life in which
he would earn a living through his own labors. He took a
position as an official in the Ministry of Finance, but
quickly found his new life tedious and dull. As the scene
opens, Layevsky is reading a letter. He puts it away quickly
as Samoilenko enters.*

*(For more information see other scenes from this play in
other sections of this book.)*

....

SAMOILENKO: So early, Ivan Andreich? Is this for professional reasons or just to visit? Are you ill?

LAYEVSKY: I'm sorry. I wasn't able to sleep. Is it too early
for you? Shall I come back later?

SAMOILENKO: No, no, my friend, sit down. In fact, I've meant to tell you to come by for an examination. I've noticed that you've been nervous lately, and distracted. That's not usual for you, and quite frankly, you look rather pale to me.

LAYEVSKY: I've been having trouble sleeping lately. Sasha, have you some vodka?

SAMOILENKO: Vodka? This early in the day?

LAYEVSKY: Never mind, never mind . . . Sasha . . .

SAMOILENKO: Sit, sit . . . one moment, let me get my instruments.

LAYEVSKY: Aleksandre Davidych, I'm just tired. I'm sure my physical health is sound.

SAMOILENKO: One should not take sleeplessness lightly. There are many physical ailments that can cause insomnia without your even suspecting they are there. It's probably nothing serious, but it certainly pays to be cautious. No arguments! Let's have a little look. Unbutton your shirt. There. Good. Does this hurt?

LAYEVSKY: No.

SAMOILENKO: Here?

LAYEVSKY: No.

SAMOILENKO: Good. Now turn your head sideways, take a deep breath, and hold it.

(During most of the ensuing scene, SAMOILENKO continues to examine LAYEVSKY, palpating, listening with stethoscope, checking eyes, ears, nose, throat, etc.)

LAYEVSKY: Sasha . . .

SAMOILENKO: Breathe . . . hold. . . .

LAYEVSKY: Aleksandre Davidych, answer one question for me. Suppose you had fallen in love with a woman, had lived with her, say for over two years, and then as often happens, fell out of love . . .

SAMOILENKO: One second, turn to the other side. Breath . . . hold.

LAYEVSKY: Aleksandre Davidych . . .

SAMOILENKO: Wait, let me look in your mouth. Tongue out— good. Go "ah."

LAYEVSKY: Ah.

SAMOILENKO: Again.

LAYEVSKY: Ah.

SAMOILENKO: A little infection there. Too much smoking. I'll mix up a gargle for you, and make sure you take it. Of course, a sore throat can interfere with sleep.

LAYEVSKY: Aleksandre Davidych, please . . . can I speak to you frankly, as a friend?

SAMOILENKO: Of course.

LAYEVSKY: Things are going badly with Nadyezhda Fyodorovna and me . . . in fact, very badly! Forgive me for discussing my private life with you, but I've lived with her for two years now and have stopped loving her; or perhaps there never was any love. These two years have been a delusion. Sasha, talk to me. I know perfectly well you can't help me, but I'm desperate and I'm ineffectual, and conversation is my only comfort. I have to find an explanation and justification for my absurd life in talk, in someone else's theories, even in literary types; in the notion, for instance, that we noblemen are degenerating, and so on. Last night, for example, I kept consoling myself by thinking: Ah, how right Tolstoy was, how fundamentally right! And that made me feel better.

SAMOILENKO: Yes, all the other authors write from imagination, while he writes straight from nature . . .

LAYEVSKY: My God, we have been mutilated by civilization!

SAMOILENKO: Yes, I'm listening to you, but turn around.

LAYEVSKY: I fell in love with a married woman and she fell in love with me. In the beginning there were the kisses, intimate evenings, vows; there was Spencer and ideals, and common interests . . . What a deception! We lied to ourselves that we were running away from the emptiness of our lives, when we were actually only running away from her husband—it was a game, an adventure . . . an entertainment to break the tedium. What fantasies we had about our future. We would rush off here to the Caucasus and I would launch my life of usefulness by entering the civil service. Then, in time, we'd find a plot of land and with the sweat of our brows work the land: plant a vineyard, fields, and so on. If it had been you or that zoologist of yours, Von Koren, you would have lived with Nadyezhda Fyodorovna for thirty years, perhaps, and left your heirs a rich vineyard and three thousand acres of maize. As for me, from the very first I knew my ideas about farming and a life of labor were worthless and self-deceiving. I found the heat here unbearable, the town dull, barren; you go out into the country and under every bush and stone there's an insect or a scorpion or a snake ready to bite you; and beyond the fields—mountains, desert. Alien people, alien nature, a pitiful culture ... All this, my friend, is not so easy as it seemed then in Petersburg, strolling along the Nevsky in a fur coat, arm in arm with Nadyezhda, dreaming of the sunny south. I am a misplaced person. And as for love, I can tell you that living with a woman who has read Spencer and has followed you to the ends of the earth is no more exciting than living with any other woman. There's the same smell of ironing, of powder, of medicines, the same curl papers every morning, the same self-deception ...

SAMOILENKO: You can't run a household without ironing. You're out of sorts today, Vanya, I can see that. Nadyezhda Fyodorovna is a fine woman, very beautiful, well educated, and you—you're a man of the greatest intelligence ... Of course, the two of you can't be married but that's not your fault and, besides, one must be able to rise above such outdated conventions, one must move with the times. I believe in free love, myself; yes ... but in my opinion, once you've lived together you ought to go on living together for the rest of your lives.

LAYEVSKY: Without love?

SAMOILENKO: Now let me explain something to you. Lean forward a bit ... fine. (*Checking his eyes.*) Eight years ago we had an old fellow, an agent here—a man of the greatest intelligence. He used to say: the major ingredient in a marriage is patience. Do you hear, Vanya? Not love, but patience.

LAYEVSKY: You may believe your old agent, but to me his advice is absolute nonsense. One can only exercise patience by treating a person you no longer love as an object, something indispensable to one's routine; but I haven't fallen that low yet. If I want to exercise patience I'll take up chess or buy an unruly horse and leave human beings in peace ... Enough of this! Where is my vest?

SAMOILENKO: Wait, I haven't checked your pressure.

LAYEVSKY: Right now, it's quite high; believe me, quite high ...

SAMOILENKO: Vanya, you misunderstand what I'm saying . . .

LAYEVSKY: Just answer one question for me—a technical question.

SAMOILENKO: Ask.

LAYEVSKY: What does softening of the brain mean?

SAMOILENKO: It's . . . how can I explain it to you? . . . It's a disease in which the brain becomes softer . . . as if it were dissolving. Why do you ask? You don't think your sleeplessness is . . . Are you having headaches?

LAYEVSKY: No, no, no, my friend, no . . . Sasha, can't you appreciate the position I'm in? On the one hand I can't live with her, I simply cannot. And at the same time it's impossible to leave her. She's alone, she can't work, neither of us has any money . . . What would become of her? Whom could she turn to? This awful indecision . . . How true was Shakespeare's observation, oh, how true. . . . There's nothing I can think of . . . Advise me: what am I to do?

SAMOILENKO: Does she love you?

LAYEVSKY: Yes, she loves me, for all that means. Given her age and temperament she needs a man. It would be as hard for her to give me up as it would be to give up her powder or her curl papers. I'm an indispensable part of her boudoir.

SAMOILENKO: You're not yourself today, Vanya. It's probably the lack of sleep.

LAYEVSKY: Yes . . . altogether I feel miserable, empty, numb. I feel a kind of weakness . . . I must get away.

SAMOILENKO: Where to?

LAYEVSKY: The north. To the pines, to the crisp air, to people, ideas . . . I'd give half my life to be bathing right now in some little stream near Moscow or Tula, to feel chilly, and then to stroll about for a few hours with even the worst student, talking and talking; and the scent of hay! Do you remember? And evenings, walking in a garden and hearing the sound of a piano in the house, hearing a train pass . . .

SAMOILENKO: I haven't been in Russia for eighteen years. I've forgotten what it's like. In my opinion, there's not a place on earth more magnificent than the Caucasus.

LAYEVSKY: If I were offered my choice of being a chimney sweep in Petersburg or a prince here, I'd take the chimney sweep.

SAMOILENKO: My dear, sad friend . . . Is your mother living? Can you turn to her?

LAYEVSKY: She's living, but we are not on good terms. She couldn't forgive me for this affair. She still fancies herself an aristocrat and insists that I've disgraced the family name by running off with a married woman. Aleksandre Davidych, there is something else, but it must remain between you and me. I'm keeping it from Nadyezhda Fyodorovna for now so don't let it slip out in front of her. I received a letter this morning telling me her husband had died of softening of the brain.

SAMOILENKO: May the kingdom of heaven be his. Why are you keeping it from her?

LAYEVSKY: To show her that letter would simply mean "Let's go to the church and get married." Before I show it to her we must clarify our relations. When she understands that we can't go on living together, I'll show her the letter. It will be safe then.

SAMOILENKO: Do you know what, Vanya? Marry her, my dear boy.

LAYEVSKY: Why?

SAMOILENKO: Fulfill your obligation to that splendid woman. Her husband has died. This is the hand of providence showing you what to do.

LAYEVSKY: But don't you understand that this is impossible . . . deceitful . . . ?

SAMOILENKO: But it is your duty.

LAYEVSKY: Why is it my duty?

SAMOILENKO: Because by taking her away from her husband you assumed responsibility.

LAYEVSKY: But I'm telling you in plain Russian, I don't love her!

SAMOILENKO: All right, there's no love, but you can respect her, show her consideration . . .

LAYEVSKY: Respect her, show her consideration . . . you'd think she was an abbess . . . You're a poor psychologist and physician if you think that all a woman wants from a man she is living with is respect and consideration. The most important thing for a woman is what happens in the bedroom.

SAMOILENKO: Vanya, Vanya . . . Shush!

LAYEVSKY: You think like a child, you're unrealistic, and we shall never understand each other. Let's end this conversation.

SAMOILENKO: You're spoiled, my friend. Fate has sent you a young, beautiful, cultivated woman, and you refuse the gift; while I—if God were to give me some lopsided old woman—so long as she was kind and affectionate, I'd live with her in my own little vineyard and . . . and the old witch could at least look after the samovar for me. I am truly fond of you. We drink, we laugh together. But I simply do not understand you. You are an educated man, but you foolishly discount the many simple pleasures this life has to offer you: the pride that comes from putting on a new white tunic and freshly polished boots and then strolling down the boulevard and being greeted with respect by passing friends; the contentment that comes from feeling the warm ocean breeze and observing that the cypresses and eucalyptuses have grown taller and fuller since last you noticed them; of awakening to the smell of strong coffee and looking forward to a small glass of cognac after breakfast. For me it is doing a day's work and feeling satisfied at the end of the day knowing that the patients have been treated and the infirmary is empty. My advice to you is to marry Nadyezhda Fyodorovna, to devote yourself to her and to your work, and to open your eyes to the many small wonders that you are now blind to.

LAYEVSKY: I can only reply to you that everything she does or says seems to me to be a lie or the equivalent of a lie, and everything unpleasant I have ever read about women and love seems to apply perfectly to myself, to Nadyezhda Fyodorovna, and to her husband. At this moment what I detest above all about her is her bare white neck with the little curls at the nape. Remember when Anna Karenina stopped loving her husband what she disliked most were his ears. Tolstoy! How right Tolstoy was! You see, my friend, I am not insensitive to the small details in life. On the contrary, they constantly remind me of my present unhappiness . . . I will go home now (*Spot on LAYEVSKY as he crosses away from SAMOILENKO. The lights fade on SAMOILENKO as they come up on NADYEZHDA FYODOROVNA seated at a table on the other side of stage.*) and when I get there Nadyezhda Fyodorovna will be sitting at the window already dressed, her hair done and with a preoccupied expression on her face, drinking coffee and leafing through a thick magazine. Drinking coffee is clearly not a sufficiently remarkable event to warrant such a preoccupied expression. She will have wasted her time on such a fashionable coiffure since there is no one to attract and no occasion for it. The magazine, too, represents a lie—she will have dressed and arranged her hair in order to appear beautiful and she will be reading—not for pleasure or enlightenment—but so that she will give the impression that she is intelligent.

BREAKING THE CODE

by Hugh Whitemore

ACT I, SCENE 8

This play is based on the life of Alan Turing, the brilliant, eccentric English mathematician who broke the Nazis' secret code (the Enigma) *during World War II, enabling Allied forces to anticipate and prepare for all major German war strategies. Despite the debt owed Turing by England and the entire civilized world, he was arrested in 1952 in Manchester for breaking another code, a sexual code. Turing was arrested for homosexuality. Turing's contribution to the war effort was little known at the time; nor had he received recognition for his seminal work that led to the development of the computer.*

At the time of his arrest, Turing was teaching at the University of Manchester. He had reported a robbery and, not nearly as wily socially as he was mathematically, gave the investigating detective (Sergeant Ross) some confusing information. He said that he knew that the thief's name was George because he had been told by someone who might have been a brush salesman that he had overheard that a man named George was planning a robbery in the neighborhood. In this scene, Sergeant Ross returns with more questions. (After his conviction, Turing was jailed and given hormone treatments that were supposed to eliminate his homosexual inclinations. He became depressed, physically debilitated, and eventually committed suicide.)

....

At rise: (The rat-a-tat-tat of a front door knocker. TURING enters; he is wearing running shorts and a singlet; he opens a door; ROSS enters.)

TURING: (*Some surprise.*) Sergeant Ross.

ROSS: Sorry to bother you at home, sir.

TURING: It's no bother. Please come in.

ROSS: Thank you, sir. (*TURING closes the door; he feels obliged to explain his mode of dress.*)

TURING: I've just been, uh . . . I do a bit of running.

ROSS: Ah.

TURING: I can't do as much as I used to, alas. (*Small smile.*) Middle-age creeping on.

ROSS: What were you: long distance, sprinter or what?

TURING: Long distance. Marathon, actually.

ROSS: God, I couldn't run that far when I was twenty, let alone now. (*TURING smiles; he and ROSS stand facing each other.*)

TURING: Do you, um . . . do you want to ask me some more questions?

ROSS: Yes, sir, I do; but first of all, I think we should try to clear up this story of yours.

TURING: What story?

ROSS: The one about a young man coming to your house to sell things; brushes, I think you said . . . ?

TURING: Yes?

ROSS: We have good reason to believe that you were lying. (*No response.*) Were you lying?

TURING: (*Hesitates.*) Yes.

ROSS: Why?

TURING: I'm sorry. It was very foolish of me.

ROSS: Would you like to tell me what really happened?

TURING: There was no brush salesman. I, uh . . . a friend told me about the burglar. George.

ROSS: A friend . . . ?

TURING: Yes.

ROSS: How did this friend know about the burglary?

TURING: He didn't know, exactly; he guessed.

ROSS: How did he guess?

TURING: He was having a drink with George, you see; in a

milk bar, and, uh . . . he mentioned me, my friend mentioned me, and told George where I lived. (*ROSS looks; waits.*) He'd been to dinner, you see. My friend. He'd been to dinner just a few days before, and he was telling George all about it. And then, um . . . after the burglary—I told my friend what had happened and he said it might've been George. He knew that George was a petty thief, or whatever the expression is. It was just a guess.

ROSS: Well, your friend was right.

TURING: Was he?

ROSS: Detectives found some fingerprints here in your house. This man George has a criminal record.

TURING: Oh, I see. So that proves it? (*No response.*) Yes, I see. (*Brief pause.*)

ROSS: This friend of yours: what's his name?

TURING: Ron. Ron Miller.

ROSS: A colleague of yours at the university?

TURING: Well, no.

ROSS: A social acquaintance?

TURING: In a way.

ROSS: Have you known him long?

TURING: Not long.

ROSS: How long?

TURING: Three or four weeks.

ROSS: And in those three or four weeks, how many times have you seen him?

TURING: About once a week.

ROSS: How did you meet?

TURING: Just—you know, casually.

ROSS: He's just a casual, social acquaintance?

TURING: Yes.

ROSS: Not what you'd call a close friend?

TURING: Oh no.

ROSS: So why did you lie to conceal his identity?

TURING: I, um . . . I didn't want to get him into trouble.

ROSS: Why not?

TURING: Well . . .

ROSS: He was, after all, partly responsible for your house being burgled.

TURING: I wouldn't say that.

ROSS: Wouldn't you, sir?

TURING: I wouldn't say, responsible.

ROSS: Partly responsible.

TURING: It's difficult to say. I mean, it's difficult to say exactly what his involvement in all this actually was—is.

ROSS: He told George your address.

TURING: Yes.

ROSS: And presumably he knows that George has got a criminal record.

TURING: Well, yes.

ROSS: So why go to all these lengths to protect him?

TURING: (*Blurting it out.*) The truth is, I'm having an affair with him. (*Pause.*)

ROSS: With Miller?

TURING: With Ron, yes.

ROSS: You're having a sexual relationship with this man?

TURING: Yes.

ROSS: What sort of sexual relationship?

TURING: How many sorts are there?

ROSS: You tell me, sir.

TURING: What exactly do you want to know?

ROSS: I need to understand the precise nature of this sexual relationship.

TURING: You mean you want to know what we did?

ROSS: That would help.

TURING: Well—since you ask—it wasn't much more than mutual masturbation.

ROSS: Did penetration occur?

TURING: No.

ROSS: You do realize, don't you, sir, that this is a criminal offense?

TURING: Look, isn't this rather beside the point? I thought we were trying to establish who had burgled my house.

ROSS: That's part of it, yes.

TURING: "Part of it" . . . ? Part of what?

ROSS: You've just told me that you've committed a criminal offense. I can't ignore that, can I?

TURING: What criminal offense?

ROSS: Gross indecency.

TURING: Oh, now look—I didn't corrupt him—Ron knew what he was doing—he came to my house—*my* house, don't forget—he came here perfectly well aware that we'd almost certainly go to bed together—it didn't come as any great surprise to him—he'd had other homosexual experiences—I mean, it's ludicrous to talk about criminal offenses—and, as I say, everything happened here, in private, in my own house, in private—if I hadn't told you, you wouldn't have known anything about it.

ROSS: But you did tell me.

TURING: Can't you forget about it? (*No response.*) Can't you? (*Pause.*)

ROSS: How old is this man, Miller?

TURING: I don't know. Nineteen, twenty.

ROSS: And how old are you, sir?

TURING: Thirty-nine. (*Brief pause.*) Obviously I shouldn't have told you. I'm always saying things I shouldn't say. (*No response.*) Look—surely there's no need to make a fuss about this? I mean, surely you can forget what I told you. Can't you? It's not asking much, after all. Please. (*ROSS remains silent; pause.*) What's the position if I make a statement? Shall I?

ROSS: That's up to you, sir. (*TURING hesitates for a moment.*)

TURING: Anyway . . . all right . . . yes, I'll make a statement. (*Looks at ROSS.*) You'll want me to go to the police station. I'd better get dressed. (*TURING exits briskly.*)

BENT

by Martin Sherman

ACT I, SCENE 6

*Max and Horst are prisoners in Dachau, the German con-
centration camp. They are imprisoned because they are homosexual. Horst was arrested because his name was on a
petition to legalize homosexuality. Max was arrested with
his long-term lover, Rudy, because the authorities became
aware of their homosexual activities when Max picked up
and brought home (for a threesome) a man the Nazis were
looking for.*

*Before his arrest, Max, who came from a wealthy family,
led an open and flamboyant homosexual life among Berlin's sophisticates. After he learned the authorities were
looking for him, Max could have escaped from Germany
through the use of family connections, but he would not
abandon Rudy.*

*On the train to Dachau, Rudy was brutally beaten by the
Nazi guards. It was on the train that Max first met Horst,
who saved his life by advising him not to come to Rudy's
aid. Max listened to Horst and sat silently—in terror and
anguish—as he heard Rudy screaming. When the Nazi
guard told Max to hit Rudy, he complied over and over
again, and Rudy soon died from his beatings.*

*Horst told Max that the Nazis treated homosexuals even
worse than they treated Jews, so Max managed to get himself categorized as a Jew and was given a yellow star to
wear on his uniform instead of a pink one.*

Just prior to the scene below, Horst complained to the

*prisoner in charge of doling out the soup that he had not
received any meat or vegetables in his bowl, only water.
The prisoner pushed Horst away and called him a "fucking
queer." Max saw the incident and after getting his soup,
followed Horst into the barracks.*

....

MAX: Hi.
  (*HORST looks at him; says nothing; MAX holds up his bowl.
  MAX looks at HORST's bowl. He gives him some vegetables.*)
  Here.
HORST: Leave me alone.
MAX: I got extra. Some vegetables. Here. (*Drops some veg-
  etables from his bowl in HORST's bowl.*)
HORST: (*HORST looks in his own bowl.*) Thanks.
  (*They eat quietly.*)
  (*HORST looks up. Stares at MAX's uniform.*)

HORST: (*HORST does not look at MAX.*) Yellow star?
MAX: What?
HORST: Jew?
MAX: Oh. Yeah.
HORST: I wouldn't have figured it.
  (*Silence.*)

  I'm sorry about your friend.
MAX: Who?
HORST: Your friend.
MAX: Oh.
  (*Silence.*)

HORST: It's not very sociable in these barracks. (*Laughs.*) Is
  it?
MAX: (*MAX slides into HORST and indicates the triangle.*)
  How'd you get the pink?
HORST: I signed a petition.
MAX: And?
HORST: That was it.
MAX: What kind of petition?
HORST: For Magnus Hirschfield.
MAX: Oh yeah. I remember him. Berlin.

HORST: Berlin.

MAX: He wanted to . . .

HORST: Make queers legal.

MAX: Right. I remember.

HORST: Looked like he would too, for a while. It was quite a movement. Then the Nazis came in. Well. I was a nurse. They said a queer couldn't be a nurse. Suppose I had to touch a patient's penis! God forbid. They said rather than be a nurse, I should be a prisoner. A more suitable occupation. So. So. That's how I got my pink triangle. How'd you get the yellow star?

MAX: I'm Jewish.

HORST: You're not Jewish, you're a queer.

(MAX looks right and left to see who might have heard.)
(Silence.)

MAX: I didn't want one.

HORST: Didn't want what?

MAX: A pink triangle. I didn't want one.

HORST: Didn't *want* one?

MAX: You told me it was the lowest. So I didn't want one.

HORST: So?

MAX: So I worked a deal.

HORST: A deal?

MAX: Sure. I'm good at that.

HORST: With the Gestapo?

MAX: Sure.

HORST: You're full of shit.
(Silence.)

MAX: I'm going to work a lot of deals around here. They can't keep us here forever. Sooner or later they'll release us. I'm only under protective custody, that's what they told me. I'm going to stay alive.

HORST: I don't doubt it.

MAX: Sure. I'm good at that.

HORST: Thanks for the vegetables. *(HORST starts to rise. He hunches over.)*

MAX: Where are you going?

HORST: *(HORST pauses in movement.)* To sleep. We get up at four in the morning. I'm on stone detail. I chop stones up. It's fun. Excuse me . . .

(*HORST starts again to rise. MAX stops him with his right hand. HORST sits back on haunches.*)

MAX: Don't go.

HORST: I'm tired.

MAX: I don't have anyone to talk to.

HORST: Talk to your lansmen.

MAX: I'm not Jewish.

HORST: Then why are you wearing that?

MAX: You told me pink was the lowest.

HORST: It is, but only because the other prisoners hate us so much.

MAX: (*MAX holds out and indicates bowl.*) I got meat in my soup. You didn't.

HORST: Good for you. (*HORST rises and crosses left of MAX.*)

MAX: Don't go.

HORST: (*HORST goes into deep knee position.*) Look, friendships last about twelve hours in this place. We had ours on the train. Why don't you go and bother someone else.

MAX: You didn't think I'd make it, did you? Off the train?

HORST: I wasn't sure.

MAX: I'm going to stay alive.

HORST: Yes.

MAX: Because of you. You told me how.

HORST: Yes. (*Pause.*) I did. (*Pause.*) I'm sorry.

MAX: About what?

HORST: I don't know. Your friend.

MAX: Oh.
(*Silence.*)
He wasn't my friend.
(*Silence.*)

HORST: You should be wearing a pink triangle.

MAX: I made a deal.

HORST: You don't make deals here.

MAX: I did. I made a deal.

HORST: Sure. (*HORST rises and crosses left corner of right wall. Starts to leave again.*)

MAX: They said if I . . . I could . . . they said . . .

HORST: (*HORST takes a step in toward MAX.*) What?

MAX: Nothing. I could prove . . . I don't know how . . .

HORST: What? (*Stops, sits next to* MAX.)
MAX: Nothing.
  (*Silence.*)

HORST: (HORST *moves into* MAX *and kneels to him.*) Try.
  (*Silence.*)

  I think you better.
  (*Silence.*)

               Try to tell me.
MAX: Nothing.
  (*Silence.*)

HORST: O.K. (HORST *stands to leave. Moves away.*)
MAX: I made ...
  (MAX *pulls* HORST *down. The next lines do not relate to*
  HORST. *He finds it exceptionally difficult to tell.*)

  they took me ... into that room ...
HORST: (*Stops.*) Where?
MAX: Into that room.
HORST: On the train?
MAX: On the train. And they said ... prove that you're ...
  and I did ...
HORST: Prove that you're what?
MAX: Not.
HORST: Not what?
MAX: Queer.
HORST: How?
MAX: Her.
HORST: Her?
MAX: They said, if you ... and I did ...
HORST: Did what?
MAX: Her. Made ...
HORST: Made what?
MAX: Love.
HORST: Who to?
MAX: Her.
HORST: Who was she?
MAX: Only ... maybe ... maybe only thirteen ... she was
  maybe ... she was dead.
HORST: Oh.

MAX: Just. Just dead, minutes . . . (*MAX indicates a gun at the temple.*) bullet . . . in her . . . they said . . . prove that you're . . . and I did . . . prove that you're . . . lots of them, watching . . . laughing . . . drinking . . . he's a bit bent, they said, he can't . . . but I did . . .

HORST: How?

MAX: I don't . . . I don't . . . know. I wanted . . .

HORST: To stay alive.

MAX: And there was something . . . (*MAX holds his head in his hands.*)

HORST: Something . . .

MAX: Exciting . . . (*MAX raises his head.*)

HORST: Oh God.

MAX: I hit him, you know. I kissed her. Dead lips. I killed him. Sweet lips. Angel.

HORST: God.

MAX: Angel . . . She was . . . like an angel . . . to save my life . . . little breasts just beginning . . . her breasts . . . just beginning . . . they said he can't . . . he's a bit bent . . . but I did . . . and I proved . . . I proved that I wasn't . . .
  (*Silence.*)

And they enjoyed it.

HORST: Yes.

MAX: And I said, I'm not queer. And they laughed. And I said, give me a yellow star. And they said, sure make him a Jew. He's not bent. And they laughed. They were having fun. But . . . I . . . got . . . my . . . star . . . (*MAX fingers his star.*)

HORST: (*Gently.*) Oh yes.

MAX: I got my star.

HORST: Yes. (*HORST reaches for MAX.*)

MAX: *Don't do that!* (*MAX pulls away right.*) You mustn't do that. For your own sake. You mustn't touch me. I'm a rotten person.

HORST: No . . .
  (*HORST reaches for MAX again. MAX strikes out at and crawls right.*)

MAX: Rotten.
  (*HORST stares at MAX.*)

HORST: No.
>   (*HORST pauses then stands. He exits between walls and out U.C. There is a silence. MAX leans against wall. He closes his eyes, takes a deep breath.*)

MAX: One. Two. Three. Four. Five. (*MAX takes another breath.*) Six. Seven. Eight. Nine. Ten.

BLOBO'S BOY

by Albert J. Zuckerman

*Eighteen-year-old George has returned home mid-semester
from Annapolis, the Naval Academy, the school he had always dreamed of attending. His father, Morris, a gruff,
blustery, self-made man with a questionable past as an executive in the butcher's union, can't understand why. He
feels that he has given Morris everything and is angry that
his son has not been able to overcome whatever problems
he was having at school. George reveals that he was hu-
miliated and harassed by the other midshipmen because
Morris is being investigated by a Senate committee for his
illegal political influence in a New York City mayoral elec-
tion twenty years ago (the hearings have been showing on
national TV).*

*George's mother Shirley has just tried to convince Mor-
ris that he must contain his anger and do what he can to
help his son through this terrible ordeal. Morris has just
telephoned the Commandant at Annapolis to make sure that
George will be readmitted if he returns.*

....

MORRIS: George! George, come on in here! (*After a moment,
GEORGE appears.*) Come in! Sit down, George!
GEORGE: Yes?
MORRIS: Look, uh . . .
GEORGE: I'm sorry. Okay?
MORRIS: That's not what I called you in here for. If I got

started, *I* could do some apologizin', too. George, your ma and me want you should go back right away.

GEORGE: To Annapolis?

MORRIS: Right.

GEORGE: Don't you understand? I can't.

MORRIS: Shut up! Never mind: you wanna say something, go ahead and say it. Okay, this is the first time things gone bad on you, ain't it? Really bad, I mean? Well, it is, ain't it?

GEORGE: I guess so.

MORRIS: Up till now me and your ma, we done pretty good for you. The Thunderbird, cashmere suits, whatever you wanted. You wanted Annapolis; we seen to it you got there. You think my parents, or your ma's, ever did any of that stuff for us?

GEORGE: I'm grateful. But I'm your son. It just won't work.

MORRIS: Why not? You think your old man's not as good as the next guy? You never been outa kindergarten. I never gave you that spiel about the birds and the bees that kids are supposed to get from their fathers, did I? The facts of life, I suppose you think you know them.

GEORGE: Yes. I'm afraid I do.

MORRIS: So I'm no angel! I never said I was. George, when I got off that boat in 1921, I was sixteen, I had two quarters in my pocket, and I didn't speak a word of English. The best job I could get paid four bucks a week, nights, cleaning out elevators in an office building. Maybe I'd be a janitor now if I'd stuck it. But I got tired eating beans all the time, and cleaning other people's mess. The liquor business was a good business then. Illegal, sure, but the same judge that was throwing guys in the clink, that come into his court, was buying plenty of the stuff from me at home. All your hoity-toity buddies at the Naval Academy—all their fathers were buying it when I was selling it, and it was just as illegal . . . Only I made some money out of it and they didn't. That's the only real bitch they got.

GEORGE: I know. I understand that, but . . .

MORRIS: You don't understand. You don't like to hear your own name, you said. It makes you feel dirty. Well, you're gonna live with that name for a long time, so you better understand it. I worked hard for what I got, and what you got.

GEORGE: I don't want any of it.

MORRIS: You don't, huh? So act like it. Stand up on your own two feet! . . . You get knocked down, you don't whine, you don't quit, you get back up.

GEORGE: Just like that! Sending me back there is going to straighten everything out. People don't bother *you.* You don't give a damn what anybody says. But me? If you have me around, you'll know our lives are a mess. All the time you'll know, and that's the one thing you don't want.

MORRIS: You finished?

GEORGE: Yes. Before I ever began.

MORRIS: Son, I'm sorry about what happened to you down there. But it woulda been my fault, too, if I never got nowhere and you was just one more East Side bum of a kid like I was. Where'd you get all your fancy ideas? Kids on the East Side don't have them, because they cost. I paid for 'em, with sweat and boot licking, but I ain't sorry. You're better than them. There's some ways you're better than me, 'cause I wanted you to be. You got that: because I wanted you to be. But there's one big way you ain't yet. Guts! You grow up where it's tough, and you learn to fight back without even thinkin' about . . . You want to go back there, don't you?

GEORGE: Maybe. Yes, if I could be someone else.

MORRIS: You know what that means you're sayin', don't you? If you can't be yourself there, you can't be yourself no place else, either. You're throwin' in the towel right after your first big bout. Everybody loses, some time; but that don't mean you give up.

GEORGE: I guess I lost before I ever got in the ring.

MORRIS: Kid, if you give up now, you're dead. Listen! First time I went in the liquor business, it took a week, and some rough-housers come down at night, smashed every penny's worth of the stuff I had, and beat up the guy I had watching it. So where'd I be now if I chickened out then, like I was supposed to? You think it was easy? Every cent I'd saved and borrowed, money from my kid sisters, Uncle Jake, my Chinese laundryman, was in that smashed pile of stinking glass. I begged and borrowed all over again. The second time, I didn't have so much. I hid it better, watched it myself. Then when they found out, they knew I was in that business for real, and I stayed. You see what I'm talkin' about?

GEORGE: Sure. Only the Naval Academy's not a bootleggers' club, and I'm not you.

MORRIS: Who are you, then? Chew on that! You don't know, and you never will if you don't go back and look 'em all in the eye. Then they'll know and you'll know.

GEORGE: I do know, though, and you do, too, and I wish to hell I didn't.

JULIUS CAESAR

by William Shakespeare

ACT IV, SCENE 3

*Soon after Brutus, Cassius, and their co-conspirators killed
Julius Caesar, all of Italy became consumed by civil war,
with Mark Antony and Octavius Caesar allied against Brutus and Cassius. Brutus is honest and noble, concerned
about the good of the country, while Cassius is wily and
self-serving. And now their alliance is beginning to crum-
ble. Both men lead their armies in the field and Cassius
comes to Brutus, enraged that Brutus has condemned one
of Cassius's subordinates for taking bribes. Brutus tells
Cassius to lower his voice and join him in his tent, lest
their men become demoralized by the rift that has grown
between them. They enter Brutus's tent.*

....

(Enter BRUTUS and CASSIUS.)

CASSIUS: That you have wrong'd me doth appear in this:
            You have condemn'd and noted Lucius Pella
            For taking bribes here of the Sardians;
            Wherein my letters, praying on his side,
            Because I knew the man, were slighted off.
BRUTUS: You wrong'd yourself to write in such a case.
CASSIUS: In such a time as this it is not meet
            That every nice offence should bear his comment.
BRUTUS: Let me tell you, Cassius, you yourself
            Are much condemn'd to have an itching palm,

To sell and mart your offices for gold
To undeservers.

CASSIUS: I an itching palm!
You know that you are Brutus that speaks this,
Or, by the gods, this speech were else your last.

BRUTUS: The name of Cassius honours this corruption,
And chastisement doth therefore hide his head.

CASSIUS: Chastisement!

BRUTUS: Remember March, the ides of March remember:
Did not great Julius bleed for justice' sake?
What villain touch'd his body, that did stab,
And not for justice? What, shall one of us,
That struck the foremost man of all this world
But for supporting robbers, shall we now
Contaminate our fingers with base bribes,
And sell the mighty space of our large honours
For so much trash as may be grasped thus?
I had rather be a dog, and bay the moon,
Than such a Roman.

CASSIUS: Brutus, bait not me;
I'll not endure it; you forget yourself,
To hedge me in; I am a soldier, I,
Older in practice, abler than yourself
To make conditions.

BRUTUS: Go to; you are not, Cassius.

CASSIUS: I am.

BRUTUS: I say you are not.

CASSIUS: Urge me no more, I shall forget myself;
Have mind upon your health, tempt me no farther.

BRUTUS: Away, slight man!

CASSIUS: Is't possible?

BRUTUS: Hear me, for I will speak.
Must I give way and room to your rash choler?
Shall I be frighted when a madman stares?

CASSIUS: O ye gods, ye gods! must I endure all this?

BRUTUS: All this! ay, more: fret till your proud heart break;
Go show your slaves how choleric you are,
And make your bondmen tremble. Must I budge?
Must I observe you? must I stand and crouch
Under your testy humour? By the gods,
You shall digest the venom of your spleen,

Though it do split you; for, from this day forth,
I'll use you for my mirth, yea, for my laughter,
When you are waspish.

CASSIUS: Is it come to this?

BRUTUS: You say you are a better soldier:
Let it appear so; make your vaunting true,
And it shall please me well: for mine own part,
I shall be glad to learn of noble men.

CASSIUS: You wrong me every way; you wrong me, Brutus;
I said, an elder soldier, not a better:
Did I say, better?

BRUTUS: If you did, I care not.

CASSIUS: When Cæsar lived, he durst not thus have moved
me.

BRUTUS: Peace, peace! you durst not so have tempted him.

CASSIUS: I durst not!

BRUTUS: No.

CASSIUS: What, durst not tempt him!

BRUTUS: For your life you durst not.

CASSIUS: Do not presume too much upon my love;
I may do that I shall be sorry for.

BRUTUS: You have done that you should be sorry for.
There is no terror, Cassius, in your threats;
For I am arm'd so strong in honesty,
That they pass by me as the idle wind
Which I respect not. I did send to you
For certain sums of gold, which you denied me:
For I can raise no money by vile means:
By heaven, I had rather coin my heart,
And drop my blood for drachmas, than to wring
From the hard hands of peasants their vile trash
By any indirection. I did send
To you for gold to pay my legions,
Which you denied me: was that done like
Cassius?
Should I have answer'd Caius Cassius so?
When Marcus Brutus grows so covetous,
To lock such rascal counters from his friends,
Be ready, gods, with all your thunderbolts,
Dash him to pieces!

CASSIUS: I denied you not.

BRUTUS: You did.

CASSIUS: I did not: he was but a fool
    That brought my answer back. Brutus hath rived
      my heart:
    A friend should bear his friend's infirmities,
    But Brutus makes mine greater than they are.

BRUTUS: I do not, till you practise them on me.

CASSIUS: You love me not.

BRUTUS: I do not like your faults.

CASSIUS: A friendly eye could never see such faults.

BRUTUS: A flatterer's would not, though they do appear
    As huge as high Olympus.

CASSIUS: Come, Antony, and young Octavius, come,
    Revenge yourselves along on Cassius,
    For Cassius is aweary of the world;
    Hated by one he loves; braved by his brother;
    Check'd like a bondman; all his faults observed,
    Set in a note-book, learn'd and conn'd by rote,
    To cast into my teeth. O, I could weep
    My spirit from mine eyes! There is my dagger,
    And here my naked breast; within, a heart
    Dearer than Plutus' mine, richer than gold:
    If that thou be'st a Roman, take it forth;
    I, that denied thee gold, will give my heart:
    Strike, as thou didst at Cæsar; for I know,
    When thou didst hate him worst, thou lovedst him
      better
    Than ever thou lovedst Cassius.

BRUTUS: Sheathe your dagger:
    Be angry when you will, it shall have scope;
    Do what you will, dishonour shall be humour.
    O Cassius, you are yoked with a lamb,
    That carries anger as the flint bears fire,
    Who, much enforced, shows a hasty spark
    And straight is cold again.

CASSIUS: Hath Cassius lived
    To be but mirth and laughter to his Brutus,
    When grief and blood ill-temper'd vexeth him?

BRUTUS: When I spoke that, I was ill-temper'd too.

CASSIUS: Do you confess so much? Give me your hand.

BRUTUS: And my heart too.

CASSIUS: O Brutus!
BRUTUS: What's the matter?
CASSIUS: Have not you love enough to bear with me,
         When that rash humour which my mother gave
             me
         Makes me forgetful?
BRUTUS: Yes, Cassius, and from henceforth,
        When you are over-earnest with your Brutus,
        He'll think your mother chides, and leave you so.

MONOLOGUES FOR WOMEN

A COUPLA WHITE CHICKS SITTING AROUND TALKING

by John Ford Noonan

ACT II, SCENE 1

Hannah Mae and her husband, Carl Joe, have just moved from Austin, Texas, to an upscale suburban community in Westchester County, near New York City. Hannah Mae is big hearted, intense, and forceful and has intruded herself into the home and life of her conservative, uptight neighbor, Maude Mix, visiting her every day uninvited.

Yesterday Maude told Hannah Mae that Carl Joe had visited her too, and he too was forceful and intrusive, so much so that they had sex on the kitchen table. After getting the details, Hannah Mae concluded that Carl Joe only did it to break up their friendship, and she determined to get even. She arrives the next morning with a large white cast on her left arm and a severely bruised right eye. She has also brought two cups of coffee. Maude (whose husband has recently run off to Puerto Rico with his secretary) assumes that Carl Joe has beat her up, but Hannah Mae corrects her.

(To use as a monologue, omit Maude's lines.)

....

HANNAH MAE: Self inflicted wounds, Honey, self inflicted.

MAUDE: I don't believe you.

HANNAH MAE: Carl Joe arrives on the five-forty-seven. I'm dressed perfect. Dinner's a killer. He stuffs his face. I wipe his mouth. My plan's going perfect, I'm leading the sucker to slaughter! Next I take off his shoes—I'm on the verge of doing a job on his insteps—only I can't hold my anger back another second. I smash his shoes to the floor and I scream, ''Lug, the wandering hands is one thing but this next-door hustling's gotta stop!'' He screams back, ''What next-door hustling?!'' I smile and say real quiet and slow, ''I know about you and Miss Maude.'' He smiles and says real quiet back, ''Nothing happened between us. She's got no proof!''

MAUDE: No proof? There's me.

HANNAH MAE: I grab his shoe and wack him hard on the side of his head. ''Goddang liar!'' He bolts out of the chair. For twenty years every day I've been afraid of pushing him too far . . . I mean, to live all that time threatened by something that never comes but at any minute could . . . only now it's here! Before he can even make a fist, *WHAP!* I get him with the shoe again. It's him that's afraid of me. Twice more I hit him. *WHAP, WHAP*. He rolls over and the chase begins. Ain't never felt so good in my life. Only trouble is I wrecked my eye falling against the coffee table in the living room and my wrist, well, that got broke falling down the back stairs trying to tackle the lug. Self inflicted, but sure feels good.

ABSENT FRIENDS

by Alan Ayckbourn

ACT I

Diana and Paul have invited friends this afternoon to their comfortable, modern home and tea sandwiches and cakes are set out. Evelyn is the first to arrive and Diana suspects that she is having an affair with Paul (who has not yet returned from playing squash). In truth, Evelyn did have sex with Paul once, but found the experience "horrible. Worse than my husband and that's saying a lot." Ayckbourn describes Diana as "mid to later thirties. She always gives the impression of being slightly fraught. She smiles occasionally but it's painful. Her sharp darting eyes don't miss much after years of suspicions both genuine and unfounded."

(See other scene from this play in another section for more information.)

....

DIANA: No, there are times when I think that's the principal trouble between Paul and me. I mean, I know now I'm running myself down but Paul basically, he's got much more go—well, I mean let's face it, he's much cleverer than me. Let's face it. Basically. I mean, I was the bright one in our family but I can't keep up with Paul sometimes. When he has one of his moods, I think to myself, now if I was really clever, I could probably talk him round or something but I mean the thing is, really and truly, and I know I'm running myself down when I say this, I don't think I'm really enough for him. He needs me, I can tell that; he doesn't say as much but I know he does. It's just, as I say, I don't think I'm really enough for him. (*She reflects.*) But he couldn't do without me. Make no mistake about that. He's got this amazing energy. I don't know where he finds it. He goes to bed long after me, he's up at dawn, working down here—then off he goes all day. . . . I need my eight hours, it's no good. What I'm saying is really, I wouldn't blame him. Not altogether. If he did. With someone else. You know, another woman. I wouldn't blame him, I wouldn't blame her. Not as long as I was told. Providing I know, that I'm told—all right. Providing I feel able to say to people—"Yes, I am well aware that my husband is having an affair with such and such or whoever . . . it's quite all right. I know all about it. We're both grown-up people, we know what we're doing, he knows I know, she knows I know. So mind your own business." I'd feel all right about it. But I will not stand deception. I'm simply asking that I be told. Either by him or if not by her. Not necessarily now but sometime. You see.

(*A pause. EVELYN is expressionless.*)

I know he is, you see. He's not very clever and he's a very bad liar like most men. If he takes the trouble, like last Saturday, to tell me he's just going down the road to the football match, he might at least choose a day when they're playing at home. (*She lifts the tablecloth and inspects the sandwiches.*) I hope I've made enough tomato. No, I must be told. Otherwise it makes my life impossible. I can't talk to anybody without them. . . . I expect them, both of them, at least to have some feeling for me. (*She blows her nose.*) Well.

(*The doorbell rings.*)

Excuse me. . . .

(*DIANA goes out.*)

MASTER CLASS

by Terrence McNally

ACT I

In this play, based on the life of Maria Callas, Maria is teaching a master class in opera. She is fabulous and imperious. As she listens to her pupil (the soprano) sing Amina's aria from La Sonnambula, *she recalls her own performances and reminisces about her life (while we hear her singing this aria in the background).*

....

MARIA: I keep thinking of a pretty, slim blonde girl back at the conservatory in Athens. Madame de Hidalgo gave her the part of Amina at the student recital. I was so heartbroken but I wanted to scratch her face with my nails at the same time, too. I was cast as a nun in *Suor Angelica* instead. But I want to sing Amina in *Sonnambula*, Madame de Hidalgo. With your voice and figure you're better off as a nun, my child. Look at me now, Madame de Hidalgo. Listen to me now. Sometimes I think every performance I sing is for that pretty, slim blonde girl taking all those bows at the Conservatory. Whatever happened to her with her freshly laundered blouses and bags full of oranges? My sister was another slim pretty blonde. They're not up here, either one of them. I'm up here. The fat ugly greasy one with the thick glasses and bad skin is up here, and she's dressed by Piero Tosi and she's wearing so many diamonds she can scarcely move her arms and she is the absolute center of the universe right now.

I know they're all out there in the dark. My enemies. My mother. My sister. The other singers. Smiling. Waiting for me to fail. The dare-devil stuff is coming up. The hullaba-loo. I'm not afraid. I welcome it. Reckless. You bet I'm reckless! Someone said I'd rather sing like Callas for one year than like anyone else for twenty!

Now the embellishments. The second time around. Never do it the same way twice. Flick your voice here. Lighten it. Shade it. Trill. Astonish.

(She listens.)

AN IDEAL HUSBAND

by Oscar Wilde

ACT II

It is the height of the social season in London at the turn of the century and we are in the splendid home of Sir Robert Chiltern. His young sister Mabel is complaining to her sister-in-law, Gertrude, about Tommy Trafford, a young man who works for Sir Robert as a secretary. Mabel Chiltern, as Wilde describes her, "is a perfect example of the English type of prettiness . . . (with) the fascinating tyranny of youth, and the astonishing courage of innocence."

(See other scene from this play for more information.)

....

MABEL CHILTERN: Well, Tommy has proposed to me again. Tommy really does nothing but propose to me. He proposed to me last night in the Music-room, when I was quite unprotected, as there was an elaborate trio going on. I didn't dare to make the smallest repartee, I need hardly tell you. If I had, it would have stopped the music at once. Musical people are so absurdly unreasonable. They always want one to be perfectly dumb at the very moment when one is longing to be absolutely deaf. Then he proposed to me in broad daylight this morning, in front of that dreadful statue of Achilles. Really, the things that go on in front of that work of art are quite appalling. The police should interfere. At luncheon I saw by the glare in his eye that he was going to propose again, and I just managed to check him in time by assuring him that I was a bimetallist. Fortunately I don't know what bimetallism means. And I don't believe anybody else does either. But the observation crushed Tommy for ten minutes. He looked quite shocked. And then Tommy is so annoying in the way he proposes. If he proposed at the top of his voice, I should not mind so much. That might produce some effect on the public. But he does it in a horrid confidential way. When Tommy wants to be romantic he talks to one just like a doctor. I am very fond of Tommy, but his methods of proposing are quite out of date. I wish, Gertrude, you would speak to him, and tell him that once a week is quite often enough to propose to any one, and that it should always be done in a manner that attracts some attention.

ANTON CHEKHOV'S "THE DUEL"

adapted by Michael Schulman and Eva Mekler
from the translation by Ann Dunnigan

ACT I, SCENE 4

*Nadyezhda Fyordorovna was a young married woman in
St. Petersburg when she met Layevsky and fell in love with
him. They read poetry together, dreamed of a better world
and a more meaningful life for themselves, and ran off together to a small village on the Black Sea in the Caucasus.
It didn't take long for both Nadyezhda and Layevsky to tire
of their new life and each other.*

*Their relationship has grown cold, but neither can speak
aloud about their changes of heart. Neither wants to openly
betray the dreams they wrought together. So Layevsky expresses his trapped feelings in petty criticisms of Nadyezhda, and Nadyezhda expresses hers by having brief and
not very satisfying affairs.*

*At a picnic, Nadyezhda reveals some of her frustrations
and longings to the Deacon, a young man who was recently
assigned to the local parish.*

*(To form Nadyezhda's conversation with the Deacon into
a monologue, the Deacon's lines have been omitted and
slight adjustments were made in Nadyezhda's speeches.)*

(For more information about these characters, see other scenes from this play in other sections of the book.)

....

NADYEZHDA: Vanya's become cold, even insulting at times, but I don't mind anymore. On the contrary, I find it preferable this way now. At first . . . oh, at first I reacted with tears, reproaches, and even threatened to leave him. But no longer. Now I respond to his indifference with silence. I withdraw. Yes, in fact I'm glad he no longer treats me with affection. . . . Because I've disappointed him. In what way? you wonder. By no longer sympathizing with his dreams. He gave up Petersburg to come here to the Caucasus for a life of meaningful work, and I thought I would find a little cottage on the shore, a cozy little garden, birds, a stream, a place where I could entertain neighbors, nurse the poor peasants, and distribute little books among them. But the Caucasus turned out to be nothing but mountains, forests and huge stifling valleys. There are no interesting neighbors of any kind and one has even to worry about being robbed. As it turned out there seems to have developed between us a tacit agreement never to mention farming and the life of labor. He is silent, I believe, because he is angry with me for being silent. I know I still love Vanya since I get jealous of him and miss him when he is away. But life is so tedious here. One day is so much like the next. When I see the foreign steamers and the sailors in white, I remember . . . I remember a vast ballroom . . . and music mingled with the sound of French; a waltz strain begins to throb in my ears and my heart races with joy. I want to dance, I want to dance, I want to speak French . . . *(She has begun to cry and runs off.)*

A MONTH IN THE COUNTRY
by IVAN TURGENEV

translated by Richard Freeborn

ACT III

It is the 1840s in Russia on the country estate of Arkady Islaev. His wife, Natalya Petrovna, has realized that she has fallen in love with her son's handsome, young tutor, Belyaev. She has become jealous of Belyaev's friendship with her seventeen-year-old ward, Vera, and has just asked Vera about their feelings for each other. Vera acknowledged her love for Belyaev and expressed her belief that he might love her. Natalya Petrovna did not take this news well and, feeling faint, asked Vera to leave her alone. Rakitin, whom she mentions in the monologue, is a family friend and confidant, who has told Natalya Petrovna of his love for her.

(See other scene from this play in another section for more information.)

....

NATALYA PETROVNA: (*Alone, remaining for a short while quite still.*) Now I see it clearly—these children love each other. (*Stops and draws her hand across her face.*) What of it? So much the better! God grant them happiness! (*Laughing.*) And I . . . I could think . . . (*Again stops.*) She came out with it so quickly, I confess I hadn't suspected, I confess the news shocked me . . . But wait a moment, everything's not over yet. My God, what am I saying? What's wrong with me? I don't recognize myself, I don't know what I've come to! (*A pause.*) What *have* I been doing? I've been trying to marry the poor young girl—to an old man! I send for the doctor, he insinuates this, hints at that . . . Then there's Arkady and Rakitin . . . And me . . . (*Gives a shudder and suddenly raises her head.*) What's it all about after all? Am I jealous of Vera? I'm really in love with him, am I? (*A pause.*) You can't go on doubting it, can you? You are in love, you wretched woman! I don't know how it happened. It's as if I'd been given poison . . . Suddenly everything's gone to pieces, scattered, done with . . . He's afraid of me . . . Everyone's afraid of me. What am I to him? What's a creature like me mean to him? He's young and she's young. And me! (*Bitterly.*) How can he appreciate me? They're both of them silly, as Rakitin says . . . Oh, how I hate that clever-clever man! But Arkady, my trustful, kind Arkady! My God, my God, I'd be better off dead! (*Stands up.*) I think I'm going out of my mind. Oh, stop exaggerating! Well—in a state of shock, then, astonished, amazed that for the first time—yes, for the very first time—I'm in love for the very first time in my life! (*She sits down again.*) He must leave. Yes. And Rakitin too. The time's come for me to sort myself out. I've gone down a notch—and look where it's got me! And what on earth did I see in him? (*After a moment's reflection.*) But it's frightful what I'm feeling now . . . Arkady! Yes, I'll fling myself into his arms, I'll beg him to forgive me, beg him to protect me and save me, him and no one else! All the others are no part of me and must remain like that. But surely . . . surely there's another way? That girl—she's just a child. She may be mistaken. It's all childishness anyhow . . . Which means I'll—I'll have it out with him myself, I'll ask him . . . (*Reproachfully.*) Ah, so you're still hoping, are you? You're still living in hope? Oh, what's the point of my hoping! My God, don't let me despise myself! (*Drops her head into her hands.*)

SAY GOODNIGHT, GRACIE

by Ralph Pape

*It is the 1970s and Bobby, Jerry, and their friends are soon
to go off to their high school reunion. They have gathered
at Jerry's rundown East Village apartment, and with some
time to kill before they have to leave, have brought out the
pot and begun to chat and joke about their lives. Catherine
is Bobby's new girlfriend. She is an airline stewardess and
appears more level headed and comfortable with herself
than Bobby and the others. During a discussion of crushes
on TV personalities, she mentioned her attraction to JFK
during the Cuban missile crisis, and this brought back
memories of when her life took a dramatic turn. She tells
her story to the group.*

(To use as a monologue, omit Bobby's line.)

....

CATHERINE: I was in high school during the Cuban missile
crisis. When the blockade went into effect, they led us
downstairs into the basement, and the nuns stood around
and everyone had to say the rosary because people really
believed that a nuclear war could have broken out that
morning. I didn't want to stay there. I didn't want to die
like that. I was near a flight of steps that led upstairs and
when no one was looking, I snuck out. I just . . . wanted to
be outside. I had never been disobedient or questioned au-
thority before that moment.
BOBBY: (*Appreciatively.*) All right . . . !
CATHERINE: It was cold outside and there was an incredible

blue sky and no wind. There were no people. I walked around the empty schoolyard. I was so afraid. There were tears in my eyes because I really believed I was looking at everything for the last time. It was so beautiful. I felt like a little girl. I began to touch things. The brick wall of the school. The iron railing of the fence that ran around the yard. The bicycle rack. Everything was so cold and yet so beautiful. I filled my lungs with air. I was alive. I had never admitted to myself how much I loved just being alive. And I knew if I survived, I would never forget that morning when I had wanted to touch and feel everything around me. I was sixteen at this time. A virgin . . . After the crisis had passed, I still felt like I was moving through a very beautiful dream. I had a date with Greg Sutton, the captain of the basketball team, very soon after. That night, without even realizing that I was saying the words, I begged Greg to fuck me. He couldn't believe it. He was probably a virgin, too. I said, Greg, all of us are on this earth for only a short while, and we can't be afraid, we have to open ourselves up to every moment . . . so Greg fucked me in the back seat of his car that cold winter's night at the drive-in. Moonlight shone through the windows. I can't begin to describe what it was like. I can only ask you to imagine it. In and out. In and out. In and out. I wrapped my legs around him and I remembered how beautiful and precious the world had seemed to me that morning and I grabbed at him repeatedly and plunged my tongue deep inside his mouth. My breasts were heaving up and down. I was so hot and wet. It was indescribable . . . I can only ask you to try and imagine this. Anyway, after that night, Greg must have done some bragging to his friends, because the next week I was literally besieged with requests for dates. All of which I accepted. Greg became jealous, but I explained to him that I needed to reach out and touch everyone for myself, just as, that morning, I had wanted to touch every leaf on the big oak tree outside the school when I thought the world would perish in a fiery holocaust. Before the term was over, I had gone to bed with over twenty different boys. And my geometry teacher, Mr. Handfield. That summer, I took a house with some girls down at the Jersey shore. College boys were in and out of that house every night, and I denied myself nothing. At long last, I became a stewardess and travelled all over the world and had innumerable sexual experiences with men of every race and culture imaginable . . . also, I was able to see the clouds close up, which I had always wanted to do. I wanted to reach out and touch them. I still do. Perhaps some day I will . . . But I have never lost the joy of just being alive ever since that morning in 1962. Bobby always tells me I'm the most passionate person he knows, in or out of bed, and he understands why, although I love him, I have to have the freedom to reach out and touch and commune with my fellow human creatures. Because we are all on this earth for only a very short while . . . And I just can't get depressed by that . . .

DOUBLE SOLITAIRE

by Robert Anderson

*In this short play about the disappointments and discontents
of married life, an elderly couple is about to celebrate their
fiftieth wedding anniversary with their son and daughter-
in-law, whose marriage we soon learn is on the rocks. This
ostensibly happy occasion quickly deteriorates into a series
of confrontations, exposing the loneliness and unfulfilled
longings of each character. As if to highlight the woes of
married life, at a certain point in the play, Sylvia, described
as a stylish woman of around forty, appears "from the
shadows" and tells the audience why she would never get
married again. At the end of her speech she merely "drifts
off into the shadows" and the play proceeds.*

....

SYLVIA: I wouldn't get married again for a million dollars. I
was a very boring wife. I came to know exactly what I was
going to say on every occasion and said it . . . Oh, I read all
the books on how to be a thousand different women for
your husband . . . On one occasion I even suggested an in-
novation or two in our sex life which had the unfortunate
effect of blocking him completely for two weeks. So I finally persuaded him to divorce me (sans alimony, of course.
I have my own shop, and I wasn't going to fleece him because I was a frumpy bore). I lost ten pounds and immediately became more attractive and interesting . . . at least to
myself.

"Don't you get lonely?" they ask me. Who has time to

UNCLE VANYA
by ANTON CHEKHOV

translated by Ann Dunnigan

ACT III

As a young student, Elena Andreyevna fell in love with one of her professors, a distinguished older man. Now, some years later, she is still young and beautiful, but he has become cranky and ill. She has been a faithful wife, but during their years together she found him to be far less brilliant than she once believed and grew increasingly bored with their life. They have returned to his estate in the country and Elena has managed to overcome the distance that had grown between herself and her husband's daughter, Sonya. Sonya, who has worked laboriously (with her uncle, Vanya) to keep the estate solvent, has just confided to Elena that she is in love with Astrov, the handsome, idealistic doctor who is visiting the family. Sonya is in despair because she believes she in not pretty and because the doctor pays no special attention to her. Elena, sympathetic to Sonya's plight, says that she will try to discover what the doctor feels for her and sends Sonya out to get him. She waits in the drawing room, alone, and begins to realize that she too has feelings for the doctor.

....

ELENA ANDREYEVNA: (*alone.*) There is nothing worse than knowing someone's secret and not being able to help. (*Musing.*) He is not in love with her—that's clear, but why shouldn't he marry her? She isn't beautiful, but for a country doctor, and at his age, she would make an excellent wife.

She's clever, and so kind, so pure.... No, that's wrong, wrong.... (*Pause.*) I understand that poor girl. In the midst of desperate boredom, with some sort of gray shadows floating around her instead of people, and hearing only the banalities of those who can do nothing but eat, drink, and sleep—he sometimes appears, unlike the rest, handsome, interesting, fascinating, like a bright moon rising in the darkness.... To yield to the charm of such a man, to forget oneself ... It seems that I, too, am somewhat carried away. Yes, I am bored when he's not here, and I smile just thinking of him.... Uncle Vanya says I have mermaid's blood in my veins. "Let yourself go for once in your life" ... Well? Perhaps that's what I ought to do.... To fly, free as a bird, away from all of you, away from your sleepy faces and your talk, to forget you even exist in the world.... But I'm a coward, timid.... My conscience would torment me. ... He comes here every day, I can guess why, and even now I feel guilty. I am ready to fall on my knees before Sonya, and ask her to forgive me ... to weep....

THREE TALL WOMEN

by Edward Albee

ACT II

In the first act of this play a young female attorney, C, tries in vain to get A, a frail but cantankerous 92-year-old woman, to cooperate with her in arranging her finances. The old woman's paid companion, B, a middle-aged woman, joins in the bickering. In the second act of the play, the three women, A, B, and C, turn out to represent different phases of the same life (but don't recognize that they are the same character). As in act one, A is bitter about her life and losing touch with reality; B is a domineering matron in her middle years; and C is a flirtatious woman of 26. They each reveal their stories to each other and the audience. C has been insisting that she won't turn into her two companions and tries to explain herself to the audience. She tells about how elegant she feels modeling clothing (with her sister) in the fanciest dress shop in town, acknowledging that she sometimes flirts with the husbands who have accompanied their wives to the shop. But she maintains that she is a "good girl."

(To use as a monologue, omit all but C's lines.)

....

C: I'm a good girl. I know how to attract *men*. I'm *tall*; I'm striking; *I* know how to do it. Sis slouches and caves her front in; I stand tall; breasts out, chin up, hands . . . just so. I walk between the aisles and they know there's somebody coming, that there's somebody *there*. But, I'm a *good girl*. I'm not a virgin, but I'm a good girl. The boy who took me was a good boy.

(C *does not necessarily hear—or, at least, notice—the asides to come.*)

B: Oh, yes he *was*.

A: Yes? Was he?

B: *You* remember.

A: (*Laughs.*) Well, it *was* a *while* ago.

B: But you *do* remember.

A: *Oh* yes, I remember him. He was . . .

C: . . . sweet and handsome; no, not handsome: beautiful. He was beautiful!

A: (*To* B). He was; yes.

B: (*To* A *and herself.*) Yes.

C: He has coal-black hair and violet eyes and such a smile!

A: Ah!

B: Yes!

C: His body was . . . well, it was thin, but *hard*; all sinew and muscle; he fenced, he told me, and he was the one with the megaphone on the crew. When I held him when we danced, there was only sinew and muscle. We dated a lot; I liked him; I didn't tell Mother, but I liked him a lot. I like him, Sis, I said; I really like him. Have you told Mother? No, and don't *you*; I like him a lot, but I don't *know*. Has he? . . . *you* know. No, I said; no, he hasn't. But then he did. We were dancing—slowly—late, the end of the evening, and we danced so close, all . . . pressed, and . . . we were pressed, and I could feel that he was hard, *that* muscle and sinew, pressed against me while we danced. We were the same height and he looked into my eyes as we danced, slowly, and I felt the pressure up against me, and he tensed it and I felt it move against me.

B: (*Dreamy.*) Whatever is *that*, I said.

A: Hmmmmmmmm.

C: Whatever is *that*, I said. I *knew*, but whatever is that, I said, and he smiled, and his eyes shone, and it's me in love with you, he said. You have an interesting way of showing it, I said. Appropriate, he said, and I felt the muscle move again, and . . . well, I knew it was time; I knew I was ready,

and I knew I wanted him—whatever that *meant*—that I
wanted *him*, that I wanted *it*.

B: (*Looking back; agreeing.*) Yes; oh, yes.

A: Hmmmmmmmmm.

C: Remember, don't give it away, Mother said; don't give it
away like it was nothing.

B: (*Remembering.*) They won't respect you for it and you'll
get known as a loose girl. *Then* who will you marry?

A: (*To* B.) Is that what she said? I can't remember.

B: (*Laughs.*) *Yes* you can.

C: They won't respect you for it and you'll get known as a
loose girl. *Then* who will you marry? But he was pressed
against me, exactly against where he wanted to be—we
were the same height—and he was *so* beautiful, and his eyes
shone, and he smiled at me and he moved his hips as we
danced, so slowly, as we danced, and he breathed on my
neck and he said, you don't want me to embarrass myself
right here on the dance floor, do you?

B: (*Remembering.*) No, no; of course not.

C: I said, no, no; of course not. Let's go to my place, he said,
and I heard myself saying (*Incredulous.*) I'm not that kind
of girl? I mean, as soon as I said it I blushed: it was so . . .
stupid, so . . . expected. Yes, you are, he said; *you're* that
kind of girl.

B: And I was, and my God it was wonderful.

A: It hurt! (*Afterthought; to* B.) Didn't it?

B: (*Admonishing.*) Oh . . . well, a little.

C: You're that kind of girl, and I guess I was. We did it a
lot. (*Shy.*) I know it's trite to say your first time is your best,
but he was wonderful, and I know I'm only twenty-six now
and there've been a few others, and I imagine I'll marry,
and I'll be very happy.

B: (*Grudging.*) Well . . .

A: We'll talk about happy sometime.

C: I *know* I'll be very happy, but will I ever *not* think about
him? He was long and thick and knew what I wanted, what
I needed, and while I couldn't do . . . you know: the thing
he wanted . . . I just *couldn't*: I *can't*.

B: (*Stretches.*) Nope; never could.

A: (*Sort of dreamy.*) I wonder why.

C: (*Very agitated; upset.*) I tried! I wanted to do what . . . but

I choked, and I ... (*Whispered.*) I threw up. I just ... couldn't.

A: (*To* C.) Don't worry about it; don't worry about what can't be helped.

B: *And* ... there's more than one way to skin a cat.

A: (*Puzzles that.*) Why?

B: Hm?

A: *Why* is there more than one way to skin a *cat*?

B: (*Puzzles that.*) Why not?

A: Who needs it!? Isn't one way *enough*?

C: (*To the audience; still; simply.*) I just want you to know that I'm a good girl, that I was a good girl.

SEXUAL PERVERSITY IN CHICAGO

by David Mamet

This play is about two young men and two young women making their way through the sexual and emotional minefields of the singles scene in Chicago. On the surface Joan appears to be a young woman who knows her way around. At a singles bar she can quickly put a man in his place and with friends she can say clever things about relationships. But underneath the surface she is finding life very confusing, especially with regard to men and sex. And she is not having any relationships. Her confusions even spill over into her job as a kindergarten teacher, where the children seem to have an easier time with sex than she does. In the following monologue, she has just caught two of her kindergartners engaging in some sexual exploration.

....

JOAN: What are you doing? Where are you going? What are you doing? You stay right there. Now. What were the two of you doing? I'm just asking a simple question. There's nothing to be ashamed of. (*Pause.*) I can wait. (*Pause.*) Were you playing "Doctor"? (*Pause.*) "Doctor." Don't play dumb with me, just answer the question. (You know, that attitude is going to get you in a lot of trouble someday.) Were you playing with each other's genitals? Each other's ... "pee-pees"?—whatever you call them at home, that's what I'm asking. (And don't play dumb, because I saw what you were doing, so just own up to it.) (*Pause.*) Alright ... no. No, stop that, there's no reason for tears ... it's perfectly . . . natural. But . . . there's a time and a place for everything. Now . . . no, it's alright. Come on. Come on, we're all going in the other room, and we're going to wash our hands. And then Miss Webber is going to call our parents.

SEASCAPE WITH SHARKS AND DANCER

by Don Nigro

SCENE 5

The play takes place in "a small decrepit house on Cape Cod." The owner of the house is a young man named Ben, a writer in his late twenties. One night he fishes Tracy, an attractive young woman, out of the ocean. She is naked and clearly trying to kill herself—although she denies it (she says she was dancing). Tracy is a drifter who, as she puts it, is "a very bright little girl, and rather wicked [who has] wandered all over the country hitching rides and shacking up "until she'd done just about everything and been almost everywhere," (although she is in fact only twenty and a half years old.)

During their very first moments together Tracy begins heaping a torrent of abuse on Ben. She almost breaks his nose, kicks him in the groin, and calls him every insulting name she can think of. But Ben sees something worthwhile in her and understands the depth of her pain. Over the next few months he continues to care for her—and continues to endure her insults. After Tracy discovers that she is pregnant she tells Ben she intends to have an abortion. He demands that she not do it. "It's my baby. . . . If you do that you can forget all about me," he threatens.

Tracy does have the abortion. She returns, looking tired, and crosses to the couch where Ben is sitting. She sits, "not close to him." She asks him if he hates her. He responds by asking her why she tries to make him hate her. She denies that she does, but he pushes her for an answer. She replies with a story about her childhood.

....

TRACY: When you were little did your parents always keep giving you these animals and things, like they thought you looked like you had to have something to be grabbing onto all the time or you'd fall over or blow away or something? Well, don't look at me like that. Listen, if you don't want to hear this I can just leave, if you think this is stupid or something. I mean, you asked me a question and now I'm going to answer it, whether you like it or not. So my parents kept giving me these animals, see, not just like cats and dogs but also a pregnant racoon and two ducks named Mickey and a deflowered skunk and a chicken named Arnold and all kinds of things like that. They were really dumb. Not the animals, my parents. Well, you know how dumb they are. And the house we lived in was too close to the road, and what happens when you live too close is that all of your animals get splattered always on the road, and your brothers are always having to go out with a shovel and scrape them off and take them someplace to bury. And sometimes if they're all squashed but not quite dead your brother has to hit them with the shovel until they stop screaming or quacking or squawking or whining or meowing as the case may be. And giving them names makes it worse but I loved to and I couldn't help it and I did and when they got squashed then it wasn't just the cat or the duck it was somebody with a name that you'd lived with and slept with and talked at and listened to and fussed over and took care of and accepted you and then it was the mess that was left on the road. And after the last one was squashed which was a small bowlegged Persian kitten named Clarence aged six months who was sort of dumb and loved me a lot and never wanted any more than to just be alive and play with some piece of string or something, after that last one I made my stupid parents promise me they would never get me another thing that was alive because I had figured out what was true and still is true that there is no excuse and no way ever to make up for the millions and millions and millions of innocent betrayed and squashed up dead, and nobody's parents and nobody's God was ever going to be able to explain that to me and make it all right, and the only way not to go crazy if you had the misfortune to be a compulsive namer and lover was if you never hooked yourself up with splatterable things then it can never be your fault for needing them and having them because if you don't give you can't hurt and you don't get guilty because you can't betray if you never gave to begin with. Doesn't that make sense to you? It does make sense. It does.

EAT YOUR HEART OUT

by Nick Hall

ACT II

The scenes of this play take place in various restaurants in Manhattan. It is now winter. A woman has entered the restaurant and started up a conversation with Charlie, the waiter, and a young man at a nearby table (he is referred to as "Boy," but is described as in his late twenties). The woman is over 40 and described as "stout, puffing unhealthily with some respiratory problem. She wears thick lensed glasses. Although she lacks taste and is not spectacularly dressed, her wealth shows, when she takes off her mittens and scarf, in a couple of very large diamond rings and, possibly, a necklace or earrings or broach." She is smoking and is drinking tea. She has asked the young man his sign and he has told her his birthday.

(To use as a monologue, omit the Boy's lines.)

....

WOMAN: (*Nods.*) Gemini. (*Pause.*) I was born at exactly midnight on April nineteenth or twentieth, depending how you look at it. And it's been a terrible problem. I was born on the cusp.

BOY: Hunh?

WOMAN: The cusp. That means I'm between Aries and Taurus. Between a ram and a bull. It's very awkward.

BOY: Yeah. (*The* WOMAN *sips her tea and smokes. The* MAN *reads. The* BOY *smokes and drinks coffee.* CHARLIE *mops.*)

WOMAN: Every morning down at the office, during coffee break, they'd read the horoscopes, and they'd ask me what I was and I'd say, "I'm on the cusp." After a while they didn't ask me anymore. They gave up. After they'd had their little jokes like saying, "my cusp runneth over," they stopped. I pretended I wasn't interested, but I was. I wanted to know my fortune just like the rest of them. There were four other girls at the office and they were all Virgos. Well, Elsie Flemming wasn't a Virgo, but at least she wasn't on the cusp. The other girls were all married, but not me. Well, Elsie Flemming wasn't married either, but she went out a lot. The thing is, they got married by following the advice in the horoscope. How could I do that? Under Aries it would say, "Romance finally comes out from its elusive hiding and is within reach;" and under Taurus, "Be careful not to add new dimensions to what is already a satisfactory relationship;" so when Ernie who ran the Seven-Eleven superette at the corner, asked me to go with him on his bowling team's annual picnic, what could I do? There I was caught on the horns of a dilemma, or, in this case, the horns of a ram and a bull. Well, I worried over that decision till I was all over red blotches, and Ernie didn't want to take me anyway. So there I was with my nerves gone and all over red blotches and the girl who did my hair was away that week and a new girl did it and made a mess. I was so upset, I went right off my food, and Mother, who's a Libra, said I'd pine away. That's when I came across this book—*An Astrological Guide to Diet*—so I bought it. Well, nowhere under either Aries or Taurus is there anything recommended for red blotches. But they did have good dietary tips for each. And so, being on the cusp, I followed both. For example, for Aries you should eat lots of liver, kidneys, raw nuts, apricots, mushrooms and navy beans. And be sure and drink plenty of herb tea. And for Taurus, who need extra iodine, they should have wheat germ, peppermint, buckwheat pancakes, lamb, avocados and spinach juice. (*Beat.*) So I did all that. Well, the red blotches didn't go away and I got fat. By this time even Ernie's assistant, Rodriguez, wasn't interested in me. But somewhere, I vowed, somewhere in the stars there was an answer for me. So I read and read everything about astrology and made notes on it, trying to find out what to do, if you're caught between a ram and a bull. There was no answer. Romance stayed in its elusive hiding. I ruined my eyes with so much reading and now I have to wear these thick, corrective lenses, and the joints in my right thumb and forefinger enlarged from making all those notes. And I'm still fat and have red blotches and Ernie ... (*Trails off momentarily.*) But there is hope in the stars. I never gave up that belief. And now that I'm a fat, arthritic, blotchy, bespectacled, old maid, I still won't give it up. Finally I knew so much about astrology, I was asked to do the horoscope for a little newspaper. So I did. Well, strangely enough, my column became syndicated. (*Fingering her jewelry in bitter triumph.*) And now I know. Even for those born on the cusp, there is a fortune in the stars. (*Pause.*) How much for the tea, love?

THE FACULTY LOUNGE

by Michael Schulman

SCENE 1

The play consists of a series of short scenes, all taking place in the faculty lounge of a small New England high school. It is the first day of school and the clock reads 8:15 AM, just before classes are to begin. Linda, a teacher, enters. She takes a moment to decide whether to make a phone call, then does. She is calling her ex-husband, Richard, with whom she has just spent the night. They had a lovely time and Linda, who was the one who initiated the breakup of the marriage, now thinks that she wants Richard back. She soon learns that that isn't going to happen easily.

....

LINDA: It's me. I'm sorry I made such a fuss this morning. I know I called you a dickhead, but I was hurt. Well, after we had such a nice weekend and such a really swell time in the shower this morning, I was angry that you were busy tonight. (*Cutting him off to repeat what he's saying, as if she's heard it a hundred times.*) Yes. Yes. I know. We're not married anymore and I have no right to make demands on you. Yes. And *you* didn't divorce me. *I* divorced you. I know. I know. But now I want you back. So, I changed my mind. You used to say that's what attracted you to me— my whimsy. Why do I want you back? A tough one. Let's see. (*Not seriously.*) Because you make a really great omelet, that's why. That omelet this morning had just the right amount of cheese and . . . Yes. I know. I never take anything seriously. (*Heavenward.*) God, tell my why I had to fall in love with someone so tedious and boring—and why twice, God? (*To Richard.*) Only kidding. Do you accept my apology for this morning? Good. Wait. Talk to me. It's always a little depressing the first day of school. Sure I know there are worse jobs—like being a taxi cab driver or a proctologist. But, still, it's a little depressing on the first day. Well, at least they painted the hallways over the summer. Mucus green, of course. Oh, and listen to this: The semester hasn't even begun and our local book burners have already descended on the library. They're purging the new acquisitions. Yes, I saw them there as I came in. Diligent little, self-righteous bastards. The only book they approved of last year was the *Mobil Travel Guide to the Southwest.* Tell me I'm living a useful life, that forcing Keats and Shelley down the throats of ninth graders is keeping the world safe for democracy or something. Come on. Wait. I have only three more minutes before I have to greet the darlings. How's the writing coming? What does "not bad" mean? A page? No. A paragraph? Hmm. (*Repeating.*) You have all the words but you're still not sure of the order to put them in. Clever. Not original, but clever. It really has been hard for you lately, hasn't it? Don't worry, you'll pull out of it. You're a good writ . . . What's that? What's that? My little friend, did I just hear a woman's voice in the background? Huh? Hey, I'm talking to you—you! The once sensitive and no longer young poet I married and divorced. (*Southern accent.*) I take it from your silence, Sir, (*Own voice, harshly.*) that I did just hear a woman's voice in the background. Yes, that's right: You don't have to explain your comings and goings to me anymore. Is that what this call interrupted— some imminent comings and goings? I left you at 7:45. It's now 8:10. What time did she arrive? God, if I had wanted 8-minute eggs this morning I would have screwed up your whole schedule. I can just picture the three of us slurping our yolks together in your cheery little breakfast nook. You bastard! I'll bet you're making *her* an omelet, too. Well, I guess it simply is not true what they say about the best laid plans of men and rats. What timing. They could schedule the trains in Switzerland around your hard-ons. And to think I was feeling sorry for you for having writer's block. What's the matter? A smart guy like you should be able to write and fuck at the same time. You wait one second, Richard. There's one more thing I have to say to you before you hang up. (*Can't find what she wants to say, so.*) DICK-HEAD!

(*LINDA hangs up.*)

WHISKEY

by Terrence McNally

The Lush Thrushes is a cowboy singing group on the most popular television show in the country and each member of the group is named after his or her favorite liquor. They have just had a disastrous live appearance at the Astrodome and are now in their hotel room, licking their wounds and getting drunk. Southern Comfort, a very sexy young woman, has just persuaded Jack Daniels to have sex with her. But just as they are getting into it, she pulls away and reveals that she is frigid and can't have a climax. He's all for proceeding anyway, but she goes on to explain the reason for her sorry condition.

(To use as a monologue, leave out Jack Daniels's lines.)

....

SOUTHERN COMFORT: There's something about me you don't know.

JACK DANIELS: Can't it wait?

SOUTHERN COMFORT: It's too important.

JACK DANIELS: Go ahead then.

SOUTHERN COMFORT: I'm frigid, Johnny.

JACK DANIELS: I don't mind.

SOUTHERN COMFORT: I can't have a climax. I can lie there and go through the motions but I can't have a climax.

JACK DANIELS: That's okay, too.

SOUTHERN COMFORT: It's not a very pretty story. I grew up right here in Houston. I was pretty, I was the national champion baton twirler and I only dated football players. Sound familiar? The typical American girl. The first boy I went all the way with was Bobby Barton. Bobby was the state champion high school quarterback and since I was a champion, too, only a national one, it was pretty natural that we should get together. It was in the back seat of his daddy's Ford Fairlane on our eleventh date. Remember them? They were two-toned with a chrome trim that made kind of a dip along the door. Anyway, I really enjoyed it and Bobby did, too. I started going all the way with him on every date we had. Gee, it was swell. Then one day after school during football practice somebody tackled Bobby and he just didn't get up. I mean he was dead. So then I started dating Bobby's best friend, Terry Walsh, who played right guard and who'd been the one who'd accidentally killed Bobby when he tackled him during practice that time. I went all the way with him on the fourth date. He had a sports car, a reptile-green MG, so we had to spread blankets on the ground first. Terry got killed during the game with Lubbock for the state quarter finals down in Austin. Spontaneous concussion. My senior year at Sunset I started dating and going all the way with Tiny Walker, who played left end and who used to be Terry and Bobby's real good friend. He drove a blood-red, chopped down Plymouth Fury with dual carburetors and two front seats that you could make go flat down like a dentist's chair. Tiny was small but powerful and he'd been tackled lots of times by bruisers a whole lot bigger than that linebacker from Sweetwater. But when Tiny died like that I stopped dating football players. I felt like a jinx on 'em, you know what I mean? And I knew people were starting to say things about me behind my back. I stopped twirling, started drinking, got to hate Houston so much I couldn't stand it here any longer, ran away from home and got into show business. Now I sleep around a lot, but only with musicians; they don't die on you like football players. (*A pause.*) I told you it wasn't a very pretty story.

IVANOV
by ANTON CHEKHOV

translated by Ann Dunnigan

ACT I

Anna Petrovna married Nikolai Alekseyevich Ivanov five years ago when he was an exciting, idealistic young man. She still loves him but he has plunged into a deep depression and now neglects her, just as he neglects his estate. Now he spends his time complaining about everything and feeling sorry for himself, confused about why his emotional life has deteriorated so precipitously. Anna Petrovna gave up her family and religion to marry Nikolai (she was Jewish), and now feels lost and alone. He has gone out for the evening, as he does most evenings, and has told her, apologetically, that when he is depressed he does not feel love for her.

Anna Petrovna is sick and has been coughing. Her sympathetic young doctor, Lvov, has not had the heart to tell her that she is dying, but she can sense that her illness is serious and yearns to recapture the joy and love she once knew. As Anna Petrovna and Lvov talk in the garden, they hear the song "Greenfinch" coming from the kitchen where the servants are having a party. Lvov, who is appalled by the behavior of Nikolai and others in his family, can't understand how Anna Petrovna, "an intelligent, honest, almost saintly woman" has allowed herself to be "so brazenly deceived and dragged into this owl's nest." Anna, feeling melancholy, recalls something said earlier.

(To use as a monologue, omit Lvov's lines and Anna's next to last speech.)

....

ANNA PETROVNA: The flowers return in the spring, but not the joy. Who said that to me? Why can't I remember? . . . I think it was Nikolai himself who said it. *(Listens.)* The owl is screeching again!

LVOV: Well, let it screech.

ANNA PETROVNA: I am beginning to think that fate has cheated me, Doctor. There are a great many people, perhaps no better than I, who are happy without having had to pay for their happiness. But I have paid for everything, absolutely everything! . . . And so dearly! Why should I have had to pay such terribly high interest? . . . My dear friend, you are always so considerate of me, so tactful, you are afraid to tell me the truth, but do you think I don't know what my illness is? I know perfectly well. However, it's boring to talk about it . . . *(With a Jewish accent.)* 'Shcuse plees! Can you tell funny stories?

LVOV: No, I can't.

ANNA PETROVNA: Nikolai can . . . I am beginning to be amazed at the unfairness of people; why do they not respond to love with love, and why should truth be answered with lies? Tell me: how long will my father and mother go on hating me? They live about fifty versts from here, but I can feel their hatred day and night, even in my sleep. And what am I to make of Nikolai's depression? He says it's only in the evening that he doesn't love me, when he feels depressed. I understand that, I think it's probably true, but suppose he has stopped loving me altogether! Of course, that's impossible, but—what if he has! No, no, I mustn't even think of it. *(Sings.)* "Greenfinch, greenfinch, where have you been?" *(Shudders.)* What frightening thoughts I have! . . . You have no family of your own, Doctor, and there are a great many things you can't understand. . . .

LVOV: You are amazed. . . . *(Sits down beside her.)* No, it's I who am amazed, amazed at you! Now, explain it to me, help me to understand: how is it that you, an intelligent, honest, almost saintly woman, have allowed yourself to be so brazenly deceived and dragged into this owl's nest? Why are you here? What have you got in common with that cold, heartless—but let's leave your husband out of it—what have you in common with this futile, vulgar environment? Oh, my God! . . . That perpetually grumbling, moth-eaten, lunatic count, that thorough fraud and swindler, Misha, with his hideous face? Explain it to me, what are you doing here? How did you ever come to be here?

ANNA PETROVNA: (*Laughs.*) You're talking exactly the way he used to talk . . . exactly. . . . Only his eyes are larger, and when he spoke with passion about anything, they glowed like coals. . . . Go on, go on talking!

LVOV: (*Gets up with a gesture of impatience.*) What's the use? Please go on. . . .

ANNA PETROVNA: You say that Nikolai is this or that, one thing and another. How can you know him? Is it possible to know a man in six months? That is a remarkable man, Doctor, and I am sorry you didn't know him two or three years ago. Now he's depressed, he doesn't talk, he doesn't do anything, but then . . . how fascinating he was! I fell in love with him at first sight. (*Laughs.*) I just looked at him and the trap was sprung! He said: come . . . and I cut myself off from everything; it was just like cutting off dead leaves with a scissors, and I went. . . . (*Pause.*) But now it's different. . . . Now he goes to the Lebedevs' to amuse himself with other women, and I . . . I sit in the garden and listen to the owl screech.

TWELFTH NIGHT; OR, WHAT YOU WILL

by William Shakespeare

ACT II, SCENE 2

Viola washed up on an unfamiliar shore after the ship she was traveling in sunk in a storm. Afraid of what might happen to her as an unprotected young woman in a strange land, she disguised herself as a man, called herself Cesario, and found employment in the service of the handsome Duke Orsino, with whom she immediately fell in love. But Orsino loves the beautiful Countess Olivia, who has refused all his overtures. He has sent Viola with a message of love to Olivia, but Olivia remains unmoved and Viola heads back to the Duke. Soon Malvolio, Olivia's steward, catches up with her and tries to give her a ring that Olivia said "he" (Viola) left behind. Viola denies leaving the ring and refuses to take it. Malvolio tosses it on the ground and departs. Viola soon realizes that something totally unexpected has happened.

(See other scene from this play in another section for more information.)

....

VIOLA: I left no ring with her: what means this lady?
       Fortune forbid my outside have not charm'd her!
       She made good view of me; indeed, so much,
       That methought her eyes had lost her tongue,
       For she did speak in starts distractedly.
       She loves me, sure; the cunning of her passion
       Invites me in this churlish messenger.

None of my lord's ring! why, he sent her none.
I am the man: if it be so, as 'tis,
Poor lady, she were better love a dream.
Disguise, I see, thou art a wickedness,
Wherein the pregnant enemy does much.
How easy is it for the proper-false
In women's waxen hearts to set their forms!
Alas, our frailty is the cause, not we!
For such as we are made of, such we be.
How will this fadge? my master loves her dearly;
And I, poor monster, fond as much on him;
And she, mistaken, seems to dote on me.
What will become of this? As I am man,
My state is desperate for my master's love;
As I am woman,—now alas the day!—
What thriftless sighs shall poor Olivia breathe!
O time! thou must untangle this, not I;
It is too hard a knot for me to untie!

THE TWO GENTLEMEN OF VERONA

by William Shakespeare

ACT I, SCENE 2

Julia's waiting-woman Lucetta has brought her a letter from Proteus, the young man she secretly loves. But Julia, impetuous and headstrong, does not want to appear interested in Proteus. So she tears the letter into pieces, throws them to the ground, and tells Lucetta to leave her alone. Lucetta, who thinks that Proteus is quite a catch, does not understand Julia's reaction and, as she departs, remarks that Julia would be better off if her anger were directed at another letter rather than this one. Alone, Julia acknowledges that she is not at all angry at the letter, and, eager to know what the letter says, proceeds to piece it back together.

....

JULIA: Nay, would I were so anger'd with the same!
      O hateful hands, to tear such loving words!
      Injurious wasps, to feed on such sweet honey,
      And kill the bees, that yield it, with your stings!
      I'll kiss each several paper for amends.
      Look, here is writ 'kind Julia.' Unkind Julia!
      As in revenge of thy ingratitude,
      I throw thy name against the bruising stones,
      Trampling contemptuously on thy disdain.
      And here is writ 'love-wounded Proteus.'
      Poor wounded name! my bosom, as a bed,
      Shall lodge thee, till thy wound be throughly heal'd;

And thus I search it with a sovereign kiss.
But twice or thrice was 'Proteus' written down.
Be calm, good wind, blow not a word away,
Till I have found each letter in the letter,
Except mine own name: that some whirlwind bear
Unto a ragged, fearful-hanging rock,
And throw it thence into the raging sea!
Lo, here in one line is his name twice writ,
'Poor forlorn Proteus, passionate Proteus,
To the sweet Julia':—that I'll tear away.—
And yet I will not, sith so prettily
He couples it to his complaining names.
Thus will I fold them one upon another:
Now kiss, embrace, contend, do what you will.

ROMEO AND JULIET

by William Shakespeare

ACT II, SCENE 2

*The family feud between the Montagues and the Capulets,
two prominent families of Verona, has reached the point
where the Prince has threatened severe punishment to
members of either family who disturb the peace of the city.
Romeo is a Montague and Juliet is a Capulet, but they fell
in love instantly upon their meeting earlier in the evening
at a huge masked banquet thrown by Juliet's father for his
friends and family (Romeo and his companions went uninvited). After the party, Romeo, to get away from his companions who have been teasing him, climbs over a wall and
discovers that he is in Capulet's garden. He sees Juliet on
her balcony and overhears her rhapsodizing about her love
for him. He declares that he loves her too (startling her)
and soon the lovers exchange vows.*

*In the following speech, Juliet explains to Romeo that
ordinarily she would not have revealed her love so quickly,
but now there is no sense denying her feelings since he has
already heard what is in her heart.*

....

JULIET: Thou know'st the mask of night is on my face,
   Else would a maiden blush bepaint my cheek
   For that which thou hast heard me speak to-night.
   Fain would I dwell on form, fain, fain deny
   What I have spoke: but farewell compliment!
   Dost thou love me? I know thou wilt say "Ay,"

And I will take thy word: yet, if thou swear'st,
Thou mayst prove false: at lovers' perjuries,
They say, Jove laughs. O gentle Romeo,
If thou dost love, pronounce it faithfully:
Or if thou think'st I am too quickly won,
I'll frown and be perverse and say thee nay,
So thou wilt woo; but else, not for the world.
In truth, fair Montague, I am too fond;
And therefore thou mayst think my 'haviour light:
But trust me, gentleman, I'll prove more true
Than those that have more cunning to be strange.
I should have been more strange, I must confess,
But that thou overheard'st, ere I was ware,
My true love's passion: therefore pardon me,
And not impute this yielding to light love,
Which the dark night hath so discovered.

A MIDSUMMER-NIGHT'S DREAM

by William Shakespeare

ACT III, SCENE 2

Lysander and Demetrius both love Hermia, and Hermia loves Lysander. Hermia's best friend Helena loves Demetrius, but he has no interest in her. Hermia's father insists that she marry Demetrius, so she and Lysander conspire to meet in the woods and elope. Helena passes the information on to Demetrius, hoping he will switch his affections to her. Instead, Demetrius takes off to the woods to prevent Hermia's and Lysander's marriage, and Helena follows after him. In a mixup, a wood sprite anoints both Lysander's and Demetrius's eyes with a love potion and both men fall madly in love with Helena. Hermia doesn't understand why Lysander has turned away from her, and Helena thinks all three have conspired to make fun of her.

....

HELENA: Lo, she is one of this confederacy!
Now I perceive they have conjoin'd all three
To fashion this false sport, in spite of me.
Injurious Hermia! most ungrateful maid!
Have you conspired, have you with these
    contrived
To bait me with this foul derision?
Is all the counsel that we two have shared,
The sister's vows, the hours that we have spent,
When we have chid the hasty-footed time
For parting us,—O, is all forgot?

All school-days' friendship, childhood innocence?
We, Hermia, like two artificial gods,
Have with our needles created both one flower,
Both on one sampler, sitting on one cushion,
Both warbling of one song, both in one key;
As if our hands, our sides, voices, and minds,
Had been incorporate. So we grew together,
Like to a double cherry, seeming parted,
But yet an union in partition;
Two lovely berries moulded on one stem;
So, with two seeming bodies, but one heart;
Two of the first, like coats in heraldry,
Due but to one, and crowned with one crest.
And will you rent our ancient love asunder,
To join with men in scorning your poor friend?
It is not friendly, 'tis not maidenly:
Our sex, as well as I, may chide you for it,
Though I alone do feel the injury.

THE WINTER'S TALE

by William Shakespeare

ACT II, SCENE 2

Leontes, King of Sicilia, obsessed by his belief that his wife, Hermione, has betrayed him with his close friend, and that the young princess is not really his daughter, orders the child abandoned in a deserted place and sets up a public trial to expose Hermione's perfidy. At the trial the king is unmoved by Hermione's protestations of her innocence and he refuses to accept the findings of the oracle of Apollo that his wife is chaste and his daughter truly his. Nor does he heed the warning from the oracle that he shall live without an heir until the lost daughter is found. As the raging king declares the oracle false and demands that the trial proceed, word comes that his beloved son has died. Hermione, unable to bear this new grief, collapses in a deathlike swoon. She is taken off by Paulina, a lady of the court and her friend, with the help of other attendants.

The death of his son brings Leontes to his senses and he vows to make amends, but Paulina returns brimming over with anguish and rage, which she directs at the king.

(To use as a monologue, omit all but Paulina's lines.)

....

PAULINA: Woe the while!
              O, cut my lace, lest my heart, cracking it,
              Break too!
FIRST LORD: What fit is this, good lady?

PAULINA: What studied torments, tyrant, hast for me?
           What wheels? racks? fires? what flaying?
              boiling?
           In leads or oils? what old or newer torture
           Must I receive, whose every word deserves
           To taste of thy most worst? Thy tyranny
           Together working with thy jealousies,
           Fancies too weak for boys, too green and idle
           For girls of nine, O, think what they have
              done
           And then run mad indeed, stark mad! for all
           Thy by-gone fooleries were but spices of it.
           That thou betray'dst Polixenes, 'twas nothing;
           That did but show thee, of a fool, inconstant
           And damnable ingrateful: nor was 't much,
           Thou wouldst have poison'd good Camillo's
              honour
           To have him kill a king; poor trespasses,
           More monstrous standing by: whereof I reckon
           The casting forth to crows thy baby-daughter
           To be or none or little; though a devil
           Would have shed water out of fire ere done 't:
           Nor is 't directly laid to thee, the death
           Of the young prince, whose honourable
              thoughts,
           Thoughts high for one so tender, cleft the
              heart
           That could conceive a gross and foolish sire
           Blemish'd his gracious dam: this is not, no,
           Laid to thy answer: but the last,—O lords,
           When I have said, cry "woe!"—the queen,
              the queen,
           The sweet'st, dear'st creature's dead, and
              vengeance for 't
           Not dropp'd down yet.
FIRST LORD: The higher powers forbid!
PAULINA: I say she's dead, I'll swear 't. If word nor
              oath
           Prevail not, go and see: if you can bring
           Tincture or lustre in her lip, her eye,
           Heat outwardly or breath within, I'll serve you

As I would do the gods. But, O thou tyrant!
Do not repent these things, for they are
   heavier
Than all thy woes can stir: therefore betake
   thee
To nothing but despair. A thousand knees
Ten thousand years together, naked, fasting,
Upon a barren mountain, and still winter
In storm perpetual, could not move the gods
To look that way thou wert.

MONOLOGUES FOR MEN

UNCLE VANYA
by ANTON CHEKHOV

translated by Ann Dunnigan

ACT I

Mikhail Lvovich Astrov is a country doctor, filled with passion and ideals. He has come to attend to Aleksandr Vladimirovich Serebryakov, an elderly professor who has returned to his country estate with his beautiful, intelligent young wife, Elena. The professor had been ill, but is feeling better today, and Astrov, who had planned to stay the night, was just told by a workman that he is needed to treat someone at the factory. He is perturbed that he must leave so quickly and sends the workman to get him a glass of vodka. It is clear that Elena and Astrov are attracted to each other and are enjoying each other's conversation and company. She has asked him about his great interest in preserving the forests of Russia, and Voinitsky (Uncle Vanya) has engaged in some friendly mockery by asserting that he must still "go on heating my stoves with logs and building my barns with wood." Astrov replies.

(See other scene from this play in another section for more information.)

....

ASTROV: You can heat your stoves with peat and build your barns with brick. Now I could accept the cutting of wood out of need, but why devastate the forests? The Russian forests are groaning under the ax, millions of trees are being destroyed, the dwellings of wild beasts and birds are despoiled, rivers are subsiding, drying up, wonderful landscapes vanish never to return, and all because lazy man hasn't sense enough to stoop down and pick up fuel from the ground. (*To ELENA ANDREYEVNA.*) Isn't that true, my lady? One would have to be a reckless barbarian to burn this beauty in his stove, to destroy what he cannot create. Man is endowed with reason and creative powers so that he may increase what has been given to him, but up to now he has not created but only destroyed. There are fewer and fewer forests, rivers are drying up, wild life is becoming extinct, the climate is ruined, and every day the earth gets poorer and uglier. (*To VOINITSKY.*) You give me that ironical look of yours, what I say doesn't seem very serious to you, and . . . and maybe I am just a crank, but when I walk by a peasant's woodland which I have saved from being cut down, or when I hear the rustling of young trees which I have planted with my own hands, I realize that the climate is somewhat in my power, and that if, a thousand years from now, mankind is happy, I shall be responsible for that too, in a small way. When I plant a birch tree and then watch it put forth its leaves and sway in the wind, my soul is filled with pride, and I . . . (*Seeing the workman who has brought a glass of vodka on a tray.*) however . . . (*Drinks.*) Time for me to go. All that is very likely my eccentricity, after all.

THE THREE SISTERS
by ANTON CHEKHOV

---

translated by Ann Dunnigan

ACT IV

Like his sisters, Andrei Sergeyevich Prozorov is unhappy with his life. He was a young man of great potential, with dreams of becoming a scientist and professor. Instead, he has become a bureaucrat on the District Board, is dominated by his vulgar wife, and has had to mortgage the family home to pay off gambling debts. He has even alienated his sisters, who once doted on him. In the following scene, he is walking in the garden, pondering his life as he pushes a baby carriage. He is followed by Ferapont, a porter for the District Board, who has been trying to get him to sign some papers.

....

ANDREI: Oh, where is it, where has it all gone, my past, when I was young, gay, clever, when I dreamed and thought with grace, when my present and my future were lighted up with hope? Why is it that when we have barely begun to live, we grow dull, gray, uninteresting, lazy, indifferent, useless, unhappy.... Our town has been in existence now for two hundred years, there are a hundred thousand people in it, and not one who isn't exactly like all the others, not one saint, either in the past or in the present, not one scholar, not one artist, no one in the least remarkable who could inspire envy or a passionate desire to imitate him.... They just eat, drink, sleep, and then die ... others are born and they, too, eat, drink, sleep, and to keep from being stupefied by boredom, they relieve the monotony of life with their odious gossip, with vodka, cards, chicanery, and the wives deceive their husbands, while the husbands lie and pretend not to see or hear anything, and an overwhelmingly vulgar influence weighs on the children, the divine spark is extinguished in them, and they become the same pitiful, identical corpses as their fathers and mothers. . . . (*Angrily, to* FERA-PONT.) What do you want?

CONVERSATIONS WITH MY FATHER

by Herb Gardner

ACT II

Eddie Goldberg is a Jewish immigrant who left Russia with his father when he was ten years old and who now owns a bar in lower Manhattan. Eddie has been trying hard to put the old world behind him and become a success in America. This scene takes place in July 1944 during the last year of World War II. Eddie's son Joey is eighteen, bright and attractive, and an up-and-coming boxer. Eddie is frantic because Joey didn't show up for his big fight tonight (which Eddie and the bar patrons learned about when they tuned in the fight on the radio).

Before Joey left for the fight, accompanied by his younger brother Charlie, he was troubled by a story in the Jewish newspaper, The Forward, *about the number of Jews being killed by the Nazis. Eddie tried to downplay the story, arguing that if it were true it would be in* Life *magazine and President Roosevelt would be "doing something about it this* minute, guaranteed!''

Eddie assumes something terrible has happened to Joey (whom he loves dearly), otherwise he would never have missed the fight. As he is about to telephone Bimmy's boxing gym, Joey bursts into the bar, followed by Charlie. In the following monologue, Joey explains why he didn't show up for the match.

(To use as a monologue, omit all but Joey's lines.)

JOEY: (*Moving towards him.*) Please, ya gotta be quiet, Pop. That's maybe two thousand just while I'm workin' out. Seventeen thousand five hundred a day. No, it's impossible, I figure; Pop's *right*, it's nuts. I keep punchin' the bag. I come back to pick up Charlie, we're headin' over, not Seven yet; then I hear people hollerin', I look up, I see it. Top of *The Forward* buildin', tallest damn buildin' around here, there's the ''Jewish Daily Forward'' sign, y'know, big, maybe thirty feet high and wide as the buildin', electric bulbs, ya can see it even deep into Brooklyn, *forever*, Pop. What they did is they took out the right bulbs, exactly the right bulbs, gotta be hundreds of 'em, so instead of ''Jewish Daily Forward'' the sign says: ''Jew is For War''; it's Goddamn blazin' over the city, Pop, and Charlie and me start runnin' towards it, we're still maybe eight blocks away, we're passin' alotta people and kids on Canal, pointin' up, laughin', some cheerin', ''Son of a *bitch*, son of a *bitch*, we fight the *war* and the Jews get *rich*,'' a guy grabs my arm, smilin', musta seen me box, guy my age, he says, ''Pete, Pete, let's go get us some Yids, Pete!'' and I know that second for sure they are doin' seventeen thousand five hundred a day, somewhere, seventeen thousand five hundred a day and I'm a guy spends his time boppin' kids for a silver-plated watch from Big Mike, hockable for fifteen dollars; right now I wouldn't hock me for a dime. Point is, I'm goin' in, Pop. I'm gettin' into this war and I need your help, now. (*EDDIE is silent.*) Army don't register me till next month, then it could be a year, more, before they call me. *Navy*, Pop, Navy's the game; they take ya at seventeen with a parent's consent. Eight AM tomorrow I'm at Ninety Church, I pick up the consent form, you fill it out, sign it, ten days later Boot Camp at Lake Geneva, September I'm in it, Pop. Korvette, Destroyer, Sub chaser, whatever, in the Goddamn thing.

EDDIE: (*After a moment.*) Your mother will never—

JOEY: I just need you, Pop. One parent. One signature. (*Silence for a moment.*) Do me a favor; take a look outside. Just turn left and look at the sky.

SAY GOODNIGHT, GRACIE

by Ralph Pape

Steve and other friends are gathered in Jerry and Ginny's apartment, planning to attend their high school reunion later in the evening. As they wait for the time to leave, they chat, joke, and get high. The discussion wanders into many areas and when one of the group mentions the movie 2001, Steve is reminded of Laura, the girl he saw the movie with. He was in love with her and went out with her for about a year. Jerry remembers receiving a letter from Steve that he intended to ask Laura to marry him and Steve describes what happened after that.

(To use as a monologue omit Ginny's lines.)

....

STEVE: Right, right—it was a pure Hollywood ending. I mean, our last day together. The final scene. In the rain, no less. And her telling me with tears in her eyes that I was living in this fantasy world. Right? Now, you have to picture this: the rain, the two of us standing together on the sidewalk, not moving, just looking at each other, in close-up, the camera cutting back and forth between our faces. This warm Spring rain . . .

GINNY: *(Shutting her eyes.)* Yes, I can see it!

STEVE: *(He's having fun, still in control, the Movie Director—but as he continues, it is clear that the memory controls him.)* And then she said goodbye, and turned, and walked away. And as I watched her, I could feel the camera pulling back for a long shot ...

GINNY: (*With eyes still closed.*) I can see it.

STEVE: ... and I felt her about to become a memory and I remembered watching her walking with her friends, it was like a slow-motion flashback you know, in the rain, or singing, the wind blowing her hair ... and I ran after her and I held her shoulders and ... I turned her around and I said to her: the very first time I saw you, you were walking in the rain, I saw you from a window in the library, and you were soaked and you looked so helpless, the leaves were all over you, and even though I didn't know who you were, I wanted to take off my coat and put it around you, which you would never have let me do, but I thought at that moment ... that it would have been possible not to be afraid of anything ... if only I could place my coat around someone I loved ... and pretend that I could protect her ... I just wanted to tell you that ...

THE HOUSE OF BLUE LEAVES

by John Guare

ACT II

Ronnie needs attention and he's going to get it by blowing up the Pope when he visits New York later today. He is eighteen, "his hair is cropped close and he wears big glasses. He wears a heavy army overcoat and under that a suit of army fatigue clothes." He is in his father's apartment and stares out at the audience. "He takes two hand grenades out of the pockets of his fatigues, wire, his father's alarm clock. He wires them together, setting the alarm on the clock" and puts the whole device into a gift box.

....

RONNIE: My father tell you all about me? Pope Ronnie? Charmed life? How great I am? That's how he is with you. You should hear him with me, you'd sing a different tune pretty quick, and it wouldn't be "Where Is the Devil in Evelyn?"
(He goes into his room and returns carrying a large, dusty box. He opens it and takes out an altar boy's bright red cassock and white surplice that used to fit him when he was twelve. As he puts them on, he speaks to us.)

I was twelve years old and all the newspapers had headlines on my twelfth birthday that Billy was coming to town. And *Life* was doing stories on him and *Look* and the newsreels, because Billy was searching America to find the Ideal American Boy to play Huckleberry Finn. And Billy came to New York and called my father and asked him if he could stay here—Billy needed a hide-out. In Waldorf Astorias all over the country, chambermaids would wheel silver carts to change the sheets. And out of the sheets would hop little boys saying, "Hello, I'm Huckleberry Finn." All over the country, little boys dressed in blue jeans and straw hats would be sent to him in crates, be under the silver cover covering his dinner, in his medicine cabinet in all his hotel rooms, his suitcase—"Hello, Hello, I'm Huckleberry Finn." And he was coming here to hide out. Here—Billy coming here—I asked the nun in school who was Huckleberry Finn—

The nun in Queen of Martyrs knew. She told me. The Ideal American Boy. And coming home, all the store windows reflected me and the mirror in the tailor shop said, "Hello, Huck." The butcher shop window said, "Hello, Huck. Hello, Huckleberry Finn. All America Wants to Meet Billy and He'll Be Hiding Out in Your House." I came home—went in there—into my room and packed my bag . . . I knew Billy would see me and take me back to California with him that very day. This room smelled of ammonia and air freshener and these slipcovers were new that day and my parents were filling up the icebox in their brand-new clothes, filling up the icebox with food and liquor as excited as if the Pope was coming—and nervous because they hadn't seen him in a long while—Billy. They told me my new clothes were on my bed. To go get dressed. I didn't want to tell them I'd be leaving shortly to start a new life. That I'd be flying out to California with Billy on the H. M. S. Huckleberry. I didn't want tears from them—only trails of envy . . . I went to my room and packed my bag and waited.

The doorbell rang. (*He starts hitting two notes on the piano.*) If you listen close, you can still hear the echoes of those wet kisses and handshakes and tears and backs getting hit and Hello, Billys, Hello. They talked for a long time about people from their past. And then my father called out, "Ronnie, guess who? Billy, we named him after your father. Ronnie, guess who?"

I picked up my bag and said good-bye to myself in the mirror. Came out. Billy there. Smiling.

It suddenly dawned on me. You had to do things to get parts.

I began dancing. And singing. Immediately. Things I have never done in my life—before or since. I stood on my head and skipped and whirled—(*He cartwheels across the stage.*)—spectacular leaps in the air so I could see veins in the ceiling—ran up and down the keys of the piano and sang and began laughing and crying soft and loud to show off all my emotions. And I heard music and drums that I couldn't even keep up with. And then cut off all my emotions just like that. Instantly. And took a deep bow like the Dying Swan I saw on Ed Sullivan. I picked up my suitcase and waited by the door.

Billy turned to my parents, whose jaws were down to about there, and Billy said, "You never told me you had a mentally retarded child."

"You never told me I had an idiot for a godchild," and I picked up my bag and went into my room and shut the door and never came out the whole time he was here.

My only triumph was he could never find a Huckleberry Finn. Another company made the picture a few years later, but it flopped.

My father thinks I'm nothing. Billy. My sergeant. They laugh at me. You laughing at me? I'm going to fool you all. By tonight, I'll be on headlines all over the world. Cover of *Time*, *Life*. TV specials. (*He shows a picture of himself on the wall.*) I hope they use this picture of me—I look better with hair—Go ahead—laugh. Because you know what I think of you? (*He gives us hesitant Bronx cheers.*) I'm sorry you had to hear that—pay seven or eight dollars to hear that. But I don't care. I'll show you all. I'll be too big for any of you.

A DELICATE BALANCE

by Edward Albee

ACT I

Tobias, about 60, is leading a comfortable life in his comfortable home with his devoted wife, Agnes. But Agnes doesn't always understand him. For example, she can't imagine why he is so indulgent with her alcoholic sister, Claire, who lives with them. Nor why he doesn't take a stronger role in the life of their daughter Julia, who is returning home again after her fourth divorce. Agnes and Claire have just raised issues about love and wishing someone dead, leading Tobias into recollections about a cat he had when he was a young man.

(To use as a monologue, omit Agnes's and Claire's lines and adjust for Tobias's responses to them.)

....

TOBIAS: The cat that I had . . . when I was—well, a year or so before I *met* you. She was very old; I'd had her since I was a kid; she must have been fifteen, or more. An alley cat. She didn't like people very much, I think; when (*AGNES crosses to L. chair.*) people came . . . she'd . . . pick up and walk away. She liked *me*; or, rather, when I was alone with her I could see she was content; she'd sit on my lap. I don't know if she was happy, but she was content.

AGNES: Yes.

TOBIAS: And how the thing happened I don't really know. She . . . one day she . . . well, one day I realized she no longer liked me. No, that's not right; one day I realized she must have stopped liking me some time before. One evening I was alone, home, and I was suddenly aware of her absence, not just that she wasn't in the room with *me*, but that she hadn't been, in rooms with me, watching me shave . . . just *about* . . . for . . . I couldn't place *how* long. She hadn't gone *away*, you understand; well, she *had*, but she hadn't run off. I knew she was *around*; I remembered I had caught sight of her—from time to time—under a chair, moving out of a room, but it was only when I realized something had happened that I could give any pattern to things that had . . . that I'd noticed. She didn't like me any more. It was that simple.

CLAIRE: Well, she was old.

TOBIAS: No, it wasn't that. She didn't like me any more. I tried to force myself on her.

AGNES: Whatever do you mean?

TOBIAS: I'd close her in a room with me; I'd pick her up, and I'd *make* her sit in my lap; I'd make her stay there when she didn't want to. But it didn't work; she'd abide it, but she'd get down when she could, go away.

CLAIRE: Maybe she was ill.

TOBIAS: No, she wasn't; I had her to the vet. She didn't like me any more. One night—I was *fixed* on it now—I had her in the room with me, and on my lap for the . . . the what, the fifth time the same evening, and she lay there, with her back to me, and she wouldn't purr, and I *knew*: I knew she was just waiting till she could get down, and I said, "Damn you, you like me; God damn it, you stop this! I haven't *done* anything to you." And I shook her; I had my hands around her shoulders, and I shook her . . . and she bit me; hard; and she hissed at me. And so I hit her. With my open hand, I hit her, smack, right across the head. I . . . I *hated* her!

AGNES: Did you hurt her badly?

TOBIAS: Yes; well, not badly; she . . . I must have hurt her ear some; she shook her head a lot for a day or so. And . . . you see, there was no *reason*. She and I had lived together and been, well, you know, friends, and . . . there was no *reason*. And I hated her for that. I hated her, well, I suppose because I was being accused of something, of . . . failing. But, I hadn't been cruel, by design; if I'd been neglectful, well, my life was . . . I resented it. I resented having a . . . being judged. Being *betrayed*.

CLAIRE: What did you do?

TOBIAS: I had *lived* with her; I had done . . . *everything*. And . . . and if there was a, any responsibility I'd failed in . . . well . . . there was nothing I could *do*. And, and I was being accused.

CLAIRE: Yes; what did you do?

TOBIAS: (*Defiance and self-loathing.*) I had her killed.

AGNES: (*Kindly correcting.*) You had her put to sleep. She was old. You had her put to sleep.

TOBIAS: (*Correcting.*) I had her killed. I took her to the vet and he took her . . . he took her into the back and (*Louder.*) he gave her an injection and killed her! I had her *killed*!

AGNES: (*After a pause.*) Well, what else could you have done? There was nothing to be done; there was no . . . meeting between you.

TOBIAS: I might have tried longer. I might have gone on, as long as cats live, the same way. I might have worn a hair shirt, locked myself in the house with her, done penance. For *something*. For *what*. God knows.

THE SUBSTANCE OF FIRE

by Jon Robin Baitz

ACT I

Isaac Geldhart's children are rising up against him, pooling their shares in the family publishing company to force him into retirement. He and his children are gathered for a meeting in his office where they tell him that the company can no longer pass up commercial manuscripts in order to publish the kinds of unprofitable literary and scholarly works that Isaac loves. Isaac is a Holocaust survivor who has built his life in the U.S. around great books—reading them, publishing them, cherishing them—and he has run the business with an autocratic hand. His children accuse him of being remote and imperious, more responsive to literature than to their feelings. In the following monologue, his son Martin, who teaches landscape architecture at Vassar, is telling Isaac that neither he nor books will dominate his life anymore.

(To use as a monologue, omit Isaac's lines.)

....

MARTIN: I counted my books last week. Do you know how many I have? Want to take a guess? (*No one says anything.*) Fourteen thousand, three hundred, and eighty-six. The sixty crates of books that Mom left me. Well, I finally had them carted up the Hudson, but I had to have shelves built. The whole house. Every room. And instead of just guessing—I was, I mean—speechless. A wreck of a life. It just flashed before my eyes. No sex, no people, just books 'til I die. Dickens. In *French*. The bastard didn't write in French. What the fuck am I doing with "Dombey and Son" in French? The twelve-volume "Conquest of Mexico." Two hundred cookbooks. The "Oxford World Classics," the little ones with the blue bindings, you know?

ISAAC: You got that?

MARTIN: They're all just words. And this is life, and besides, I hear the book chains are now selling pre-emptive strike video games, so why bother anyway? I'm out.

ISAAC: But really, there are limits, sweetheart.

MARTIN: Yes. That's exactly right. There are limits. I believe I know that. Hey, I spent most of my sixteenth year getting chemotherapy, remember? And it's not that long ago, I can still feel it. I cannot waste my life. I feel you people dragging me into this thing. You want this confrontation, Dad. You want nothing more than your children gathered around you, fighting. Well forget it. You don't know what I feel in my back, in my bones. I wake up some days and I'm crying. I think I'm still at Sloan-Kettering, lying there hairless and white and filling up with glucose from a drip. Hey! I can't get that time back. I feel all the needles, some days, my lymph nodes swollen, and I'm sweating. And part of my life is spent in fear, waiting. I know none of us has forever, know that very well, and I care very much how I spend my time. And involved in an internecine war over a publishing house, is, by my reckoning, Father, a dead waste. *And* if I choose to live with plants as an assistant lecturer at an over-rated seven-sisters school, *that* is my goddamn choice. But let's clear up something finally: I am not a goddamn gardener, and you are never going to goad me back into this life by calling me one. And Sarah is not a clown at children's birthday parties, Dad, and Aaron isn't a fucking accountant. You are really charming about your superiority, Dad. But you're really alone, too. This Nazi book jag of yours—it scares me.

STEAMBATH

by Bruce Jay Friedman

ACT II

*Tandy died in an accident and finds himself in a kind of
waiting area that resembles a steambath, with God in the
guise of a tough Puerto Rican attendant who communicates
with the outside world through a TV monitor. Tandy, who
had lived self-indulgently, doesn't want to accept that his
life is over and tries to convince the attendant and others
in the steambath that he deserves another chance at living
because he has finally gotten "past all that baloney" and
is on the verge of some real emotional and creative break-
throughs. But in truth, nothing has been going well in
Tandy's life, and the more he argues for another chance
the more fully he comes to realize that he wasted the one
life he was given.*

(To use as a monologue, omit other characters' lines.)

....

TANDY: I told you I'm not accepting this.

P. R. ATTENDANT: You want me to get rough? (*As he turns
to* TANDY, MEREDITH *runs* U., *hiding behind* L. *pillar and
then, when she finds the moment, crossing to behind the* R.
pillar.)

TANDY: (*Hiding* R. *of pillar.*) No, just reasonable . . . Let's say
you're having a Chinese dinner. . . . You've had your won
ton soup, a few spareribs, you're working up a terrific ap-

petite.... And, bam, you're thrown out of the restaurant. You never get to eat the won shih pancakes ...

P. R. ATTENDANT: (*Puts basket D. L. of R. pillar, picks up candy wrapper from floor.*) I can get any kind of food I want up here ... except lox. The lox is lousy, pre-sliced ... the kind you get in those German delicatessens.... I can't get any fresh lox.... I don't know why that is. (*Takes basket to alcove. Goes to sink and puts head under tap.*)

TANDY: (*Moving around pillar to C.*) It's like a guy about to have some terrific operation. The odds against him surviving are ridiculous, Newton High School against the Kansas City Chiefs. They're working on his eyes, ears, nose, throat and brains. A whole squadron of doctors is flown in from the Caucasus where they have all these new Caucasus techniques. He's hanging by a hair—and, miracle of miracles, he makes it. Gets back on his feet, says good-bye to the doctors, goes home and gets killed by a junkie outside of Toots Shor's.... That's the kind of thing you want me to accept.

P. R. ATTENDANT: (*Wiping hands, he writes on a clipboard hanging above the sink.*) That's a pretty good one. I'm gonna use that.... Yes, come to think of it, that is the kind of thing I want you to accept.

TANDY: Well, I can't. I worked too hard to get where I am. ... You know about Wendy Tandy, my ex-wife?

P. R. ATTENDANT: Sure I know about her.... Good-looking broad.

TANDY: That stunt she pulled?

P. R. ATTENDANT: That was a good one.... Gottlieb, you got to hear this.

(*GOTTLIEB has entered with dirty towels and gathered more from U. bench. He crosses D. to listen. MEREDITH moves D. from behind the R. pillar.*)

TANDY: (*Moving C. More to MEREDITH than anyone.*) She's an unfaithful wife. Fine. You put up with it, you don't. I did. Fair and square. So then we meet a retired hairdresser who has become an underground film-maker.... He shoots his film through these filters of teased hair ... it's a new technique. This is the guy Wendy falls madly in love with. And she moves out—to live with him. Fair and square. She prefers him, she's got him. (*GOTTLIEB puts the towels down U. and then moves D. L. of TANDY.*) Swingin'. I'm getting along fine—got a few deals of my own cooking—and all of a sudden I get an invitation to go see a film that this hairdresser has put Wendy in—down on Charles Street. And I find out—in one of the Village papers—that what he's done is make a huge blow-up—in one of the scenes—I don't know how to say this—of her private parts. It's very artistic, don't get me wrong. . . . The audience thinks it's a Soviet train station. . . .

MEREDITH: God, I'd never do that. How did he get her to do that? She must have really loved him.

P. R. ATTENDANT: (*Sitting on sink, cleaning his nails with pocket knife.*) Hey, Gottlieb, what did I tell you? (*GOTTLIEB gestures for quiet.*)

TANDY: Well, that makes me the supreme schmuck, cuckold, whatever you want to call it, everybody agreed? Half the city sitting in a theater, looking at my wife's box—sitting inside it, for Christ's sakes . . .

MEREDITH: (*Moving to him.*) For heaven's sake, what did you do?

TANDY: That's what I'm getting at. The old me would have come in with guns. I'm a very good shot—at under seven feet—there's a technique I learned over at the Bureau. You run into a little room after this cornered guy and as you shoot you're supposed to start screaming these animal sounds. (*Demonstrates, crossing D.*) YI, YI, YI, YI, YI, YI. That's in case you miss, you scare the shit out of him. But I finally figured, what the hell, it's got nothing to do with me. She's that kind of a girl. I knock off this guy, the next one'll be Xeroxing her pussy all over Times Square. So I said the hell with it and I went to the movie.

ONE FOR THE ROAD

by Harold Pinter

In this short play, Pinter conveys the essential horrors of living in a totalitarian state—the degradation, the isolation, the uncertainty, the utter helplessness. Nicolas, a cunning and sadistic official in an unnamed state, is interrogating Victor, who was arrested with his wife and seven-year-old son in a brutal raid at their home. Victor is bruised and his clothes are torn and he has not seen his wife and son since they were brought to this building. Nicolas is drinking whisky as he continues his questioning of Victor about some vague offense that he is alleged to have committed against the state and its supreme leader. But Nicolas's goal is not really a confession; he will not be satisfied until Victor recognizes that he has absolute control over his life.

....

NICOLAS: Well now . . .
  (Pause.)

What do you say? Are we friends?
  (Pause.)

I'm prepared to be frank, as a true friend should. I love death. What about you?
  (Pause.)

What about you? Do you love death? Not necessarily your own. Others. The death of others. Do you love the death of

others, or at any rate, do you love the death of others as much as I do?
(Pause.)

Are you always so dull? I understood you enjoyed the cut and thrust of debate.
(Pause.)

Death. Death. Death. Death. As has been noted by the most respected authorities, it is beautiful. The purest, most harmonious thing there is. Sexual intercourse is nothing compared to it.
(He drinks.)

Talking about sexual intercourse . . .
(He laughs wildly, stops.)

Does she . . . fuck? Or does she . . . ? Or does she . . . like . . . you know . . . what? What does she like? I'm talking about your wife. Your *wife*.
(Pause.)

You know the old joke? Does she fuck?
(Heavily, in another voice.)

Does she fuck!
(He laughs.)

It's ambiguous, of course. It could mean she fucks like a rabbit or she fucks not at all.
(Pause.)

Well, we're all God's creatures. Even your wife.
(Pause.)

There is only one obligation. *To be honest.* You have no other obligation. Weigh that. In your mind. Do you know the man who runs this country? No? Well, he's a very nice chap. He took me aside the other day, last Wednesday, I think it was, he took me aside, at a reception, visiting dignitaries, he took *me* aside, *me*, and he said to me, he said, in what I can only describe as a hoarse whisper, Nic, he said, Nic (that's my name), Nic, if you ever come across anyone whom you have good reason to believe is getting

on my tits, tell them one thing, tell them honesty is the best policy. The cheese was superb. Goat. One for the road.
(He pours.)

Your wife and I had a very nice chat but I couldn't help noticing she didn't look her best. She's probably menstruating. Women do that.
(Pause.)

You know, old chap, I do love other things, apart from death. So many things. Nature. Trees, things like that. A nice blue sky. Blossom.
(Pause.)

Tell me . . . truly . . . are you beginning to love me?
(Pause.)

I think your wife is. Beginning. She is beginning to fall in love with me. On the brink . . . of doing so. The trouble is, I have rivals. Because everyone here has fallen in love with your wife. It's her eyes have beguiled them. What's her name? Gila . . . or something?
(Pause.)

Who would you prefer to be? You or me?
(Pause.)

I'd go for me if I were you. The trouble about you, although I grant your merits, is that you're on a losing wicket, while I can't put a foot wrong. Do you take my point? Ah God, let me confess, let me make a confession to you. I have never been more moved, in the whole of my life, as when— only the other day, last Friday, I believe—the man who runs this country announced to the country: We are all patriots, we are as one, we all share a common heritage. Except you, apparently.
(Pause.)

I feel a link, you see, a bond. I share a commonwealth of interest. I am not alone. I am not alone!

LIPS TOGETHER, TEETH APART

by Terrence McNally

ACT II

John and his brother-in-law Sam just had an argument that developed into a wrestling match, during which John almost broke Sam's arm. He twisted it to try to force Sam to say, "I give up" (which he did), and then to get him to say, "I admit I'm a stupid piece of shit." This Sam refused, instead challenging John to "break my fucking arm." At that moment, John felt ashamed of how far his "passion" had carried him; he released Sam, apologized to him, and went off to be alone.

John, Sam, and their wives (Chloe and Sally) are spending the July 4th holiday together at Sally's Fire Island beach house (which she inherited from her brother who died of AIDS). It has not turned into a happy outing for any of them, especially since both men have little inclination to cover their intense dislike for each other. Among the complications is the fact that John has had an affair with Sam's wife and would like to repeat the experience (which she refuses). Also, John recently learned that he has cancer.

In the following monologue, John is alone, speaking his thoughts to the audience.

(To use as a monologue, omit Chloe's calls to John and his responses.)

JOHN: The weekend's ruined. The four of us can never look at each other the same way again. I hate what happened back there. I overpowered another man, fairly, and I had reason, but it wasn't enough. I wanted to humiliate him in front of his wife. I wanted him to feel small about himself in front of me. I could feel the bone in his arm about to snap like a dry, brittle wishbone. "Break the fucking arm." When he looked at me and said "Break the fucking arm" I didn't know who he was talking to. "Break the fucking arm." Jesus. Where was I? Whose arm was it? That could have been Chloe or one of the kids or one of them. In my head, I do it all the time. Cut ahead of me in traffic. Check your bank balance and start paying bills on the quick cash machine when there's a line. Say "Hunh?" with an accent when I ask you a question in perfectly good English. Fucking nigger, dumb cunt, idiot faggot. I kill a couple of hundred of them a day in my impotent fashion.

CHLOE: (*From within.*) John!

JOHN: In a minute! When I turned 40, my mother gave me a baby picture of myself. Everyone cooed and aahed but I took it as a reproach. There I am, golden curls, laughing, chipped front tooth, holding an apple. And now look at me. I've become a stranger to the very woman who bore me. I just wish I knew the precise moment I stopped being that laughing child with apple and turned into this. I would go back there again and again until I understood it. I know the precise moment I almost broke my brother-in-law's arm.

CHLOE: (*From within.*) John!

JOHN: I'm on my way! Sally will never let me fuck her again. That pisses me off as much as it saddens me. We gave each other great pleasure. We can never talk about these things the way they really happened and what they really meant. There's no apology deep enough to undo what I did to Sam. None. I will say "I'm sorry" and he will accept my apology but they will just be words and lies to get us through the business of living.

LOLITA

by Edward Albee

ACT I, SCENE 1

Lolita is adapted from Vladimir Nabokov's novel about a middle-aged man's sexual obsession with an eleven-year-old "nymphet." Humbert Humbert, an educated and refined middle aged man, finds himself "besotted with love and lust for that treasure of heaven," Lolita Haze. Here he explains to the audience the beginnings of his lustings for young girls, or what he calls "nymphets." It started with his first love and sexual partner, Annabel, when they were both about thirteen. To make his point clear, Humbert summons Annabel (who has long since died) to appear so the audience can see her.

(To use as a monologue, tie together the three speeches to the audience, leaving out Annabel's lines and Humbert's responses to her.)

....

HH: *(To the audience. HH will indicate ANNABEL from time to time.)* It is my belief that between the ages of nine and fourteen there occur—little girls—who, to certain bewitched travellers, twice or many times older than they, reveal their true nature—which is not human, but demonic. They are . . . nymphets. Well, you may ask, between those age limits, are not *all* girls nymphets? Of course not! If they were, those of us in the know, we lone voyagers, would have long ago gone insane. And, a normal man, looking at photographs of a group of Girl Scouts, say, would not be able to pick out the nymphet of the group. To do that you have to be an artist or a madman, a creature of infinite melancholy. To sense the deadly little daemon among the wholesome children you have to have a hot bubble of poison in your loins and a super-voluptuous flame permanently aglow in your supple spine. Annabel here was no nymphet to me, when she and I were both children.

ANNABEL: A what? Nymphet?

HH: That's right. (*To the audience again.*) After all, I was a faunlet in my own right; we loved each other with a premature love; I was strong, and I survived.

ANNABEL: I didn't. Can I go?

HH: All right.

ANNABEL: (*As she skips off.*) Thanks.

HH: You're welcome. (*To the audience again.*) But I was marked, you see. Had I been older I would have seen Annabel as the nymphet she was, but I was too young to know. The poison was in the wound, though, and the wound remained open, and soon I found myself maturing in a civilization which allows a man of twenty-five to court a girl of sixteen but not a girl of twelve. In Africa, in India still— in remote areas—grown men are wed to girls of ten, and no one thinks twice, but I am a criminal. (*Shrugs.*) So be it. I am ravaged by my first encounter with that poor word, love; I seek it out, again and again. I am a criminal. Tough! I would remind you, though, that when Dante fell madly in love with Beatrice he was a grown man, and she was all of nine. (*Whispers it.*) Nine! (*Normal voice again.*) And, unless I am mistaken, Dante is still taught . . . at least in our better schools. No matter; here I stand; pedophile; nympholept, unregenerate. And there is a little girl over there (*Indicates the Haze set.*) whom I have seen, who has broken my heart and sent my blood coursing . . .

ANTON CHEKHOV'S "THE DUEL"

adapted by Michael Schulman and Eva Mekler
from the translation by Ann Dunnigan

ACT III, SCENE 2

Ivan Layevsky and Nadyezhda Fyordorovna had been passionately in love. She left her husband for him and they fled St. Petersburg to lead a useful and meaningful life doing honest labor—something neither had ever done. They came to a seaside village on the Black Sea in the Caucasus and Layevsky took a job as an official in the Ministry of Finance. But they soon wearied of the place, the people, the interminable heat—and each other. They are unable to leave, though—neither has any money. Nadyezhda has no family to turn to, and Layevsky's mother, from an aristocratic family, will have nothing to do with them because of their adultery.

Last night, Nadyezhda, desperate for some excitement in her life, had a brief, unsatisfying affair that Layevsky discovered. Also last night, Layevsky got embroiled in an argument with Von Koren, a man who has been his constant enemy in the village and he rashly accepted Von Koren's challenge to duel with pistols. Layevsky knows that Von Koren is an expert marksman, and he realizes he will probably be killed.

His primary concern, though, is what will happen to Nadyezhda if he dies, how she will fare with no money. He feels that he is to blame for her seeking out another man— that he brought her to an arid place, then lost interest in her and, after that, either ignored or criticized her. It is late at night, just a short while before the duel is to take place. Layevsky is seated at a desk, writing a letter to his mother, asking her to take care of Nadyezhda.

(For more information, see other scenes from this play in other sections of this book.)

....

LAYEVSKY: Dear Mother . . . Whether they kill me tomorrow or make a mockery of me—that is, leave me my life—I am ruined in any case. Whether this dishonored woman kills herself from shame and despair or drags out her pitiful existence, she is ruined in any case . . . I ask you in the name of a merciful God to give shelter and a little warmth and kindness to this unfortunate woman whom I have dishonored, and who is now alone and impoverished and weak; to forget and forgive everything . . . everything, and by your charity to atone, at least in part, for your son's terrible sin . . . *(Thunder is heard.)* A storm. *(He continues to write.)* It is storming now. I recall how as a child I always ran bareheaded into the garden when there was a storm, two fairhaired little girls with blue eyes chasing after me, and how we were drenched by the rain. The little girls would laugh with delight, but when there was a loud clap of thunder they trustingly pressed close to me as I crossed myself and repeated Holy, Holy, Holy . . . Dear Mother, where have they gone, in what sea have they drowned, those early buds of fair, pure life? I no longer fear storms nor love nature; I have no God; all the trusting little girls I have ever known have been ruined by me and my contemporaries . . . In my entire life I have never planted one tree nor grown a single blade of grass in my own garden. Surrounded by living things, I have never saved so much as an insect, but have only destroyed, ruined, lied, and lied, and lied. Mother, I am not sure if you can understand all this or even if you really care . . . *(He stops writing and reading, and tears up letter on the line.)* What a fool!

DEATH OF A SALESMAN

by Arthur Miller
ACT II

*Biff Loman has come home to visit his family again, and
again he finds himself caught up in dreams of staying in
New York and becoming a success in business and, more
importantly, a success in his father's eyes. His father Willy
had big dreams for Biff, as he had big dreams for himself,
and Willy still can't face the reality that neither he nor Biff
has been able to find much success in life. Biff, his younger
brother Happy, and his mother Linda have always helped
Willy maintain his illusions but tonight Biff must demand
that Willy recognize the truth. He knows he will not get the
job that Willy had hoped he would get, and he knows that
Willy (who has just lost his own job as a salesman and is
also losing his grasp on reality) is planning to commit suicide so that Linda will get his insurance money.*

*Willy believes that Biff has purposely led a life of failure
to spite him because during his last days of high school
Biff learned that the father he so admired was having an
affair with a woman while on a sales trip to Boston. But
Biff demands that Willy listen to what he is saying.*

(To use as a monologue leave out all lines except Biff's.)

....

BIFF: (*To* WILLY.) Now hear this, Willy, this is me.

WILLY: I know you!

BIFF: You know why I had no address for three months? I
stole a suit in Kansas City and I was in jail. (*LINDA sobs,*

turns U.S.) Stop crying. I'm through with it. (*She turns away from them, hands on her face.*)

WILLY: I suppose that's my fault!

BIFF: I stole myself out of every good job since high school

WILLY: And whose fault is that!?

BIFF: And I never got anywhere because you blew me so full of hot air I could never stand taking orders from anybody That's whose fault it is!

WILLY: I hear that!

LINDA: Don't, Biff.

BIFF: It's goddam time you heard that! I had to be boss big shot in two weeks, and I'm through with it!

WILLY: (*Rises, crosses D. to D. R. corner of kitchen.*) Then hang yourself; for spite, hang yourself!

BIFF: (*Putting tube in his pocket, crosses D. to L. of WILLY.*) No! Nobody's hanging himself, Willy! I ran down eleven flights with a pen in my hand today ... and suddenly I stopped, you hear me? And in the middle of that office building ... I saw ... do you hear this!—I stopped in the middle of that building and I saw ... the sky. I saw the things that I love in this world; the work and the food and time to sit and smoke. And I looked at the pen and said to myself what the hell am I grabbing this for? Why am I trying to become what I don't want to be? What am I doing in an office building making a contemptuous, begging fool of myself, when all I want is out there, waiting for me the minute I say I know who I am! Why can't I say that, Willy (*He tries to turn WILLY to him to face him, but WILLY pulls away and moves to L., with hatred and threat.*)

WILLY: (*Crossing below table to L. end of kitchen.*) The door of your life is wide open!

BIFF: (*Crosses to R. of table.*) Pop! I'm a dime a dozen and so are you!

WILLY: (*At L. of kitchen. Turning on him now in an uncontrolled outburst.*) I am not a dime a dozen! I am Willy Loman, and you are Biff Loman!

BIFF: (*Crosses above toward WILLY, but HAPPY grabs him above table.*) I'm one dollar an hour, Willy! I tried seven states and couldn't raise it. A buck an hour, do you gather my meaning? I am not a leader of men, Willy, and neither are you; you were never anything but a hard-working drummer who landed in the ashcan like all the rest of them! I'm not bringing home any prizes any more and you're going to stop waiting for me to bring them home!

WILLY: (*To his face now.*) You vengeful, spiteful mutt! (*BIFF breaks away from HAPPY and goes for WILLY, who goes to stairs to escape, but BIFF grabs him and pulls him around, shaking him.*)

BIFF: (*At the peak of his fury, shaking him.*) Pop, I'm nothing, I'm nothing, Pop! Can't you understand that? There's no spite in it any more. I'm just what I am, that's all. . . . (*His fury has spent itself and he breaks down, sobbing, holding on to WILLY, who takes him in his arms, comforting.*)

WILLY: What're you doing? What're you doing? (*To LINDA.*) Why is he crying?

BIFF: (*Crying, broken.*) Will you let me go, for Christ's sake? Will you take that phoney dream and burn it before something happens? (*Struggling to contain himself, he pulls away and moves to stairs.*) I'll go in the morning. Put him . . . put him to bed. . . . (*In exhaustion he moves out, upstairs to his room.*)

MUCH ADO ABOUT NOTHING

by William Shakespeare

ACT II, SCENE 3

The central characters in this dark comedy are Benedick, a young lord and soldier from Padua, and Beatrice, the niece of the governor of Messina. Both have scorned love and marriage, and seem to enjoy nothing more than topping each other with their wit. Eventually, their friends, recognizing that their banter is merely a way to cover up their feelings for each other, devise a plan that brings them together. The following monologue takes place before the plan has been hatched. Benedick, still smug about his invulnerability to women, has seen yet another of his buddies succumb to love. This time it is his close friend and fighting companion, Claudio. It is now mid-afternoon and with Claudio off courting, there is little for Benedick to do but sit and read in the orchard, not a very exciting activity for a man of action. Benedick has sent a servant to fetch him a book and as he awaits his return, his agitation overflows.

....

BENEDICK: I do much wonder that one man, seeing how much another man is a fool when he dedicates his behaviours to love, will, after he hath laughed at such shallow follies in others, become the argument of his own scorn by falling in love: and such a man is Claudio. I have known when there was no music with him but the drum and the fife; and now had he rather hear the tabor and the pipe: I have known when he would have walked ten mile a-foot to see a good armour; and now will he lie ten nights awake, carving the fashion of a new doublet. He was wont to speak plain and to the purpose, like an honest man and a soldier; and now is he turned orthography; his words are a very fantastical banquet,—just so many strange dishes. May I be so converted, and see with these eyes? I cannot tell; I think not: I will not be sworn but love may transform me to an oyster; but I'll take my oath on it, till he have made an oyster of me, he shall never make me such a fool. One woman is fair, yet I am well; another is wise, yet I am well; another virtuous, yet I am well: but till all graces be in one woman, one woman shall not come in my grace. Rich she shall be, that's certain; wise, or I'll none; virtuous, or I'll never cheapen her; fair, or I'll never look on her; mild, or come not near me; noble, or not I for an angel; of good discourse, an excellent musician, and her hair shall be of what colour it please God. Ha! the prince and Monsieur Love! I will hide me in the arbour. (*Withdraws.*)

KING LEAR

by William Shakespeare

ACT I, SCENE 2

Edmund, the bastard son of the elderly Earl of Gloucester, has plans to fool his father into disinheriting his legitimate and loving son Edgar. Edmund, whose father has always been kind to him, has no intentions of accepting his second-class status as an illegitimate offspring, and is determined that his father's wealth and property will come to him. He has forged his brother's handwriting on a letter that implicates the brother in a plot to murder their father. The scene takes place in the Earl of Gloucester's castle. Edmund enters, holding a letter.

EDMUND: Thou, nature, art my goddess; to thy law
My services are bound. Wherefore should I
Stand in the plague of custom, and permit
The curiosity of nations to deprive me,
For that I am some twelve or fourteen moonshines
Lag of a brother? Why bastard? wherefore base?
When my dimensions are as well compact,
My mind as generous and my shape as true,
As honest madam's issue? Why brand they us
With base? with baseness? bastardy? base, base?
Who in the lusty stealth of nature take
More composition and fierce quality
Than doth, within a dull, stale, tired bed,

Go to the creating a whole tribe of fops,
Got 'tween asleep and wake? Well then,
Legitimate Edgar, I must have your land:
Our father's love is to the bastard Edmund
As to the legitimate: fine word, 'legitimate'!
Well, my legitimate, if this letter speed
And my invention thrive, Edmund the base
Shall top the legitimate. I grow; I prosper:
Now, gods, stand up for bastards!

HAMLET

by William Shakespeare

ACT II, SCENE 2

Hamlet is furious at his mother for marrying his uncle, a loathsome man, just a month after the death of his beloved father, the King of Denmark. The uncle has now become king. Then Hamlet is told that his father's ghost walks the castle battlements at night. After the ghost tells him that he was murdered by the uncle, Hamlet vows revenge. Hamlet feigns madness as a means to carry out his vengeance, yet, because he is uncertain about whether the ghost is a benign or evil spirit, he finds himself unable to simply murder his uncle. A troupe of players comes to the castle and the lead actor gives a magnificent, tear-filled performance recounting Hecuba's agony upon seeing her husband, Priam, dismembered in battle.

Hamlet then secretly asks the player if tomorrow he will perform the play, The Murder of Gonzago, *with some additional lines that Hamlet will write for the company. The player agrees and all exit, leaving Hamlet alone.*

....

HAMLET: Ay, so, God be wi' ye! (*ROSENCRANTZ and GUILDENSTERN exit.*) Now I am alone.
O, what a rogue and peasant slave am I!
Is it not monstrous that this player here,
But in a fiction, in a dream of passion,
Could force his soul so to his own conceit
That from her working all his visage wann'd;

Tears in his eyes, distraction in 's aspect,
A broken voice, and his whole function suiting
With forms to his conceit? and all for nothing!
For Hecuba!
What's Hecuba to him, or he to Hecuba,
That he should weep for her? What would he do,
Had he the motive and the cue for passion
That I have? He would drown the stage with tears
And cleave the general ear with horrid speech,
Make mad the guilty and appal the free,
Confound the ignorant, and amaze indeed
The very faculties of eyes and ears.
Yet I,
A dull and muddy-mettled rascal, peak,
Like John-a-dreams, unpregnant of my cause,
And can say nothing; no, not for a king,
Upon whose property and most dear life
A damn'd defeat was made. Am I a coward?
Who calls me villain? breaks my pate across?
Plucks off my beard, and blows it in my face?
Tweaks me by the nose? gives me the lie i' the
    throat,
As deep as to the lungs? who does me this?
Ha!
'Swounds, I should take it: for it cannot be
But I am pigeon-liver'd and lack gall
To make oppression bitter, or ere this
I should have fatted all the region kites
With this slave's offal: bloody, bawdy villain!
Remorseless, treacherous, lecherous, kindless
    villain!
O, vengeance!
Why, what an ass am I! This is most brave,
That I, the son of a dear father murder'd,
Prompted to my revenge by heaven and hell,
Must, like a whore, unpack my heart with words,
And fall a-cursing, like a very drab,
A scullion!
Fie upon 't! foh! About, my brain! Hum, I have
    heard
That guilty creatures, sitting at a play,

Have by the very cunning of the scene
Been struck so to the soul that presently
They have proclaim'd their malefactions;
For murder, though it have no tongue, will speak
With most miraculous organ. I'll have these
    players
Play something like the murder of my father
Before mine uncle: I'll observe his looks;
I'll tent him to the quick: if he but blench,
I know my course. The spirit that I have seen
May be the devil; and the devil hath power
To assume a pleasing shape; yea, and perhaps
Out of my weakness and my melancholy,
As he is very potent with such spirits,
Abuses me to damn me. I'll have grounds
More relative than this. The play's the thing
Wherein I'll catch the conscience of the king.
    (*Exit.*)

KING HENRY IV—PART I

by William Shakespeare

ACT I, SCENE 3

Henry Percy, son of the Earl of Northumberland (nick-named Hotspur because of his fiery and fierce disposition), was instrumental in defeating the enemies of Henry Bolingbroke and placing him on the throne of England. Now Bolingbroke is Henry IV and he summons Hotspur to London to upbraid him for not turning over his prisoners to the king's ministers. Hotspur wants to use the prisoners to exchange for his captured brother-in-law, Mortimer. But the king has no interest in freeing Mortimer who may challenge him as the legitimate successor to the throne. Hotspur downplays the political implications of refusing to turn over the prisoners, explaining that, while he meant no disrespect to the king, he was enraged by the discourtesy shown him by the king's minister.

....

HOTSPUR: My liege, I did deny no prisoners.
But I remember, when the fight was done,
When I was dry with rage and extreme toil,
Breathless and faint, leaning upon my sword,
Came there a certain lord, neat, and trimly
    dress'd,
Fresh as a bridegroom; and his chin new reap'd
Show'd like a stubble-land at harvest-home;
He was perfumed like a milliner;
And 'twixt his finger and his thumb he held

A pouncet-box, which ever and anon
He gave his nose and took 't away again;
Who therewith angry, when it next came there,
Took it in snuff; and still he smiled and talk'd,
And as the soldiers bore dead bodies by,
He call'd them untaught knaves, unmannerly,
To bring a slovenly unhandsome corse
Betwixt the wind and his nobility.
With many holiday and lady terms
He question'd me; amongst the rest, demanded
My prisoners in your majesty's behalf.
I then, all smarting with my wounds being cold,
To be so pester'd with a popinjay,
Out of my grief and my impatience,
Answer'd neglectingly I know not what,
He should, or he should not; for he made me
      mad
To see him shine so brisk, and smell so sweet,
And talk so like a waiting-gentlewoman
Of guns and drums and wounds,—God save the
      mark!—
And telling me the sovereign'st thing on earth
Was parmaceti for an inward bruise;
And that it was great pity, so it was,
This villanous salt-petre should be digg'd
Out of the bowels of the harmless earth,
Which many a good tall fellow had destroy'd
So cowardly; and but for these vile guns,
He would himself have been a soldier.
This bald unjointed chat of his, my lord,
I answer'd indirectly, as I said;
And I beseech you, let not his report
Come current for an accusation
Betwixt my love and your high majesty.

KING RICHARD II

by William Shakespeare

ACT III, SCENE 2

King Richard had banished his cousin Bolingbroke and seized his lands, but now Bolingbroke has mustered an army to regain his dukedom. Richard, having just landed on the coast of Wales after a successful war in Ireland, expects to be met by his loyal forces, which he intends to lead against Bolingbroke. But his joy is short-lived as he learns that his forces have abandoned him, with many going over to Bolingbroke's side. His faithful cousin Aumerle asks Sir Scroop, one of those who has brought the bad news, where his father's forces are, but Richard already knows that his defeat is imminent. He does not allow the question to be answered.

....

KING RICHARD: No matter where; of comfort no man speak:
Let's talk of graves, of worms and epitaphs;
   Make dust our paper and with rainy eyes
Write sorrow on the bosom of the earth.
Let's choose executors and talk of wills:
And yet not so, for what can we bequeath
Save our deposed bodies to the ground?
Our lands, our lives and all are
   Bolingbroke's,
And nothing can we call our own but
   death,
And that small model of the barren earth

Which serves as paste and cover to our
  bones.
For God's sake, let us sit upon the ground
And tell sad stories of the death of kings:
How some have been deposed; some slain
  in war;
Some haunted by the ghosts they have
  deposed;
Some poison'd by their wives; some
  sleeping kill'd;
All murder'd: for within the hollow crown
That rounds the mortal temples of a king
Keeps Death his court, and there the antic
  sits,
Scoffing his state and grinning at his
  pomp,
Allowing him a breath, a little scene,
To monarchize, be fear'd and kill with
  looks,
Infusing him with self and vain conceit,
As if this flesh which walls about our life
Were brass impregnable, and humour'd
  thus
Comes at the last and with a little pin
Bores through his castle wall, and farewell
  king!
Cover your heads and mock not flesh and
  blood
With solemn reverence: throw away
  respect,
Tradition, form and ceremonious duty,
For you have but mistook me all this while:

I live with bread like you, feel want,
Taste grief, need friends: subjected thus,
How can you say to me, I am a king?

ACKNOWLEDGMENTS